2012c

Don Larson
P.O. Box 496
Ashland, WI 54806-0496

715-373-0433

D1055321

ALAN AMECHE

Terrace Books, a trade imprint of the University of Wisconsin Press, takes its name from the Memorial Union Terrace, located at the University of Wisconsin–Madison. Since its inception in 1907, the Wisconsin Union has provided a venue for students, faculty, staff, and alumni to debate art, music, politics, and the issues of the day. It is a place where theater, music, drama, literature, dance, outdoor activities, and major speakers are made available to the campus and the community. To learn more about the Union, visit www.union.wisc.edu.

ALAN AMECHE

The Story of "The Horse"

Dan Manoyan

TERRACE BOOKS

A TRADE IMPRINT OF THE UNIVERSITY OF WISCONSIN PRESS

Terrace Books
A trade imprint of the University of Wisconsin Press
1930 Monroe Street, 3rd Floor
Madison, Wisconsin 53711-2059
uwpress.wisc.edu

3 Henrietta Street
London WC2E 8LU, England
eurospanbookstore.com

Printed in the United States of America

Library of Congress Cataloging-in-Publication Data

Manoyan, Dan.
Alan Ameche : the story of "The Horse" / Dan Manoyan.
p. cm.
Includes index.
ISBN 978-0-299-29010-8 (cloth : alk. paper) — ISBN 978-0-299-29013-9 (e-book)
1. Ameche, Alan, 1933–1988. 2. Football players—United States—Biography.
3. Football players—Wisconsin—Biography. I. Title.
GV939.A595M36 2012
796.332092—dc23
[B]
2012016788

This book is dedicated to

ED, ELAINE, EDDIE, RANDY, BARB, and JUDY
and to MELBA WIXOM, my inspirational
high school English teacher at WTHS.

CONTENTS

FOREWORD

Pat Richter

Any football-minded kid growing up on Madison's East Side in the fall of 1950 was undoubtedly a huge fan of the Madison East Purgolders and the Wisconsin Badgers. The Purgolders played in the Big Eight, and one of the schools in the conference was Kenosha Bradford. Its 1950 team was regarded as one of the best ever in the state of Wisconsin.

It was an extraordinarily talented bunch, which included quarterback Mario Bonofiglio, who started college at the University of Wisconsin and then transferred to play football at the University of Miami; end Tom Braatz, who played at Marquette and in the NFL; and Bobby Hinds who accepted a boxing scholarship at the University of Wisconsin and also boxed professionally. In addition there were two other players who went on to star at the University of Wisconsin. One was guard and placekicker Paul Shwaiko, and the other was "the Horse," Alan Ameche. Ameche's successor at running back at Kenosha, Eddie Hart, was aptly named "the Pony."

Five doors down from our house on Rutledge Street lived our Purgolder hero, Gary Messner, who went on to play center on the Wisconsin football team and become a teammate of Alan Ameche. On occasion Gary would have some of the Badger players over to his house, and invariably word would get around that they were coming and that's where we headed. What a thrill it was to meet the players and get their autographs, but the guy who generated the most excitement and gave us the biggest thrill of all was the Horse. For us, he was no longer the feared running back of Madison East's rival, Kenosha. Now he was to be cheered, for he was now a Wisconsin Badger.

Alan was a great player for four years at Wisconsin, and his punishing running style gave credence to the nickname the Horse. He capped off his illustrious career by being named the recipient of the Heisman Trophy, the most coveted award in college football. He was the first player so honored from the University of Wisconsin.

We naturally followed his subsequent NFL career with the Baltimore Colts because he was still our hero, "the Horse." We were thrilled and proud of his being a Badger when he scored the winning touchdown in what has been called "the Greatest Game Ever Played," the Baltimore Colts' win over the New York Giants in 1958.

During Alan's six-year NFL career, he and teammate Gino Marchetti embarked on a very successful business career. Gino was a very tough defensive end who I played against when I joined the Washington Redskins in 1963. They made a great team, on and off the field.

On occasion, Alan would return to Madison after he retired, and it was gratifying to see that he was as genuinely gracious and humble as he was when we first met him at Gary Messner's house in the early 1950s. The humility that was his trademark, coupled with his on- and off-the-field success, had provided Alan, his wife Yvonne, and family, an opportunity to share that success with others. Their philanthropy meant as much to Alan and the family as Alan's football prowess meant to his fans.

In retirement, the Horse became an even bigger hero to us all.

~

Like Alan Ameche, Pat Richter enjoyed a legendary athletic career at the University of Wisconsin. Richter is Wisconsin's last three-sport letterman, having lettered in football, basketball, and baseball in the same school year on three occasions. As the Badgers' football tight end, Richter led the nation in receiving as a junior, was a two-time all-American, and set a Rose Bowl record with 11 receptions for 163 yards against Southern California in the 1963 game. He was Wisconsin's director of Intercollegiate Athletics for nearly fifteen years before retiring in 2004.

PREFACE

I'll never forget the day I first met Yvonne Ameche. Being the only woman in America to be the widow of two Heisman Trophy winners (Alan Ameche and Glenn Davis) and the mother-in-law of Michael Cappelletti, brother of 1973 Heisman winner, John Cappelletti, makes her a unique and interesting woman. But it was the circumstances under which we met that day that will always be indelibly etched upon my memory.

I had driven from Wisconsin to suburban Philadelphia to meet Mrs. Ameche and was delayed half a day by what some described as the blizzard of the decade in Pennsylvania. The snow had forced me to abandon the Pennsylvania Turnpike about halfway across the state and hunker down somewhere in between. The following afternoon, hours behind schedule, I arrived in a still-snow-shocked Philadelphia. After navigating the spiderweb-like roadways of that city's northern suburbs (I think the British must have designed the road patterns before retreating to Canada) to find Mrs. Ameche's cul-de-sac, I was stunned and dismayed to see that it was untouched by snow removal equipment.

I called her to inform of her of the dilemma, a situation that she was obviously well aware of. I tracked down the lone snow plow in the area, two blocks over, and asked the kind man if he could plow Mrs. Ameche's street next. I told him it was an emergency. I lied a little. He was gracious enough to comply, but there was yet another problem. Mrs. Ameche's house is half a football field off the road, and her yard was covered by nearly two feet of snow.

Wearing a pair of loafers—who, these days, plans to walk across a snow-covered yard?—I finally made it to the house, much to the amusement of Mrs. Ameche, who watched the escapade from the safety of her front window. She welcomed the stranger from Wisconsin, putting his shoes and socks on a heating vent and supplying him with a warm pair of New York Yankee logo socks. I was so grateful for the warm socks, it never occurred to me to ask why she owned Yankees socks in the first place.

After a slight delay—my tape recorder was literally frozen solid—we got into the interview. Three hours and three tape cassettes later, we were finished. Thanks to Mrs. Ameche, I had a good working background on the life and times of Alan Ameche. We would talk many more times over the course of the writing of the book, but that first meeting, when we were marooned on the same snowy island, was pretty much the foundation for everything you will read, and hopefully enjoy, in this book.

ACKNOWLEDGMENTS

First and foremost, I would like to thank Yvonne Ameche. Without her cooperation and insight, quite simply this book would not have been possible. I know there were times when she had her doubts about the project (as did I), but I think both of us now agree that it was a completely worthwhile project and a very fitting tribute to an incredible man—Alan Ameche.

The Ameche children—Brian, Alan, Catherine, Michael, and Beth—were all major contributors to the story of their father, and their insights were not only thoughtful but poignant. Brian, the Yale man, was perhaps the most skeptical that his father's story could be told in the proper light, but I hope even he will admit that the book does justice to the man.

Then, there were Ameche's Baltimore Colts teammates. What a thrill to be able to talk to NFL Hall of Famers Gino Marchetti, Lenny Moore, Art Donovan, and Raymond Berry. Jim Mutscheller is also a man with a great memory, and Lenny Lyles also provided great insight. It took me around ten phone calls to convince Moore that it was the "right" time to talk, and finally I caught him at the right moment. Berry, who was a rookie with Ameche, had some great stories to tell about "the first Italian" he ever met. Marchetti and Donovan, two of the greatest defensive linemen to ever play the game, were a delight to talk with.

I would also like thank the men who knew Ameche the longest, his high school and college teammates. Thanks to Mario Bonofiglio, Bobby Hinds, Dick Nicolazzi, Ed Ronzia, Frank Aiello, Tom Braatz, Jerry Wuhrman, Jim Temp, Mark Hoegh, and Roger Dornburg, all of whom played with Ameche at Kenosha Bradford, the University of Wisconsin, or both places.

I would be remiss without also thanking Lou Fischer, Rudy Riska, Pat Richter, Mike Klingaman of the *Baltimore Sun*, Dave Kelly of the Library of Congress, the University of Wisconsin Sports Information office, including Justin Doherty and Brian Lucas, Todd Clark of the WIAA, and the staff of the Kenosha Public Library Southwest branch.

ALAN AMECHE

1

A Man for All Seasons

AFTER THERE WAS A REAL-LIFE BRONKO NAGURSKI, but before the world had ever heard the words "Italian Stallion" thrown together as a pop-culture catchphrase, there was a man called the Horse.

Like his equine predecessor, the Horse ran hard and he ran fast, terrorizing opponents with his brute strength. Also, like Nagurski, he lugged a football for fun, and later for money. However, the only commonality he shared with the fictitious stallion of *Rocky* fame was that both were Italian through and through.

Ameche was the best football player of the mid-1950s, winning the Heisman Trophy (1954) and the NFL's first Rookie of the Year award (1955). He would be the only man to pull off that double-barreled feat in the 22 years that followed.

Not until Tony Dorsett arrived on the scene, winning the Heisman in 1976 and the NFL Offensive Rookie of the Year Award in 1977, was Ameche's feat duplicated. During that time span, such immortal players as Jim Brown, O.J. Simpson, Gale Sayers, Roger Staubach, Johnny Unitas, Mike Ditka, Jim Taylor, and Archie Griffin all failed to match Ameche.

Ameche's feats on the football field were the stuff of legends. At Kenosha High School in 1950, he was an all-state halfback, the most valuable performer in the rugged Big Eight Conference, and the most valuable performer on Kenosha's undefeated (8–0) squad, rated by some as the greatest schoolboy team in Wisconsin history. In his senior season, Ameche scored 120 points, including 108 in seven conference games, a new league scoring mark. That season the Red Devils outscored opponents 361–61, despite the fact that on only one occasion did their coach, Chuck Jaskwhich, play his starters more than one half of any contest.

Stepping up a level, Ameche was equally as dominant at the University of Wisconsin. In his freshman year, Ameche would win the starting fullback spot in the Badgers' third game of their nine-game season, and he would go on to rush for 824 yards (5.2 yards per carry), both Wisconsin records.

In his sophomore season, he would break the school rushing record again, gaining 946 yards in 205 carries. More important, he would lead Wisconsin to its first-ever Rose Bowl appearance, where it would lose to Southern California, 7–0, despite a 133-yard rushing performance by Ameche.

NCAA substitution rules, which prevented a player from leaving a game and returning in the same half, forced Ameche to play both offense and defense in his junior and senior years. The beating Ameche took at linebacker forced the Wisconsin coach Ivan "Ivy" Williamson to diversify his offense those seasons, but Ameche still finished with 801 yards rushing yards as a junior and 641 as a senior.

Ameche would earn first-team all-American honors in his final two seasons at Wisconsin and the Heisman Trophy, symbolic of the nation's top collegiate player, as a senior. His other major individual honors included two Walter Camp Memorial Trophies (1953 and 1954), two University of Wisconsin MVP honors (1953 and 1954), the UPI Back of the Year award (1954), and the Chicago Tribune Silver Football (Big Ten MVP) (1954). He would be named to the National Football Foundation's College Football Hall of Fame in 1975 as well as a first-team member of the all-time Academic All-American Team in 1997.

When he was finished at Wisconsin, he held the NCAA career rushing mark of 3,212 yards (3,345 including the Rose Bowl yardage) and every Wisconsin rushing record. He also set the NCAA record for rushing attempts—673. Despite the fact that the Badgers played just a nine-game season then, Ameche's records stood until Billy Marek broke most of them in the mid-1970s.

Ameche drew several favorable comparisons with the great Nagurski, the fullback to whom all who followed were compared. But perhaps it was said best by the legendary Iowa football coach Forrest Evashevski, after Ameche, in his senior season, had just shredded the Hawkeyes' defense for 117 yards and a touchdown in 26 carries in Iowa's 13–7 upset of the Badgers. In the postgame press conference in the Iowa locker room, Evashevski, a man not known for hyperbole, was asked his opinion of Ameche.

"I think Ameche is the greatest fullback I ever saw," he said without hesitation.

A reporter from the *Des Moines Register* by the name of Tony Cordero seemed surprised by Evashevski's rare platitude and followed up with, "Did you say the *greatest* you ever saw?"

"How can you say anything different?" Evashevski replied.

Despite the two-way pounding Ameche's body took in his final two seasons at Wisconsin, he was the third player chosen in the 1955 NFL draft. He was taken by the Baltimore Colts, a franchise that was entering its third year of existence after having gone 3–9 in each of its two previous years.

Ameche signed with the Colts for the then-princely sum of $15,000. As such a lofty draft pick, he had plenty to prove. He did just that the first time he touched the football with the Colts against the Chicago Bears. Ameche ran 79 yards from scrimmage as the Colts beat the Bears, 23–17, in the season opener.

The Colts' coach, Weeb Ewbank, who had disagreed with using the club's first draft choice on Ameche and maintained a stormy relationship with his big fullback in their six years together with the Colts, later remembered that play with fondness.

"That run by Alan took me off the hook right away for drafting him in the first round," Ewbank recalled to the *Wisconsin State Journal* after retiring. "From then on, I was a genius."

Ameche used that first game as a launching pad, leading the NFL in rushing his rookie season with 961 yards in 213 carries. He rushed for 410 yards in his first three games, which was a rookie record for fifty years until 2005, when Carnell "Cadillac" Williams of Tampa Bay rushed for 434 yards in his first three NFL games.

Ameche's pace slowed down as the years progressed and his role with the squad evolved, but in six years with the Colts, he rushed for 4,045 yards and 40 touchdowns. He was named to the NFL's All-Pro team four consecutive seasons, from 1955 through 1958, and played in five Pro Bowl games before his career ended abruptly with an Achilles tendon injury in 1960. There are those who believe that the only thing that has prevented Ameche from being named to the NFL Hall of Fame was the relatively short duration of his career.

Ameche is still remembered for scoring the winning touchdown in the Colts' 23–17 victory over the New York Giants in the 1958 NFL Championship game. The NFL's first overtime game is still referred to by many as the Greatest Game Ever Played because of the drama with which the Colts tied the game in regulation and won it in overtime. Ameche scored two touch-downs in that game.

"A lot of people just remember him for that particular run," the late Johnny Unitas, who called the winning play, would tell the Associated Press in later years. "But he was instrumental in keeping that game alive with his pass catching and running ability." Unitas said he called Ameche's number on the game-winning play because "we knew he wouldn't fumble."

Ameche was unquestionably the greatest athlete ever produced in the state of Wisconsin. At all three levels of competition—high school, college, and professional football—Ameche was dominant and his presence turned medi-ocre teams into champions. And it was his contributions to his three teams' successes that seemed to make Ameche the proudest as he reflected upon his career in his later years.

"One of the things that has happened in my football career [. . .] that has been most gratifying is that on every team that I played with we were dead last and at some point we ended up winning a championship," Ameche told Dave Klein in his book, *The Game of Their Lives*. "When I went to high school, we scored one touchdown the whole season the first year I played [1948]. One touchdown. We lost all the games.

"But by my senior year we had won the championship, we were unde-feated. Wisconsin was the same thing. And more dramatically with Baltimore."

Actually, the Badgers were 2–7 in Harry Stuhldreher's last season, 1948. But the Badgers had already begun their ascent before Ameche arrived in Madison in 1951, going 5–3–1 and 6–3 in 1949 and 1950, respectively, under Stuhldreher's replacement, Ivy Williamson. The Colts, as descendants of the defunct Dallas Texans, were a combined 6–18 in their first two seasons in Baltimore before Ameche's arrival.

"I don't want to sound like I'm blowing my own horn or anything, but [. . .] the reward is so much sweeter when you start at the bottom and you get the shit kicked into your face, then you see yourself climbing a little bit, and a little bit more. And when you make it, it's really a beautiful thing."

Ameche was a man known for his fierce competitive spirit, whether he was playing in one of the two NFL Championship games won by the Colts or a parlor game with one of his six children.

"Alan didn't want to lose at anything," said his wife, Yvonne. "Even in later years when he'd lose a tennis match, he'd be very angry if he lost.

"But Alan was also a very humble man, he never talked about his accom-plishments, even when he was playing in the pros. He knew he was good. . . . You always know when you are good."

Ameche offered a window into his mind when he described his personal philosophy of football to long-time *Baltimore Sun* Colts' beat writer John Steadman in a 1959 profile. "We backs are nothing more than parasites," he told Steadman. "We live off the linemen."

Football put Ameche center stage in the American psyche. If he wasn't already a household name after winning the Heisman, he was after he plunged into the Giants' end zone at 8:15 of the overtime, flashing across black-and-white television screens across the nation, as the underdog Colts whipped the big city Giants in the 1958 NFL title game.

"We played a pretty good game, but it wasn't the best game we played," Unitas would say in later years. "What made it the greatest game in football history was that it was the first time there was an overtime in a championship game and we drove down the field to tie the game and then win the game."

Ameche, whether he was unimpressed by the magnitude of his winning touchdown or just unaware, rolled the football away from his body as a mob of fans stormed the end zone, leaving it up to teammate Buzz Nutter to retrieve the precious cargo from a fan. Millions of Americans may have been impressed with Ameche's football prowess, but he wasn't.

"It was probably the shortest run I ever made and the most remembered," said Ameche in his most famous quote, referring to his "sudden victory" touchdown.

"Alan just didn't care to talk about himself," said his widow Yvonne. "He was a great football player, but you'd never know that from talking to him."

Art Donovan, a Hall of Fame defensive tackle with the Colts of Ameche's era, told Mark Hyman of the *Baltimore Sun* of Ameche: "He was one of the best friends I ever had in football. He was the first big star I ever played with—you can't do any better than Heisman Trophy. But he never took things seriously." In the same article Unitas took it a step further. "The awards and honors never bothered him. He was a great athlete, a super football player and a regular guy. He was there to do a job, and he did it."

The deeper one delves into Ameche's life, the overriding story becomes simplified. Football may have made him into the man everyone thought they knew, but by no means did it define who he was. Ameche's oldest son, Brian, well aware of that fact, was originally against any book being written about his father for that very reason.

"He was against it because he didn't feel any book could do justice to his father's story," Yvonne Ameche said. "Football certainly didn't define who Alan was."

Fair enough. Outside of possibly being the greatest football player of the 1950s, Ameche was also a friend, a father, a husband, a businessman, and a philanthropist. And he was hugely successful in all of those venues.

Two of his oldest friends, Mario Bonofiglio and Tom Braatz, recalled what sort of friend Ameche was in his formative years in Kenosha.

"We were out in Madison, walking down State Street right across from the capitol building . . . visiting Madison while we were still in high school," said Bonofiglio, who was the diminutive quarterback of Ameche's great Kenosha High School team. "This group of guys who we had played against from Madison East [High School] walks past us and one of the guys knocks into me on purpose.

"We said, 'Why did you do that?' and the guy says, 'Why? Do you want to make something of it?' Well, Alan grabs the kid and throws him down. He threw him down right there on the street.

"The kid got up and they all took off running. Bunch of wise guys. But that tells you what kind of friend Alan was. He would do anything for a friend."

Braatz, another high school teammate who would later go on to be, among other things, the general manager of the Green Bay Packers, grew up on the playgrounds of Kenosha with Ameche.

"If Lino knew you, and he liked you, he'd go to bat for you," Braatz said. "It wasn't that he was fighting all the time or anything like that, but we were street kids and at the playground there is always some kid there to test you.

"Most of the time Alan was the peacemaker, but let's just say that the other kids knew he was a loyal guy and would help his friends."

One of Ameche's best friends on the Colts was the legendary Unitas. Their friendship stretched so far that Unitas once installed a tile floor in the Ameche kitchen when both men were cash strapped early in the football careers.

"It was a tremendous thing to play with him," said Unitas of his friendship with Ameche. "In a time when football players were thought to be mean and ruthless, he was one of the nicest—kind and considerate."

The Ameche children, especially the family's older boys, wouldn't always have agreed with Unitas's magnanimous description of their father. But now that they are grown up, their father is on the parental pedestal, where he belongs.

"I remember going back to the University of Wisconsin to make a speech on the fiftieth anniversary of Dad's Heisman," said Michael Ameche, the family's third son. "I said if he had never touched a football, he would probably still be the greatest man I ever knew.

"He was a tough parent and he gave tough love, but the older I've gotten I see that football didn't define him by any stretch. When I think back on him, I only remember the good things now.

"He was an incredible businessman, but he didn't have an MBA or any great academic honors. His way of doing things was with a handshake. His word was his bond. He'd say if it cost him, then it cost him money, but that's the way he did things, with a ton of integrity.

"He was just a wonderful man and he was never afraid of what anybody thought about him. He was never intimidated. And he was always, *always* the first one to help anybody in need."

But Ameche was more than unselfish. He was generous almost to a fault. He became a very wealthy man after his playing days were over, teaming up with Colts teammates Gino Marchetti and Joe Campanella and associate Lou Fischer to form a chain of fast-food restaurants called Gino's.

With his newfound wealth, Ameche became a philanthropist of legendary proportions. Ameche's older daughter Catherine loved the way her father never lost his common touch, even after building Ameche-Gino Inc. into a multimillion dollar corporation.

"My dad was so well respected because he treated everybody equally," she said. "He treated the CEO the same way he treated his barber. His humble beginnings in Kenosha never left him. He was the most generous man I've ever known. . . . He wanted to like everybody."

When Ameche passed away in 1988, his second son, Alan Jr., was asked to replace his father as the chairman of the Alan Ameche Memorial Foundation, which since the 1970s has financed the education of underprivileged students in the Philadelphia area. One of the students aided by the foundation is Michael Nutter, mayor of Philadelphia.

Alan Jr. said:

My father never disappointed anybody. He never said no to the point that people took advantage of him. He would say, "It's not my place to judge. Someone else will judge someday, somewhere, but it's not me."

He was the most secure human being I've ever known; there was never any need to blow his own horn. He was literally embarrassed by attention. He wouldn't talk about his own success, a very unique man.

I've come across men in my life who I thought were at his level and literally each and every one of them ended up being other than what they seemed to be. My father ended up being exactly who he seemed to be.

Certainly, he was not a perfect man. He would be the first to admit that. He

certainly had areas where he struggled. But he worked on them to make himself
a better person and he grew tremendously. By the end of his life he was a such
a different person than he was midway through.

If football didn't define Ameche, then generosity and kindness did. His
philanthropic efforts, both through his foundation and other outlets, are the
stuff of legend. Here is a partial list of organizations he supported with his
time and financial contributions: Villanova University Development Committee; Philadelphia Orchestra (board of directors); Multiple Sclerosis Society (board of directors); Southeast Pennsylvania United Negro College Fund
(corporations chairman); Fellowship of Christian Athletes (area chairman);
and Malvern Preparatory School (board of directors).

"If I could help just one individual in the rest of my life, I would consider
that I accomplished something," Ameche told *Baltimore Sun* sportswriter
John Steadman in later years, after Ameche had retired.

Ameche's charitable work in the inner city of Philadelphia is well known.
He financially backed the renovation of many inner-city day care and community centers. He purchased several blocks of inner-city property, which he
transformed into mini-playgrounds, and financed the tuition of many underprivileged and disadvantaged youths, both white and minority.

"He felt a tremendous responsibility to help people less fortunate than
himself," Alan Jr. said. "My father's greatest gift was that he had an incredible
ability to understand what it must be like to be in someone's shoes less fortunate than himself. And I think that was because of his upbringing.

"I've never known a man who cried as much as my father, whether it was
a movie or a particular set of circumstances. He was as easily moved as any
man I've ever known. He had tremendous sympathy and empathy and it
drove him his entire life to be the man he was."

Gino Marchetti saw Ameche's generosity close up. "I heard a story just
recently, that he was coming out of a restaurant in Philadelphia and there
was a group of kids, and it was obvious that they were under the poverty
level," Marchetti said. "He gave each of them a fifty dolar bill."

"Alan was the most generous man I've ever known," said Bonofiglio, who
also was a business partner of Ameche's in a Kenosha venture. "If the man
had a fault, it was that he was too generous. He couldn't say no to anybody."

Bobby Hinds, another of Ameche's Kenosha friends and a high school
teammate, tells a very illustrative story of his buddy's generosity.

"One time we were back in Kenosha at a reunion banquet and after dinner we were talking to the parish priest at Saint Joseph's [High School],"

Hinds told Dave Zweifel, the former Madison *Capital Times* editor. "The priest happened to mention that the athletic program at the school would probably be dropped the next year unless parishioners could raise about $250,000.

"Al took out his checkbook and quietly wrote the astonished priest a check for $250,000 and never said a word to anyone about it," Hinds said. "I saw him do it, but he didn't want me to say a word to anyone. But that's the kind of guy he was. You'd be surprised how much he bought the UW [University of Wisconsin] and never wanted to take credit for it."

Although Ameche almost always insisted on anonymity, signs of generosity abound in his hometown and home state. One of the most visible is the Ameche Gym at the Christian Youth Center in Kenosha, which was built through Ameche's generosity.

"My father never said no to anything involving Wisconsin," Alan Jr. said. "They would call him constantly for stuff, and he never said no.

"He wanted no recognition; he tried to keep everything completely anonymous. That was the most beautiful thing about him. That was the only stipulation, that everything would be anonymous."

Sometimes Ameche made big donations and sometimes small ones.

"I remember once we were standing in line to go into an amusement park and Dad saw that the woman in front of us didn't have enough money to pay for her family," said Michael Ameche. "Very discreetly, Dad walked over to her and gave her enough money for her whole family.

"Another time we were in Italy and we still have a ton of relatives there. We had a party for them at the Hilton and I remember Dad shaking hands with the aunts and uncles and slipping money to them."

Alan Jr. remembers attending a class reunion and having one of his former classmates inform him about an act of generosity by his father that caught him totally by surprise.

"This fellow comes up to me and said 'Are you aware your father put me through Malvern and my sister through Notre Dame?'" Alan Jr. said. "Their father left the family and left them financially, too.

"His mother explained [to Ameche] what was going on and asked my father if he could help. He stepped up to the plate, handled all the kids' tuition, and even had the girl's teeth fixed. According to what the fellow told me, that was not rare for my father. My father felt guilty about the success he had had."

Another of Ameche's Baltimore teammates, Jim Mutscheller, tells yet another story revealing Ameche's enormous generosity.

"I was involved in this charity in Baltimore that was trying to boost things up for people in Baltimore," Mutscheller said. "It was for poor people having problems at the Lafayette Square Community Center.

"I asked Alan for a donation, not knowing what to expect. He comes back and says 'I'll give you $50,000.' Now that was 1962 and $50,000 in 1962 was a whole different ballgame from what it is today. But he said he would do it and he did. I have so much respect for that man."

"One of his favorite Gospels from the Bible was the story about how it is easier to fit a camel through the eye of a needle than it is to get a rich man into heaven," Alan Jr. said. "He took that very seriously. He felt a tremendous obligation to share his good fortune.

"I've never loved anyone more in life than my father."

Alan Jr. and his two surviving brothers and two sisters said good-bye to their father in 1988, when he died in Houston, waiting for a heart transplant at the DeBakey Heart Institute. How ironic that a man with a heart the size of Texas would die for lack of a new heart in Texas.

The man who negotiated Ameche's first professional contract with the Colts, John Walsh, a prominent Madison, Wisconsin, attorney, saw the irony, too. In an interview with *Wisconsin State Journal* sportswriter Tom Butler at the time of Ameche's death, Walsh told how Ameche had hoped to be drafted by his home state Green Bay Packers, but a short-sighted Packers scout didn't think Ameche was fast enough to play fullback in the pros.

"History records that Ameche broke off tackle against the Chicago Bears and raced 79 yards for a touchdown on his very first run from scrimmage in the pros," Butler wrote. "As Walsh put it, 'The pros thought they could judge his speed, but they couldn't judge his heart.'"

2

The Early Years

L IKE SO MANY LATE SPRING DAYS IN WISCONSIN, June 1, 1933, was unre-
markable for its cool temperatures and steady, soaking rainfall. Ordinary
Kenosha working people went about their day-to-day business, consumed by
the rigors of surviving the Great Depression. There was a cautious optimism
in those days that the newly elected president, Franklin D. Roosevelt, would
deliver on his promises of returning everyday Americans to a better standard
of living.

The big local news in the *Kenosha Evening News* that day was that the city
manager, William E. O'Brien, had been ratified to the Wisconsin State Highway Commission and would soon leave the city to accept a six-year term. The
Evening News also reported that a beer truck, en route from Milwaukee to
the Chicago World's Fair, veered off Highway 41 west of the city near the
Racine-Kenosha County line, losing 400 cases of beer.

In more mundane news, a three-year old Kenosha toddler lost the tip of
his index finger, nibbled off by a neighbor's pet rabbit. And in local sports,
Jim Anderson, Wisconsin's 1929 state amateur golf champion, led the local
qualifying at Kenosha Country Club for the prestigious Pettit Cup, carding
an even par 71.

Although it didn't register with the *Evening News* on that first day of June,
there was, in retrospect, very big news on 52nd Street, Kenosha's main east-
west street and a tavern magnet for thirsty factory workers. In an upstairs
storefront apartment, where now there is a parking lot, Lino Dante Amici,
son of Benedetta (Lentini) and Augusto Amici, was born.

But even on the little noted day of his birth, the baby who would later be
known to the world as Alan Ameche was anything but average. Since he was

home birthed, there were no records of his weight, but Benedetta would later claim that her chubby bambino came into the world weighing more than eleven pounds.

"His mother would always say that Alan weighed eleven and one-quarter pounds when he was born, and I would tell her I didn't think that was possible," said Ameche's widow, Yvonne. "But who knows? She was a very big woman."

Augusto and Benedetta, whose names were later Americanized to August and Elizabeth, or Betty, came to Kenosha from the historic Italian city of Canino in the province of Viterbo, north of Rome. Benedetta and her sons eventually decided on the more Anglicized surname of Ameche, but Augusto stubbornly remained "Amici" till the day he died.

"The old man is pretty hard-headed and he won't change his name," Alan was quoted as saying in a *Sports Illustrated* article by Booton Herndon on October 25, 1954.

Alan also said in the article that he wasn't 100 percent sure he was legally "Ameche" but it was the name he was sticking with. He said at the time that the name discrepancy was something he "intends to ask Lynn about." Lynn was Alan's older brother.

Apparently their surname wasn't the only thing the Ameche parents couldn't agree about. Their match could hardly be described as made in Heaven.

Augusto, who was twenty years Benedetta's senior, immigrated to the United States in 1914, becoming a citizen on February 21, 1921. His first stop in the United States was to visit his older brother Aresti, who had already established himself with his own landscaping company in the nearby Chicago suburb of Wilmette. Rather than follow in his brother's footsteps, Augusto moved forty miles north to Kenosha, where he was able to find work at the lakefront plant of the Simmons Mattress Company.

Augusto's decision to move to Kenosha was made easy by the fact that Kenosha had a large and vibrant community of recent Italian immigrants. He chose to live in the Columbus neighborhood, which was not only within walking distance of the Simmons plant but also just a few short blocks from the heavily Italian Mount Carmel Catholic Church.

Augusto, who spoke no English when he arrived in this country, assimilated fairly well into Kenosha but was unable to find a suitable Italian American woman with whom to share his life. So in 1927 he returned to Canino in search of a bride.

Augusto proposed to the much younger Benedetta, but she was anything but receptive to his advances. "She didn't want to leave Italy and she was fond of another man," Yvonne related.

Fortunately for Augusto, he had a powerful ally in his quest to woo his dream girl. Benedetta's father was adamant about her immigrating to the United States.

"Her father actually insisted that she move with August to America," Yvonne said. "He wanted her to move to America because he thought the streets were paved with gold here."

Actually, the streets of Kenosha were far from golden. The harsh reality of the situation was that the United States was in the throes of the Great Depression. Augusto was among the lucky ones who had a steady job, but like all laborers of that era he worked long hours for very little pay and thanked God every night for his blessings.

Augusto and Benedetta were married in Canino on June 29, 1927, and then returned to Kenosha, where Augusto reclaimed his job at Simmons. Lyndo was born in 1928 and was followed by Lino five years later. A younger sister died at birth.

In perhaps the only interview she ever gave, Elizabeth told Bill Furlong of *Sport* magazine about her big bambino, Lino. The story appeared in the magazine before the 1953 football season.

"All the time I had to take clothes a couple of sizes more than for a regular baby," said Elizabeth in broken English. "I get clothes for a four-year-old baby when Alan was only two years old. He's always been a big one."

The Ameches apparently never understood Alan's obsession with sports and weight lifting. But they did notice the results.

"All the time, [Alan] just wanted to play ball," Elizabeth was quoted in the article. "He always said to his father, 'Hey, look at my arm. Look at my muscle.'"

The Ameche parents didn't understand American football and apparently saw their son perform on the football field only on a very few occasions. It may be a cliché, but Alan was a man of few words, especially when his exploits were the topic of conversation. Most of what the Ameches learned of his exploits came from what others, especially Lynn, told them.

"Alan, he doesn't talk so much," Elizabeth said. "If he plays real good, he say, 'I think I play pretty fair.' My other son, Lynn, tells me everything.

"Alan, is he really very good?" she asked the sports writer, who described her tone as shy but proud.

Yvonne would later describe her mother-in-law as being "tall and big boned, weighing over 200 pounds. She also had really high hips and long legs."

Indeed, Elizabeth was an imposing figure of a woman. Augusto was smaller than the average-sized man, so it is not difficult to see from which side of his family Alan inherited the long legs that gave him speed and the powerful shoulders that would later help him shed would-be open-field tacklers.

"You can see where Alan and Lynn got their long legs and broad shoulders," said Mario Bonofiglio. "His father was not a big man, but his mother was a very big woman."

Elizabeth, who was a stay-at-home mother, struggled with her new life in Kenosha. Although there was a vibrant and growing Italian community in Kenosha, and Mount Carmel was within walking distance of the family's house, she longed to return to Canino.

"I imagine their life was pretty bleak," Yvonne said. "I don't think she ever wanted to leave Italy in the first place, to be honest."

The Ameches' older daughter Catherine, whose relationship with her grandmother was probably the best of anyone in the family, agreed with her mother.

"I don't think Grandmother Ameche ever wanted to be in this country," said Catherine Cappelletti. "That left a bitter woman the rest of her life."

Yvonne first met Alan in junior high school and recalls what life was like for him as a youth.

"They never owned a car or house. . . . They always rented. When I first met Alan in the 1940s they were still renting just the downstairs. A railroad went through their backyard and there were factories all over that neighborhood. Even then it was what you would call the wrong side of the tracks."

According to records unearthed from Kenosha city directories, the Amici family lived in five different locations in Kenosha's Columbus neighborhood between 1933 and 1941. When young Lino was about eight years old, the family finally settled in a rental bungalow at 5523 16th Avenue, and that was the last place he would call home in Kenosha.

The modest two-bedroom, one-bathroom house was in the heart of the Columbus neighborhood, one of city's oldest, most rundown areas when the Ameches lived there, and the passing of years hasn't been any kinder to the area.

The house was two blocks west of the Northwestern Commuter Line viaduct that bisects the city and four blocks west of the Kenosha County Courthouse and current Walter Reuther Alternative High School, which face each other across the 56th Street boulevard. An industrial trunk line of the railroad passed through the Ameches' backyard.

Reuther is housed in the imposing graystone building that evolved from Mary D. Bradford High School and from the original Kenosha High School, which Ameche attended. The Columbus neighborhood today is a hodgepodge of older rental homes, light industry, and aging houses of worship.

A previous Ameche home, at 1626 56th Street, is gone now, demolished, and a newer industrial building housing Wilmot Woodworks occupies the address. It is less than half a block away from a now-abandoned Jewish synagogue that was very active when Ameche was growing up.

"That neighborhood was probably 90 percent Italian when Alan grew up there," Bonofiglio said. "They were all hard-working people, but nobody had anything. They all looked out for each other because they were all in the same boat.

"The Italians all came to Kenosha looking for work, and there were plenty of factories and plenty of jobs for them. After they were here for a while, they branched out into other areas. My father, like Alan's, started at Simmons, then he got into the tavern business."

In the *Sports Illustrated* article, Herndon described the Ameche domicile thus: "Al grew up in a house in Kenosha surrounded by a freight yard, a junk yard and a coal yard, but it was spotless and Al was always clean and neat."

But all that mattered to Elizabeth was that the house didn't feel like her home and Kenosha wasn't Canino. She missed Italy, she missed her home, and she missed her family. So sometime in early 1937, with Lynn and Alan in tow, she returned to her homeland.

"She was still a baby and she wanted to go home," Yvonne said. "She never wanted to leave Italy in the first place and then when she came here she was homesick. The story I heard was that she didn't want to leave her family and the only reason she came was that her father insisted that she would have such a good life here."

Canino, which in 2010 had a population of 5,323, is a picturesque city that dates back to the Etruscan era of Roman history. Like much of Italy, Canino is known for its grapes and olives, but its specialty is its unique brand of olive oil—Extra Virgine, di Oliva. Napoleon Bonaparte's brother Lucien was the lord of Canino and is buried in the town.

It isn't known if Elizabeth's intentions were to return to the postcard perfect village permanently or to merely take an extended visit and eventually return to Kenosha. But something happened in Italy that forced her hand. Actually, Benito Mussolini happened.

Mussolini had come to power as the fortieth prime minister of Italy in 1922 and began using the title of Il Duce by 1925. But the ruthless dictator's predilection for Fascism and his personal delusions of grandeur were undeniable when in 1936 he gave himself the official title of His Excellency Benito Mussolini, Head of Government, Duce of Fascism, and Founder of the Empire. For good measure, he also created for himself the military rank of First Marshal of the Empire and another title—King Victor Emmanuel III of Italy.

In sleepy little Canino, the Ameches were far from immune to the nationalist fervor and winds of war that were being whipped up throughout Europe during the period. Yvonne claims she has seen old pictures of the Ameche boys wearing brown shirts and giving the infamous Mussolini fascist salute.

"Obviously they were little boys when they were [in Italy], so they didn't have any choice. They did what they were told."

Elizabeth decided that Kenosha, even with all its faults, was indeed a better alternative for raising her sons than the soon-to-be-at-war Italy. The Ameches returned to Kenosha in late 1937, and on February 21, 1938, Elizabeth made a giant step in deciding her future. She officially became an American citizen.

The consequence of Elizabeth's protracted Americanization was that the Ameche sons were slow in learning the English language. Although Elizabeth and Augusto did speak broken English later in their lives, Lynn and Alan didn't have the luxury of learning the new language at their own pace.

"I remember when Alan and I were dating, I was talking to an older Italian woman in his neighborhood who was sitting on her porch and she remembered Alan as a little boy," Yvonne said. "She spoke to him in Italian because he didn't understand any English at that point. She said to him 'Are you lost?' and he replied that he was going to see his grandmother in Italy."

Alan spoke almost no English when he enrolled at nearby Frank Grade School in 1938, but fortunately for him he wasn't alone. He was very bright and quickly picked up English, which eventually replaced Italian as his primary language.

"I first met Alan in the second or third grade at Frank School and by that time he spoke perfect English," said Ed Ronzia, who was a football teammate of Ameche's at Kenosha High School. "I never knew him to speak Italian at all to be honest.

"He was a big, strong kid. He wasn't one to just hang around with the boys all the time. He was home lifting weights with his brother, Lyndo, at an early age, or he was working so he didn't have time to be hanging out with the rest of us in the summer time especially."

Yvonne remembers that by the time she met Ameche at Washington Junior High, he spoke perfect English. Still, there were some scars from his early experience in Kenosha schools.

"I'm sure Alan remembered the trauma of being here in this country and not being able to speak English," she said. "He certainly wasn't one to complain though. He would never tell me that he struggled in school in those days. But I do know it bothered him to be in that situation, but fortunately he was a quick learner and didn't let it him sidetrack him."

According to Ronzia, Ameche spoke better English than almost any student at Frank School by the time he was a fifth grader. Ameche was chosen by his teacher to recite the Gettysburg Address from memory at a parent/teacher assembly that year.

"It was a meeting where all the parents were there, and he gave the Gettysburg Address, like a trooper, from memory," Ronzia said. "He was the one [the teachers] picked."

Although Ameche was known as a peacemaker when teenage issues would play out in his high school years and was always the gentleman in later life, Ronzia saw a side of the future Heisman Trophy winner that not many saw.

"He punched me out when we were in the fifth grade," Ronzia said. "We had a softball team at Frank, like every grade school in the city, and I was the captain of the team. Lino was never around for practice because he had a paper route, I believe, but he showed up for the first game and wanted to play.

"I said 'No, you can't play, you haven't been practicing and we already have our team picked.' So he punched me out. It's amusing because I didn't get a black eye or nosebleed, but I went down when he hit me.

"He stomped off and that was it. There was no problem after that."

Obviously, Ameche couldn't turn to his parents for help when it came to catching up in English. So he turned to Lynn, who had laid a good foundation in the English language before Elizabeth's decision to take the boys back to Italy for a year. Because Lynn had experienced all the things Alan was going through trying to assimilate, Alan leaned heavily on his brother, and the two formed a tight bond that would never be broken.

"Lynn was more like a father to Alan than a brother," Yvonne said. "When Alan was born, his father was already well into his forties and he was from a different country.

"So it was Lynn who worked with him, Lynn who taught him about being American. It was Lynn who encouraged him to play sports."

Not only did Elizabeth and Augusto not encourage Alan, but they strongly discouraged him. It was left to Lynn to nurture the budding athleticism of his younger brother.

"His parents had no background in sports whatsoever," Yvonne related. "In fact they did not want Alan to play sports at all. His parents were from the old country and all they knew was work and family.

"Lynn was Alan's friend and he was his protector. There was nothing he wouldn't do for Alan and vice versa."

According to Yvonne, Alan didn't even bother asking his parents to sign the requisite parental permission slip for football at Kenosha High School. He knew what their answer would be, so he went to Lynn.

"It wasn't that they were afraid Alan was going to get hurt or anything like that," she said. "It's just that they were older and foreign and didn't understand. They thought sports were a waste of time. When Alan needed permission to play football, he gave the form to Lynn and Lynn forged August's name."

Although standing over six feet and cutting an athletic figure himself, Lynn didn't play high school sports, but he had seen the value placed on them as he made his way through Kenosha High School and later while attending the University of Wisconsin. He recognized Alan's huge athletic potential and was determined to help his brother any way he could.

"When Alan was in high school, they couldn't afford weights, so Lynn took a couple of coffee cans, filled them with cement, and attached them with a broom stick," Yvonne said. "That was Alan's weight set. It was Lynn who worked with Alan and helped make him what he became."

It was important for Alan to have Lynn as a mentor for another reason. The Ameche home was not a happy place. Whether it was an outgrowth of Elizabeth's short-lived return to Italy in the 1930s or other reasons, the marriage of the Ameche parents was long and stormy.

"I do know that Alan's parents' marriage was not a happy one," Yvonne said. "They just never got along. I wouldn't say there was ever any physical fighting or abuse, they just didn't get along. She was never a happy woman."

Bobby Hinds was a football teammate at Kenosha High and the University of Wisconsin, who, like his good friend Ameche, came from very humble beginnings. Hinds was shuffled around as a child—by his count, attending fourteen different schools in Kenosha—and often times relied on friends' generosity to get by.

Hinds worked construction with Ameche in the summer of 1951, before going off to Madison, but he needed a place to stay. The Ameche family opened its doors and heart to the young man.

"I lived at their house that summer and they were wonderful, wonderful people, especially his mother," recalled Hinds, somewhat contradicting Yvonne's version of the family dynamic. "His father was a great guy, too. His dad worked all those years at Simmons and got his gold watch. Hardworking man."

Yvonne believes the bickering at home was the reason Ameche was ready to go off to school.

"I think that's the reason why Alan didn't like spending time at home. As long as his brother was there, Alan was all right, but when his brother left [to go to the University of Wisconsin], Alan missed him terribly when he was away at Madison."

Upon graduation from Wisconsin, Lynn married Barbara Kane, whose father was an executive at Snap-On Tools in Kenosha, and went to work for her father's company's branch office in Indianapolis. He and Alan would remain close, but the two brothers would never live in the same city again.

Bonofiglio attended a different grade school, so he didn't know Ameche till they met at Washington Junior High, one of Kenosha's three junior highs at the time. Because of their athletic inclinations, they became fast friends.

"I used to go over to their house all the time. It was a small house, like all the houses back then, but they were the nicest people you'd ever meet," Bonofiglio said. "They were so nice to me, beautiful people, treated me like a son. Alan's mom would always ask me what I want to eat because she was always cooking. Look how big Alan and Lynn were."

Yvonne saw a much different dynamic in the Ameche home, however. And to this day, it is apparent that Yvonne feels Elizabeth bears the brunt of the blame for the discord in the Ameche home.

"Alan's dad was a very, very sweet man," she said. "His mother wasn't.

"She was just very childlike. Even after she aged, she just wasn't a sweet woman. When she was older, she would say things that weren't appropriate and she was a problem."

Augusto, who suffered from chronic hypertension, died of kidney failure in 1956 and Elizabeth would marry August's brother, Aresti, shortly thereafter. After Aresti's death, Elizabeth would eventually move to the Philadelphia area to be near Alan and his family, who had moved there after his football career had ended.

"I always took care of her when she lived with us, and I always treated her with respect," Yvonne said. "She came out here after August and Aresti died and stayed in a nursing home during the week and stayed with us on the weekends.

"I did my best with her, but it wasn't easy. I remember Lynn came to visit us once and asked me 'How do you take it?'"

Yvonne claims that Alan felt pretty much the same way about his mother that she did.

"Let's put it this way," Yvonne said. "Alan always loved his father and he respected his mother when she was nice."

3

The Kenosha Kid

THE THEORIES ABOUND AS TO WHAT THOUGHTS were flowing through the sixteen-year-old's head the day he marched down 56th Street to the Kenosha County Courthouse to officially change his name from Lino Dante Amici to Alan Dante Ameche.

Was it that he didn't like the name Lino because it wasn't tough enough? Or perhaps it was a little too Italian for his taste? Or maybe he didn't like the name that Augusto and Benedetta bestowed upon him because his brother didn't like it? On the same day that Lino plunked down 50 cents to became Alan, Lyndo was by his little brother's side, officially changing his name to Lynn.

Most people who know Alan Ameche, including those who knew him best, go with the "too Italian" theory.

"That's what I think," said Dick Nicolazzi, Ameche's football teammate at Kenosha High School and the University of Wisconsin. "I think that 'Lino' just didn't sound American enough for Alan. It wasn't that he didn't like being Italian, he just wanted to be American first."

Nicolazzi's theory makes as much sense as any. Certainly if Ameche made the switch because "Lino" didn't sound tough enough, he could have found a more macho-sounding name than Alan. Rocco, Duke, or Butch come immediately to mind.

Ameche's young sweetheart at the time, Yvonne Molinaro, who eventually became his wife, is the best source for this story.

"I remember he was giving me a ride on his bicycle, and I said to him, 'You know Lino is a very strange name. It sounds like Rinso or something you would wash your clothes with.'

"You know what he said to me? He looked right at me and said 'You know what Yvonne? I think if I were you, I'd get my teeth straightened out.'"

Message received.

"That was his way of fighting back. It was his way of saying nobody is perfect and maybe I should take care of my situation before I criticize him," Yvonne said.

"To make a long story short, he changed his name and I got my teeth straightened. To be honest, I love the name Lino and I called him that till the day he died. But apparently he didn't like it and wanted it changed."

So why Alan? Yvonne knows the answer to that question as well.

"I think he changed it to Alan because I was madly in love with the actor Alan Ladd," Yvonne theorized. "It wasn't to be tougher. Alan never had to worry about that. It was about being more American. He felt 'Lino' was too foreign sounding.

"I remember we were sitting on the steps to my basement one day. We had cement walls in the basement, and Alan was writing on the wall with chalk. He wrote a bunch of names on the wall, all the different names that he was considering changing his name to.

"I always thought Lino was such a beautiful name, too. I always called him Lino.

"I don't remember what other names he was considering, but I can see him standing there with that chalk in his hand, writing names on the wall. I think maybe the reason he picked Alan was to please me."

Yvonne reflected more about the day that young Ameche was writing on the basement wall of her family's home at 4822 20th Avenue.

"I remember we laughed about the name because there is an area in Kenosha called Allendale. It's where all the wealthy people in Kenosha lived at the time."

The Molinaro home was in a better neighborhood than the Ameches', but it certainly wasn't Allendale, either. Her father, Michael Molinaro, had started as a laborer at the American Brass Company, or "the Brass" as it was known by Kenoshans, and he had worked himself up to the position of foreman.

"We lived in a little bit nicer area than where Alan lived, but it was still working class," Yvonne said. "Everybody was just happy to have a job in those days."

Although the young lovers were both born and raised in Kenosha, they never officially crossed paths until fate placed Yvonne in the seat behind Alan in Mr. Molstad's ninth-grade social studies class at Washington Junior High.

"I thought Alan was darling, even better than Alan Ladd, and I had pictures of Alan Ladd all over my room," Yvonne said. "There was just something about Alan. He was good-looking and so funny. It was just fun being around him."

There was an immediate mutual attraction, and Alan and Yvonne were soon an item. But along with the carefree laughter and cuddling that comes with young love, there was also a serious side to their relationship. Michael Molinaro was diagnosed with cancer in March 1948 and died in June of that year at the age of fifty-one.

Yvonne's only option when it came to visiting her dying father was to ride to Kenosha Memorial Hospital on the back of Alan's bicycle.

"That was a typical date for us back then," she said. "Alan would give me a ride to visit my father in the hospital after school. I remember the first time I rode on his bicycle was to go see my father in the hospital back then. I spent a lot of days on the back of his bicycle because that was the only transportation we had."

The young lovers continued their relationship throughout high school, but as in most youthful relationships, there were plenty of ups and downs. Yvonne, who was a cheerleader at Kenosha High School while Alan was playing football, recalled that there were many times when she didn't know if their relationship would survive high school.

"It was a very stormy relationship, but that's how it is in high school. Somebody gets jealous, you get mad and you break up. I honestly don't know how many times we broke up and got back together, but it was a lot.

"It was typical high school stuff. . . . It was always something. I know Alan didn't want me to smoke, so that bothered him quite a bit. It was just a lot of silliness.

"I dated other boys in high school and I'm sure he probably dated other girls."

Apparently Yvonne's smoking habits were a big issue for Ameche. High school football teammate Tom Braatz remembers the friction her smoking would create for the young couple.

"I didn't have a car of my own, but I was able to borrow my sister's car once in a while, so we would double-date," Braatz said. "Lino and Vonnie would be together, and I was with Jeri [Keckler, who would be his future wife].

"I remember how when Alan wasn't in the car, Vonnie would sneak into the backseat and have a cigarette."

Added Jeri: "It was a big deal for Alan that Vonnie smoked. When he would go over to her house, she would swing a big, wet towel in the air to absorb the smoke, so he wouldn't know."

Nicolazzi, who was not only a teammate of Ameche's but also a good friend of Yvonne's, remembers how volatile their relationship could be on occasion.

"I was in the same homeroom in high school as Yvonne, because it was alphabetical and she was an M for Molinari and I was an N," he said. "She knew Alan and I played football together, so every day, she would ask me, 'What did Alan say about me? What's going on with Alan?' They would break up but never get too far from each other."

In the end, Yvonne said their on-again, off-again relationship endured all those years for one very simple reason. "I guess you could say we liked each other a lot. No matter what happened in those days, it always came down to that."

As you might expect, Yvonne now prefers to remember the happier times.

"I'll never forget on one of my first dates with Alan. We were riding the bus, the Blue Line in Kenosha, and Alan kept waving out of the bus," Yvonne recalled. "I said 'Who are you waving to?' He said, 'Yvonne, don't you see all my fans out there?'

"He was so silly at times. He was silly, yet so charming at the same time."

One of her favorite illustrations of Alan's free-spirited nature is her story of how he would sneak into the movie theater. Spending-money for luxuries like going to the movies was in short supply in those days, but Ameche found a way to beat the system. Yvonne worked at the popcorn stand at the downtown Kenosha Orpheum Theater in high school, but that didn't translate into free passes for her friends.

"Alan had it down to such a science. He would figure out when the movie would let out, then the doors would open up and he'd walk backwards through the crowd. It was the funniest thing you've ever seen. All these people would be walking out, and Alan would walk backwards through the crowd until he got in. He'd swing his arms, just like he was walking forward.

"Then when he got in, he'd come over to the popcorn stand and I've give him free popcorn. He had it all worked out."

Whatever dating activity Ameche and Yvonne participated in, it was done on the cheap. Times were tough in Kenosha, like everywhere else at that time, and money was tight. As a freshman at Wisconsin, Ameche was asked to fill out a biographical information sheet, including a question on any adversity he may have faced in his young life.

"Financial," was Ameche's succinct, one-word answer.

"None of us had anything back then," said Braatz, whose father Myron had died of fumes inhaled at his auto-painting business when his son was just five years old. "We lived in the same kind of house Lino grew up in, two bedrooms and one bath. Nobody had any walking-around money."

But what Ameche lacked in personal finances, he made up for in charm and good humor. Apparently, Yvonne wasn't the only Kenosha High School student who was swept away by Ameche's presence. He was one of the most popular boys in the school and was even elected president of his class in his sophomore year. A short profile of Ameche in the Bradford student newspaper had this to say about the junior football player:

A 16-year-old junior, Lino packs 195 lbs. on a powerful, well-built, six foot frame. As a sophomore he was among the top KHS athletes, lettering in both football and track. A versatile, all around natural athlete, he was also a member of the KHS (basketball) squad.

Listening to classical music and eating chicken are among Lino's favorite pastimes. Attending college or working at Nash's (Motors) are two postgraduate maybes for him. He also likes his feminine acquaintances "cool." With another year of varsity high school competition ahead of him, Lino's athletic future looks bright.

An earlier indication of Ameche's popularity was demonstrated in a profile written about him in the Washington Junior High student newspaper. An anonymous column entitled "Personalities" was apparently a regular feature of the newspaper, and this particular column featured a drawing of a very well-built man with six-pack abs and an exaggerated nose.

It gives us great pleasure to introduce to you some of our Washington Junior High School students in this column. Watch in every issue—you may find out some things about yourself that you never dreamed were true—and they'll be in print, too.

That tall, dark and handsome boy you've been seeing around the school is none other than Lino Ameche.

He has a very nice build, especially his latissimus (that is from the waist up.)

His favorite movie star is Peter Lorre. His favorite subject is gym. Lino prefers concert music to popular music. His favorite singer is James Melton, and his favorite bandleader is Fred Waring.

He likes loud and silly characters like Mario Bonofiglio, so he says. He prefers brunettes to blondes or redheads.

Lino's hobbies are football and tiddlewinks. Lino, you know, is one of our football stars and football is very important to him. Going out with girls is another of his favorite hobbies.

His favorite color is black. He prefers overalls and T shirts to dress pants and starched shirts. He also likes bright colors—you know, such stuff as red flannel underwear.

Despite his burgeoning popularity, it was sports, not politics, that would be Ameche's ticket to success in high school and beyond.

There was no tackle football program in Kenosha's junior highs as there is now, only touch football. But Ameche and Bonofiglio first teamed up to play tackle football with a local traveling team called the Vagabonds. As would be their positions for the rest of their football careers, Bonofiglio was the Vagabonds' quarterback and Ameche was the team's ballcarrier.

"That was the big deal back then, the Vagabonds," recalled Bonofiglio. "I knew playing with Alan on the Vagabonds that he was going to be something special. It took three or four guys to bring him down on every play. Even for a young kid, he was so strong.

"We also played on the 'touch' team at Washington, and that's where I first met Alan. There were just three middle schools in Kenosha back then— Washington, McKinley, and Lincoln—so it was no big deal.

"I never met Alan until we were in the seventh grade. I don't really remember what my first impression was. I can't say that his reputation preceded him, because he really had never done anything before that."

But the one thing that did impress Bonofiglio, and anyone else who saw Ameche as a seventh grader, was his raw strength. All those days of hoisting the jerry-rigged coffee-can weights in his backyard with brother Lynn were apparently paying off by the time puberty arrived.

"All he did before junior high was lift weights. He and Lynn, that's all they did. He was the only kid in junior high or high school that ever lifted weights. We never had weights back then. We didn't know anything about weights."

Tom Braatz was amazed by Ameche's size when they first met as opponents in a junior high touch football game.

"I was playing for McKinley and Lino was playing for Washington," said Braatz, who after playing for the Washington Redskins and Dallas Cowboys, was an executive in the NFL, working as general manager for both the Atlanta Falcons and Green Bay Packers. "That's how we first met. I didn't really know him then, but I played against him in football and also basketball I believe.

"I thought he was way too big for his age. He was kind of like a man among boys. It looked like he had been lifting weights, and nobody lifted weights back then."

Nicolazzi didn't meet Ameche until their first year at Kenosha High School. Like Bonofiglio, he wasn't all that impressed initially.

"When I first laid eyes on Alan when we were sophomores in high school, honestly he was just one of the guys at that point in time," Nicolazzi said. "There was no tackle football in Kenosha till the tenth grade, so it wasn't like he had a big reputation or anything.

"We were all about six feet tall and around the same weight, but Alan was definitely stronger than the rest of us. He lifted weights before he got to high school, and he did a lot more once he got there, but at that point in time, weight lifting was almost unheard of.

"People would tell you, 'Don't lift weights or you'll get muscle bound.' . . . You know, you can't move, that was the thinking. You could see Alan had a nice frame, but really he was no bigger than a lot of guys on the team."

It wasn't until after the Kenosha High sophomores put on their pads that Nicolazzi and the other Red Devils soon learned that Ameche wasn't just one of the boys.

"Like I said, there were guys as tall and as big as Alan, but nobody had his kind of speed," Nicolazzi said. "You could see right away, Alan was just so quick through the hole. He didn't do a lot of faking; he was a straight line guy. You know, the shortest route from Point A to the end zone is a straight line."

Nowhere was Ameche's unrivaled combination of speed and brawn on display like it was on the unweeded old cinder track that looped around rickety Lakefront Stadium, five blocks east of the high school and just east of downtown Kenosha.

Football was his sport of choice in the fall, and track and field occupied his time in the spring season. Ameche played basketball at Washington Junior High and for one season in high school, but apparently it wasn't his favorite sport. But by all accounts, Ameche excelled at the sport, leading his Mount Carmel parish squad to the archdiocesan CYO junior championship in 1951 and the Kenosha junior CYO championship for four years running.

Mount Carmel became the first Kenosha team to win the state CYO junior title in seventeen years, according to an article in the *Kenosha Evening News* in 1951. By beating Milwaukee Saint Thomas Aquinas, 55–53, in overtime, Mount Carmel became only the third team outside of Milwaukee to win the championship. Ameche was named to the all-tournament team, averaging 14 points per game in four games.

The Mount Carmel team, coached by Aldo Madrigano, included Ameche, Edward Bonaretti, Louie DiCastri, Dario Madrigano, Nick Guarascio, Don Andreoli, Art Andreucci, George Misurelli, Vinnie Lia, and Louis Cicchini. Playing with many of the same boys for Bell Clothing in the Kenosha City League, Ameche broke a city record by scoring 287 points in 14 games, an average of 20.5 points per game. He was easily the league's leading scorer as Bell Clothing ran up a 13–1 record.

"I don't know why he didn't play on the high school [basketball] team," said Bonofiglio who was one of the stars of Kenosha High's team. "He tried basketball and played one year, but I don't think he liked it too much."

Bonofiglio was one of the most amazing athletes Kenosha has ever produced. In addition to starring in football and track, he was also Kenosha High's starting point guard in basketball. In his senior year, Bonofiglio won an unheard of four letters, the first and quite possibly the only time that has ever happened in Kenosha. While competing in track in the spring, he took days off from practice to compete in varsity golf meets and was perhaps Kenosha High's top golfer as well.

"I only went out for track because Alan went out," Bonofiglio said. "It was a way to stay in shape for football. Obviously he could have been a great thrower if he had stayed with it, but basically he just used track to keep busy and stay in shape during the spring season."

Ameche won the Wisconsin state championship in the shot put in the spring of 1950, his junior year at Kenosha High, with a toss of 50 feet 9 inches. He was even stronger as a senior, tossing a career best 53 feet 2 inches in the southeast Wisconsin sectional qualifying meet. That throw was just shy of the state record at the time, 54 feet 9 inches, which had been set by Steve Flanagan of Kaukauna.

Despite his big toss in the 1951 sectionals, Ameche failed to repeat as shot put champion that spring at the state meet. His track career ended on a down note as he finished second at the state meet with a toss of 50 feet 3 inches.

Milwaukee Washington's Dean Mielke won the 1951 shot put event in Wisconsin, throwing the 12-pound ball a state-meet record 52 feet 11½ inches, nearly 3 feet better than runner-up Ameche. Mielke broke the record of Milwaukee Washington's Bob Kalchik, set in 1940. The report of the state meet that appeared in the *Kenosha Evening News* said the meet was held in miserable conditions and that a crowd "well under 1,000 scuttled for cover when frequent showers drenched the stadium."

Ameche's last track meet was actually the Big Eight Conference meet, which inexplicably was held at Lakefront Stadium after the state meet. Ameche won shot put that day, but with a less than inspired effort of 49 feet 8½ inches.

In the course of his two seasons, Ameche set invitational meet records at Madison West, Janesville, and Kenosha Lakefront Stadium. One of his proudest achievements was a 52 foot 2½ inch toss at Lakefront, which broke Ken Huxhold's 1947 Kenosha city record of 51 feet 10 inches.

Eddie McKenna, a man known for his long-winded yet flowery prose as the sports editor of the *Kenosha Evening News* for thirty years, died unexpectedly on the Thursday before the state meet of 1951. But just weeks before his death, McKenna wrote the following about Ameche after he broke the shot put record at the Madison West Relays.

> Bull-shouldered, piston-legged Alan "Lino" Ameche, whose athletic prowess has earned him as many records as there are in a music shop, added still another standard to his glittering collection, Saturday at Madison, scene of his fabulous prep football exploits that make him the state's most sought after schoolboy halfback in college circles for the fall of 1951.
>
> With a competitive spirit that matches a stoked-up boiler factory, Ameche drew the spotlight in the annual West high school relays by setting a new shot put mark for Class A with a toss of 51 feet, ½ inches at the University of Wisconsin Fieldhouse.

Ameche also was a top-notch sprinter, posting a career best 10.2 seconds in the 100-yard dash in his junior year. He actually qualified for the state meet in Madison in 1950 as a sprinter but failed to place there.

"Alan could have been a great sprinter, but I don't know if he could have ever done better than that [10.2 seconds]," said track teammate Bonofiglio. "He was big guy, about 190 [pounds] at the time, so his starts weren't that great.

"Basically, to him, track was just something to do in the spring, rather than sit around. He always had to be doing something."

Ameche's only other incursion into the arena of sports was a short dalliance with boxing. At the age of fifteen, he entered the Kenosha Regional Golden Gloves Tournament, competing in the light heavyweight division. Registration was apparently on the low side in his division, but it got even lower when word spread that Ameche had signed up.

Every biography and short article ever written about Ameche tells the story of his Golden Gloves exploits to the point where it has become part fact, part urban legend. Bobby Hinds introduced Ameche to the sport and witnessed the story as it unfolded.

"There are a lot of stories about what happened in the Golden Gloves, but I was there and saw it," said Hinds, who was a Golden Gloves champion at 160 pounds and who later at Wisconsin fashioned a 32–0 record in dual meet bouts before injuries and illness forced him to give up the sweet science.

"There were two guys from Waukegan [Illinois] who were going to fight him in the Golden Gloves and they came down to the KYF [Kenosha Youth Foundation] where we were working out," Hinds recalled. "Now, Al was a southpaw, who was sparring with Kenny Johnson, who was the open light heavyweight champion at the time. Al was a novice, which meant that he hadn't had any [boxing matches] before.

"Al had a lot of natural ability in that his hands were so fast," Hinds said. "His hands were twice the speed of Kenny Johnson's. I remember Al throwing out a jab, but he wasn't that sophisticated.

"So instead of throwing his jab straight out, the hand kind of took a roundhouse sort of loop. So these guys from Waukegan are watching Al spar with Kenny and Al throws at jab at Kenny and misses him. But instead of going straight out and straight back, his hand kind of took that little detour, you know. So he misses with the jab but then comes back with his backhand and knocks Kenny out.

"Now, that isn't something you would recommend or show somebody to do. In fact, it's probably not legal. But the point is, he knocked Kenny out with a backhand. Think about that.

"These two guys from Waukegan saw him and the power he had and they left and never came back. That was it. The two guys were going to fight him, but when they saw him knock this guy out with a backhand, they said 'no way.' And it's a good thing they didn't come back because they would have got killed."

In later years, Ameche would joke about his successful, albeit extremely brief, boxing career. But Hinds thinks Ameche had unlimited potential had he chosen to pursue boxing as his primary sport.

"Well first, Al only got into boxing just because it was kind of the thing to do at the time," Hinds said. "It was a much bigger deal in those days than it is today.

"Al had such tremendous athletic ability, but for boxing it was kind of like when he was running with the football. He wasn't a guy you marveled at for his smoothness. Honestly, he looked uncoordinated whether it was boxing or football, but he did what he had to do, and he did it in a way that was better than anyone else.

"In boxing, he looked very awkward, but his hands were so fast and he had so much power that he could have gone places if he had wanted to. Obviously he had a lot of room for improvement—his hands weren't in the right position and he didn't punch straight out.

"He did just about everything wrong, but he could still beat you because he could overcome his shortcomings."

Hinds was at the Kenosha Eagles Club the night Ameche was scheduled to make his Golden Gloves debut.

"I'll tell you what. Al was nervous but he was anxious to fight and was disappointed when those guys didn't show up," Hinds said. "Al was fearless."

Years later, Ameche showed his sense of humor in relating his version of the story to *Parade* magazine writer Henry J. McCormick.

"I won on two byes and a forfeit," Ameche remembered. "I never lifted a glove, but they gave me a trophy. The secret of my boxing success was picking the right division."

4

Enter the Architect

B EFORE EVER SETTING FOOT IN THE STATELY GRAY stone building on
Sheridan Road that was then the home of Mary D. Bradford High
School, Alan (or Lino, as he was still called) Ameche was all about football.
The raw-boned fifteen-year-old sophomore probably had no idea what a dis-
aster the school's once-proud program had become in the fall of 1948, but it
probably wouldn't have mattered to him in the least.

His parents, Augusto and Elizabeth, knew nothing of this American game
of football and wanted their son Alan to have nothing to do with it. In their
world, school was about getting an education and achieving the American
Dream, a dream that so often in those days eluded first-generation immigrants to this country.

Although not a competitive athlete himself, Ameche's brother, Lynn, already a student at the University of Wisconsin, had seen firsthand the importance of football both in high school and on Saturday afternoons at Camp
Randall Stadium, the home of the Badgers football squad. So when his younger
brother told him that he could not play high school ball without a signed
parental permission slip, Lynn forged their father's signature on one.

As grateful as he was to his older brother, there were probably many days
when Alan wondered what his big brother had done to him. Kenosha football in 1948 was beyond terrible—it was a disaster. The varsity team was non-
competitive in the Big Eight Conference, which in those days was generally
considered the best conference in the state.

Wisconsin has never been considered a great football state, but the exception was the Big Eight, the shining star in the southeast corner of the state. At
this time, the league consisted of three Madison high schools (East, West,

and Central), two Racine schools (Horlick and Park), and the single high schools in Beloit, Janesville, and Kenosha.

The Big Eight was covered by the five cities' newspapers in the loop probably like no other high school conference in Wisconsin before or since. There was cooperation among the newspapers on Friday-night game coverage, advance game stories, and even a designated statistics keeper. It wasn't unusual for a story on the local high school team, usually written by the prolific sports editor Eddie McKenna, to appear in every fall edition of the *Kenosha Evening News*.

McKenna, although sometimes a master of hyperbole, found no fodder for sugar-coating what Kenosha's 1948 squad was about. In his 1949 season preview, McKenna had this to say about the previous season's squad: "A win over [Waukegan in season opener] the Illinois invader would pump new life and new interest in a club which floundered last season."

Waukegan, which is twenty miles south of Kenosha, in Illinois, was also Kenosha's season-opening opponent in 1948. The Red Devils managed to get on the scoreboard that night with their only touchdown of the season, but Waukegan helped start the Red Devils on their 0–8 nightmare.

There were precious few really shining moments in that 1948 season, but there were two bright spots. Three games into the season, Coach Jim Trebbin, desperate for offense, promoted three sophomores—Bonofiglio, Ameche, and Ronzia—to the varsity. The move didn't translate into instant offense for the hapless Red Devils, but it did help build a foundation for the future.

"It was pretty bad," said Bonofiglio. "Alan played a little bit as a sophomore, but I was just the back-up quarterback. Trebbin liked to play the seniors.

"But it wasn't like we were angry and said, 'Hey, we're going to transfer schools.' That may be the way things happen now, but it wasn't like that back then. We lived in Kenosha and that was where we going to play football, no matter what."

By all accounts, Trebbin was a good man and a nice person. What he wasn't, however, was a football coach.

"As a sophomore, we had the worst team in Bradford history," Bonofiglio said. "We scored one touchdown all year. *One lousy touchdown!* It was unbelievable.

"Jim Trebbin was a really nice man, but was he a football coach?"

Dick Nicolazzi saw the 1948 season from a slightly different vantage point. He was left behind on the sophomore squad after its two star players, future college all-Americans Ameche and Bonofiglio, were elevated to the varsity.

"I think we were undefeated in our first three games, with Alan and Mario still on the team," Nicolazzi said. "Then we pretty much fell apart after they left. We lost our best two players to the varsity, so it was tough after that."

There were rumblings in the community that Kenosha, which had won or shared six Big Eight titles since the league's inception in 1925, could do better. Kenosha had won outright titles in 1925, 1930, 1933, 1934, and 1945 and shared a title with Janesville in 1943. In the Big Eight's overall standings, published in the *Kenosha Evening News* just prior to the start of the 1949 season, only Beloit (87–54–16) had a better Big Eight record than Kenosha (84–54–18). Kenosha felt it could do better than it was doing under Trebbin. Much better.

Trebbin resigned after the 1948 season, and immediately a search was underway to find the right man to lead the Kenosha football team back from the depths. That man, Chuck Jaskwhich, was found in Buffalo, New York. Jaskwhich, who was born on March 4, 1911, to a Kenosha family of Polish immigrants, had the perfect pedigree to lead Kenosha back to football prominence.

The lanky yet sturdily built Jaskwhich was a John Wayne kind of figure. He was one of the greatest athletes Kenosha had ever produced. After graduating in 1929, Jaskwhich matriculated at Notre Dame, where he played quarterback for the Fighting Irish for three seasons. He also played varsity basketball.

In his first season at South Bend, Jaskwhich played for the legendary coach Knute Rockne. In 1930, a season in which Jaskwhich was the team's backup quarterback, the Fighting Irish were 10–0 and national champions. Jaskwhich played behind Frank Carideo, whom Rockne would later call the best quarterback he ever coached. Unfortunately, Jaskwhich never had the opportunity to play meaningful minutes for Rockne, who died in an airplane crash during that off-season.

Hunk Anderson replaced Rockne as head coach and installed Jaskwhich as his quarterback for the 1931 and 1932 seasons. The Irish were a very respectable 13–4–1 in the two-year Jaskwhich-Anderson era.

"A graduate of Notre Dame where he was an honor student, Jaskwhich as a sophomore was understudy to Frank Carideo at quarterback in the late Knute Rockne's last year in 1930 when the Irish won a national crown with an undefeated recorded," wrote McKenna.

"As a junior and senior, Jaskwhich was regular quarterback under 'Hunk' Anderson and was [the] high scorer of the Irish. With N.D., the Kenosha High

Alumnus was a deadly passer, tricky runner, a solid blocker and excelled in punting and kicking points after touchdowns. His main forte was the brilliance with which he engineered the plays in the long tradition of all brainy Irish quarterbacks."

His Notre Dame experience confirmed Jaskwhich as a "football man," and the end of his playing days only reinforced the importance of the game to him. Upon his graduation from Notre Dame, Jaskwhich accepted a coaching/teaching position at Holy Cross Preparatory School in New Orleans, where he won city championships in both basketball and football. From there he became the head basketball coach and football backfield coach at the University of Mississippi.

When World War II broke out, Jaskwhich enlisted in the U.S. Navy and was assigned to the Georgia Pre-Flight School. After the war and before returning to Kenosha, Jaskwhich had backfield coaching stints at the University of Iowa and with the Buffalo Bills of the short-lived (1946–49) All-American Football Conference (AAFC).

The imminent demise of the AAFC and the Bills, one of the teams that was absorbed into the NFL at that time, was perfect timing for the reunion of Kenosha and Jaskwhich. Kenosha desperately needed a program-building coach and Jaskwhich needed a job. The position of football coach/athletic director was offered, and Jaskwhich returned to his hometown.

"First of all, [Trebbin] was a nice guy, a very nice guy and I can't say anything bad about him," Nicolazzi said. "But he just wasn't in Chuck's league when it came to coaching football. It was like night and day.

"I don't know if [Kenosha's search committee] went out of its way to hire somebody who was knowledgeable in football, but Chuck was the first one in a long time in Kenosha. Number one, he was a football coach. That's why they hired him."

Like Nicolazzi, Bonofiglio wasn't certain what motivated the Kenosha powers-that-be at the time to seek out Jaskwhich, but he was certainly glad that they did.

"Half of these guys [Jaskwhich's predecessors at Kenosha High School] didn't even care about football," Bonofiglio said. "Chuck cared. Believe you me, he cared.

"Chuck was a very tough man and didn't put up with anything. We actually had a track coach who was out there smoking cigarettes on the job. Is that a coach? Can you believe that?

"Some of these guys didn't care, they just wanted a little extra money. Chuck was tough but he cared. The man loved football."

Ronzia believes that it was Jaskwhich's deep roots in Kenosha that brought him back to town.

"I don't believe Trebbin was fired, but Chuck Jaskwhich had quite a following in Kenosha from when he was an athlete," Ronzia said. "He was Polish and he was from the Northside, which is a Polish area, and he was a local hero. You're talking about a nine-letter guy in high school who went on to star at Notre Dame and coach in the pros.

"All I can say is thank God Chuck Jaskwhich came back. We went from the single wing to the T [formation], started passing more; there was more discipline. Plus we had a great group of guys who just happened to come along at the same time."

Braatz, who made his living evaluating talent and coaches at the highest level, has a more charitable view of Trebbin than most. But, then again, Braatz wasn't one of the few in that immensely talented Class of 1951 to have played football for the man.

"I played basketball for Jim Trebbin, and I thought he was your normal head coach," Braatz said. "Obviously, Chuck Jaskwhich had more of a background to be a football coach than Trebbin, but not many high school coaches had the résumé Chuck had. The other thing was Chuck was more demanding. If you had talent for the game, he was going to bring it out in you."

Certainly football talent was an abundant commodity at Kenosha High School in the classes of 1950, '51, and '52. But the class of 1951, which featured Ameche, Bonofiglio, Braatz, Nicolazzi, Hinds, Ruel McMullen, Ed Ronzia, and Frank Aiello, was the motherlode of talent for Kenosha. All except Braatz would go on to play at the University of Wisconsin in Madison. Braatz would buck the trend and play at Marquette University, which at that time fielded a very competitive Division I football program.

In their senior seasons at Kenosha High, Ameche and Bonofiglio were both first team all-staters. Only one other year, 1945, had two players from the same team been named first-team all-state in Wisconsin. Kenoshans Tom Bienneman and Joe Makarewicz, who would go on to play at Drake University, and Milwaukee Washington's Red Wilson and Lisle Blackbourn Jr., who would both play at Wisconsin, were the two all-state tandems that season.

McMullen, the team's center and punter, and Braatz, an end, would both be named to second team all-state in 1950. Teammate Vic Borowsky, a guard, would be named honorable mention.

As you might expect, Kenosha dominated Big Eight honors in 1950, as well. Of the eleven players named to the first team, six were Kenoshans—

Ameche, Bonofiglio, McMullen, Ronzia (tackle), Borowsky, and Braatz. Aiello, an end, Nicolazzi and guard Stan Demske were named to the second team.

Juniors Ray DeLaat (tackle) and halfbacks Ron Rudy and Bob Girman also received votes, as did fullback Hinds, who was injured most of the season.

It can't be denied that Jaskwhich inherited a ridiculous amount of talent, but some would say it was there all along and Jaskwhich just knew how to mine it. Certainly the truth lies somewhere in the middle.

"The timing was perfect, there is no question about that," said Hinds, an entrepreneur who stayed in Madison after his years at the University of Wisconsin. "Chuck was definitely fortunate to have all the pieces in place when he came back to Kenosha.

"I mean how many coaches come into a situation where they have two future all-Americans in Ameche and Bonofiglio, one of them who went on to win the Heisman, and another future NFL player in Braatz. Plus, we had Ruel McMullen, one of the greatest punters who ever lived and fantastic bunch of players like Nicolazzi and Ed Ronzia.

"We hadn't won a game and didn't score a point in the Big Eight the year before Chuck Jaskwhich got here. So when he came back to Kenosha, he was a bit of fresh air. He was a legend and a great coach with a long history of success.

"We scored the most points in the state as seniors. We were about as dominant as you can get. Let's be honest, the timing couldn't have been more fortunate for Kenosha and for Chuck Jaskwhich."

Good timing or not, the relatively short time that Jaskwhich needed to transform the Kenosha High School program from doormat status to one of the all-time great prep teams ever assembled is nothing short of amazing.

"When you think of it, it really was unbelievable," Bonofiglio said. "We went from scoring one touchdown as sophomores to averaging 49 points a game as seniors. And we were doing it in the best conference in the state, which at the time, was the Big Eight."

Braatz's status as a former general manager of two NFL franchises and director of scouting for a third (the Miami Dolphins) gives him a unique perspective for judging the ascendency of his old high school program.

"I don't think something like that could happen in professional football, to be honest," said Braatz, who is retired and living in Florida. "But I suppose you could see something like that happening in college, going from worst to best in a couple years, but only very rarely.

"I guess I was fortunate that I don't remember [Kenosha] being very bad, because I didn't play varsity till my junior season. I only remember us being a good team."

As well as Jaskwhich handled the football side of coaching, he was at least as adept when to it came to handling his players. To outsiders he could come across as being a bit gruff, but his players knew to a man that Jaskwhich was a classic players' coach. Maybe it was the fact that he was a Kenosha native himself and knew that most of the kids on his team came from underprivileged backgrounds, but he definitely knew how to relate.

"Before Chuck came back to Kenosha, we had old leather helmets that folded up like pancakes," said Nicolazzi, who was later a football coach and school administrator at, among other places, West Allis (Wisconsin) Central High School. "I remember walking from the high school to Lakefront Stadium with our helmets tucked inside our pants.

"We had old-fashioned wool shirts instead of the nice jerseys. He knew we were all poor kids and where we came from.

"But Chuck came in and he got the new plastic helmets which were just coming into style at that time. He got us new pants and nice new jerseys, too. I don't know where he got the money to buy all new uniforms, but he got it.

"When you give new uniforms to kids like we were, and we were basically poor Depression kids, it just makes such an impression on you. It makes you think the guy really cares about you, that he's on our side and that he's going to do something for you.

"You want to play hard for a guy like that, and we played as hard for Chuck Jaskwhich as we could; there is no question about that."

Braatz, who played for and worked for and with some of the greatest coaches of all time, such as Lisle Blackbourn at Marquette and Don Shula with the Miami Dolphins, had a very interesting relationship with Jaskwhich. Braatz said Jaskwhich was one of the most influential people in his life.

"Chuck was a huge influence in my life," Braatz related. "I had some uncles who took me fishing, but Chuck Jaskwhich helped more than anyone. He was really the first father image I had in my life after my real father died. He was a mentor. There's no question.

"If there is one thing I learned from Chuck it was to finish. Just finish what you do, whether it's finishing a block, you put the man on the ground. If it's running a pass route, you run it at full speed even if you're not involved in the play. I think the word 'finish' more than anything else summarizes what Chuck Jaskwhich's philosophy was all about."

No player had a closer relationship with Jaskwhich than Bonofiglio, his star pupil as the team's quarterback. Bonofiglio, whose best attribute may have been his slick ballhandling, was the perfect player to run Jaskwhich's offense of choice, the T formation, made famous by George Halas and the Chicago Bears in the 1930s.

Bonofiglio, who is often described as "clever," kept opponents off balance and guessing with his variety of handoffs, pitchouts, fakes, and short passes out of the T formation, which was an early version of the full house and wishbone run-oriented offenses.

"I had a great relationship with Chuck and Alan had a great relationship with Chuck," said Bonofiglio, who has lived his entire life in Kenosha. "When you played for Chuck, you were his best friend as long as you listened to Chuck because Chuck was the boss and there was no disputing that. We had a great relationship because I just kept my mouth shut and did what he said, and I became a better player for the experience.

"Chuck was not only the toughest coach I played for, he was the best coach I played for," said Bonofiglio, who played two years at Wisconsin before transferring to the University of Miami, where he achieved all-American status. "Chuck didn't take anything from anybody. If he told you to do something, you did it, no nonsense.

"If we made a mistake he'd keep us out there in the dark [at practice at Lakefront Stadium]. He'd tell us right out, 'You guys aren't going home until you get it right.' There were a couple times when he had us out there in the dark and he even turned the lights on a few times."

Bonofiglio claims that while there was a huge respect for Jaskwhich from his players, there was also a fear factor involved. Bonofiglio had an interesting answer when asked to describe Jaskwhich's personality.

"Personality? He had no personality. You walked by him, you kept your mouth shut. We were all scared to death of him.

"He was like your dad, only he hollered more than your dad. We all loved playing for Chuck. But if we weren't doing that good in a game, maybe we were beating a team by three touchdowns but we weren't playing that well, Chuck would hit the lockers and yell at us at halftime. We were scared to death of the man."

Not much was ever written about Ameche's relationship with Jaskwhich because that was not the modus operandi of sports journalists of that era. Sports writers didn't use direct quotes from high school football coaches, let alone from seventeen-year-old players.

It is doubtful that Eddie McKenna and Alan Ameche ever had a conversation about Jaskwhich for publication in the *Kenosha Evening News*, so any comments Ameche had about his high school coach came later in life.

"I know Al respected Chuck a lot," said Nicolazzi, when asked about the relationship between their coach and star player. "And Al and Mario had their picture taken with Chuck a lot for the newspaper."

Perhaps the only published comment Ameche ever made about Jaskwhich was in a *Wisconsin State Journal* story by Tom Butler published in 1975. Even at that, it was only an indirect reference.

"I think I was very fortunate to have the coaches and teammates I had in high school," Ameche said. "I learned as many fundamental things there as I did in college."

It's clear that every player on those early Kenosha High School teams respected Jaskwhich, but Nicolazzi took it a step farther.

"Chuck Jaskwhich is my hero to this day," Nicolazzi said. "I loved the man.

"Chuck did for Kenosha what nobody else has ever done. He brought us back. Before he got there, Kenosha football was terrible, but Chuck came in and turned things around.

"He knew his football, there is no question about that. And he was a stickler for details. We would run the same play in practice thirty-five times in a row if we didn't get it right. He'd make us run till we did it the right way, his way.

"He made us work, but we responded. We ran the table our senior years, something that had never been done before in Kenosha."

But Nicolazzi's respect for Jaskwhich goes much deeper than Jaskwhich's on-field expertise. As anyone who ever played for Jaskwhich knows, his relationships and responsibilities with his players didn't end when the season was over.

"I know for a fact that the only reason I got an offer from Madison [scholarship from the University of Wisconsin] was because of Chuck," Nicolazzi said. "He recommended me, told the coaches up there that it was a good move for them to offer me.

"I had offers to go to Mississippi and Temple, but he got a whole group of us into Madison. I screwed up when I was in Madison, but I graduated and eventually I got my master's degree from Madison.

"As far as I'm concerned, Chuck is my hero. There weren't many heroes in those days. We didn't know anything about the pros or colleges back then.

"Everything that I did in my life, he was my starter. I can't say enough about that man."

Braatz agrees with Nicolazzi that Jaskwhich played a big behind-the-scenes role in helping him after he was finished playing.

"You know, I don't know if Marquette would have offered me [a scholarship] if it hadn't been for Chuck," Braatz said. "I know he went out of his way to help me with the coaches at Marquette."

Added Bonofiglio on Jaskwhich's wrangling on behalf of his players: "We had seven kids get scholarships to Wisconsin. That's unheard of. You better believe Chuck had everything to do with them taking all of us."

Ronzia agrees that Jaskwhich took the player-coach relationship far beyond the playing field.

"I owe it all to Chuck Jaskwhich. We wouldn't have had the success we had. Jim Trebbin was a great guy and stayed around Kenosha for years with the Recreation Department, but Chuck was a guy who coached the pros. He did things for us kids that we will probably never know."

Perhaps Hinds sums up the Chuck Jaskwhich era best.

"Chuck was just an inspiration to all us kids back then. It all came together under him. When he came back [to Kenosha], it was just one of those moments, kind of like when [Vince] Lombardi went to Green Bay."

Jaskwhich finished his coaching career in Kenosha. He passed away January 12, 1988, just seven months before his greatest player, Ameche, would die.

5

Transitioning to Greatness

CHUCK JASKWHICH WENT INTO HIS NEW JOB well aware of what was expected of him. He knew from his playing days in the late 1920s that the city of Kenosha was a football town, and he knew the citizenry was salivating for a winner.

In 1949 high school football was literally the only game in town. Sure, there were the Packers and the Bears, but the only information fans had about the NFL was gleaned from grainy photos and sketchy write-ups in their local newspapers.

It was the same story for college football. The only way anyone would know Wisconsin's colors were cardinal and white would be if they had actually attended a game in person. In 1949 television sets were luxury items even for the very rich, and there were no black-and-white, let alone color, football telecasts to speak of on the small screens.

Kenosha had two things going for it that some of the other cities in the Big Eight didn't have. First, Kenosha had a huge immigrant population of Italians, Poles, Germans, and Irish who settled there in the early years of the twentieth century because of the city's wealth of manufacturing jobs at such factories as Simmons, Nash Motors, and American Brass. Football's brutal and uncomplicated nature provided a natural proving ground for the aspiring young Americans.

Kenosha's other asset was Lakefront Stadium. Built literally ten feet from the concrete breakers of the Lake Michigan shoreline in downtown Kenosha, Lakefront Stadium was a palace by high school standards. It had actually been home to an NFL franchise, the Kenosha Maroons, for five games in

1924. The team didn't finish its season, folding due to financial problems after going 0–4–1 in its five games.

But the Maroons—who were originally from Toledo, Ohio, and had been purchased by the City of Kenosha and sponsored by Simmons and Nash— were nice enough to leave their stadium behind. (The site is actually underwater now, torn down and dredged to make way for a pleasure-boat marina in the 1980s.) With its ornate front gate, oversized press box, and ample bleachers, the stadium was a palace by 1949 high school football standards.

But when the winds kicked up off the lake, it was an ice palace. It was a high school venue that could accommodate standing-room-only crowds of over 7,000 fans. It's doubtful there were that many in attendance to witness Jaskwhich's Kenosha debut on September 16, 1949, against Waukegan, but a good-sized crowd was on hand. They came there not knowing what to expect from the new coach and his players, who had never experienced the thrill of victory at the varsity level. What they saw was a 27–6 victory over the "Illinois invader," as McKenna called them, and Jaskwhich's exit from the field on the shoulders of his players.

"Chuck Jaskwhich, home town favorite, making the bow as coach at his alma mater where he was a great three sports star before excelling at Notre Dame, was carried off the field on the shoulders of the husky horde of Red Raiders after the game," wrote McKenna in the *Kenosha Evening News*.

"That spontaneous demonstration of jubilation reflects the new spirit that has been born during the brief time Jaskwhich has been at the helm. While the Big Eight conference schedule will be fraught with rugged assignments, there can be no doubt that the Reds will be a battling club each time out."

Carrying the coach off the field might seem a bit over the top for a victory over a nonconference opponent in the season opener, but it wasn't overkill for this group. It was the program's first victory in 10 games, dating back to October 31, 1947, when Kenosha beat Janesville, 34–0. Add that to the fact that the team had just spent three weeks preparing under the scorching late summer sun, under the critical eye of their perfectionist coach, a man they had no reason to have anything but blind faith in.

Jaskwhich had said before the season that he had no idea how long it would take to adjust to his T-formation offense, but he did know this much.

"There is a lot of rough work ahead," Jaskwhich said before the team's first practice. "I don't know how the team will function when we take the field, but I know the players will be finally conditioned physically and mentally. They will know all their plays and they will be poised for the opening kickoff."

With newly elected senior captain, Bob Carbone, at quarterback, the Red Devils were indeed well prepared for Waukegan. The steady Carbone completed three of six pass attempts in the contest, including a 14-yard touchdown strike to Keith Lindstedt, but it was obvious, even at that point, that Bonofiglio was going to challenge for the quarterback spot. The slick junior completed two of six attempts, both of them for 20-yard touchdowns to Lindstedt and Gene Fitch.

The workhorse of the contest was left halfback Ameche, who carried ten times for 44 yards. Jaskwhich was generous in his praise after the game, perhaps buoyed by his unexpected victory ride, but wasn't quite so magnanimous by Monday.

"Coach Chuck Jaskwhich said he was pleased with many phases of the Reds' style of play against Waukegan but also pointed out several weaknesses that were apparent and that these would be polished in practice this week," wrote McKenna in the newspaper.

In the opening week of the season, Big Eight teams went 7–1 against top-flight competition, with powerful Madison East, the league's only casualty, losing to perennial Illinois powerhouse, Evanston, 38–6, in the tune-up week. Kenosha would open conference play the following Friday at Janesville, which was a 30–7 winner over Beaver Dam in its opener. Jaskwhich declared that overconfidence wouldn't be a factor, with Janesville, two-time defending champion Beloit, and Madison East on Kenosha's schedule for the first three weeks of the conference season.

If there was any overconfidence in the Red Devils, they had it beaten out of them by the battling Bluebirds that Friday night at Monterey Stadium in Janesville. Despite a 95-yard kickoff return for a touchdown by Ameche, Janesville whipped the visitors, 32–19.

Bonofiglio threw a 20-yard touchdown to Lindstedt, to gain a leg up on Carbone in the by-now hotly contested quarterback competition, and Ameche added a 5-yard touchdown run for Kenosha's other points. Bonofiglio's kicking continued to be erratic, missing two of three extra-point attempts.

Things were not to get any easier for the Red Devils with two-time defending conference champion Beloit scheduled to visit Lakefront for homecoming in the third week of the season. Beloit had been roughed up by Madison East, 13–7, in its league opener, but in its season opener, the Purple Knights held Fond du Lac to -5 yards rushing in scoring a 14–6 victory.

Kenosha's last victory over Beloit had been in 1945, and the rivalry between the two state-line schools always had an unspoken undertone. Beloit, which was the only school in the conference at that time to have more than a token

African American population, was led by speedy track stars, Leon and Shelvy Bandy.

In his preview leading up to the contest, McKenna referred to the Bandys as "Negro track stars and backfield operators." Shelvy Bandy was the defending conference scoring champion and the Beloit-Kenosha contest was billed a showdown between the power running of Ameche against the sprint team of the Bandys.

As it turned out, it was no contest. The Bandys "danced through and around the Kenosha defense with the grace of ballet experts, each notching one touchdown," according to McKenna's account. "The Bandys, with their speedy spurts, paralyzed the Kenosha defense which might just as well have been trying to bottle up lightning as pursue the excursions of the elusive sepia shaded sprinters."

Shelvy carried 16 times for 134 yards and a 14-yard touchdown run, while Leon had 13 carries for 111 yards and a 10-yard score. In front of the homecoming crowd, estimated at around 6,000, Ameche was kept out of the end zone, rushing eight times for 45 yards.

Carbone continued to get the starting call at quarterback, but again it was apparent that Bonofiglio was gaining ground on the senior. Bonofiglio completed two of seven pass attempts, but the completions were for touchdowns to Lindstedt of 41 and 9 yards. Carbone was one of five for 8 yards.

Unfortunately for Carbone, it was his last start at quarterback. The following week at league coleader Madison East, Jaskwhich opened the game with Bonofiglio at quarterback, and when the junior engineered a touchdown drive that put Kenosha ahead early in the first quarter, it appeared to be a great move. Ameche's 1-yard touchdown plunge and the extra-point conversion by Bonofiglio staked the Kenoshans to a 7–0 lead.

But Madison East's powerful offense couldn't be stopped on this evening. Wendell Gulseth, who would later be a major player at the University of Wisconsin, passed for 134 yards, compared to Kenosha's 58, and East outrushed the Red Devils, 218–113 on the night en route to a 14–7 victory. Hinds was injured in the contest, but after he spent the night in a Madison hospital for observation, it was determined he was only badly bruised and was allowed to return to Kenosha.

Two things came out of Kenosha's loss at Madison East. First, it showed that despite their 1–3 record, the young Red Devils were nobody's easy mark. Although the eventual conference champion, East, would have a big edge in yardage that night, the Kenoshans moved the ball easily, piling up a 15–11 advantage in first downs.

In a sense, Carbone was a victim of injuries and the team's front-loaded schedule. When the season was over, it was clear that Kenosha's first three league opponents—Janesville, Beloit, and Madison East—were the best the league had to offer.

And despite the team's solid depth, injuries to end Aiello, linebacker/center McMullen, and tackle Fred Pauloni slowed the team's development. But with the 0–3 start in the league, it was clear that Jaskwhich was looking ahead to better things the next year with his vote of confidence in his junior quarterback.

It was a decision he would never regret, as Kenosha won its final four games of the season to finish at 4–3 in the Big Eight and 5–3 overall.

"After we lost the three games, I was lucky enough to start the rest of them," Bonofiglio would later say. "I don't know if that was the difference or not, but I'd hate to say anything like that because Bob Carbone was the team's captain and a nice guy.

"We didn't start well on the season, but once we started winning, that was it. We just knew we were going to win after that. No doubt about it."

Nicolazzi feels that the installation of Bonofiglio as starter was a clear-cut turning point in not only the 1949 season but also for the entire program.

"When Mario took over as the starting quarterback, things turned around," Nicolazzi said. "That guy was just an athlete and a half. He could do everything. His senior year the guy won letters in football, basketball and track and golf in the spring.

"When he came in, you could see the momentum building. We started scoring points, which was something new for Kenosha."

Braatz, who was on the receiving end of many of Bonofiglio's passes, especially in their senior year, proved to a great enough evaluator of talent to make a living in that field in later life. He had this to say about Bonofiglio: "Mario was just such a clever quarterback. I think 'clever' is the word most everybody uses to describe him. He was such a great ballhandler. . . . He could fake it, keep it, run with it and he was a great passer.

"Not that Alan needed any help, but I'm sure having a great quarterback like Mario in the same backfield, made things easier for Alan, too."

Hinds, who was Bonofiglio's teammate at Wisconsin as well as Kenosha High, is the most effusive in his praise.

"We had Mario Bonofiglio who I feel was the greatest f****** quarterback who ever lived," Hinds said. "He could pass, he could kick, he could handle the ball, he could lead."

Even McKenna had high praise for Bonofiglio. In a feature story the following year regarding Bonofiglio's relationship with Jaskwhich, McKenna opined:

> Jaskwhich has thoroughly schooled his quarterback Mario Bonofiglio in all the intricacies of the T formation. An apt pupil with a lot of natural athletic skill and "know-how," Bonofiglio does everything but collect tickets at the gate. Besides calling the signals, he kicks off, punts, boots the points for conversions, hurls aerials with consistency and can lay a hard block and tackle as well as break away for runs with speed and shiftiness.
>
> Mario picked up a lot of agility as a clever basketball purveyor, being a smooth floor operator on setting up plays as well as an accurate shotmaker. In baseball, he batted .424 for a high spot in the Southeastern Wisconsin circuit last season as a member of the last place United Cleaners team. His aggressiveness and trigger savvy, under a master tactician like Jaskwhich should develop Bonofiglio into one of the stick out stars of the league this season.
>
> Mario has all the attributes of a natural leader with unruffled poise under fire in "clutch" situations. He has been hailed by his teammates as a "team competitor" and on that qualification he earned their votes for the captaincy role.

Despite playing "their greatest game of the season against rugged East at Madison," according to McKenna, the Red Devils were still rated as underdogs against Racine Park (1–1–1 in conference) the following week. Likening the Kenosha-Racine rivalry to the "Hatfields and Coys" [sic], McKenna expected a crowd of 6,000 at Lakefront for the game.

McKenna noted that the Kenosha-Park series couldn't have been any more even, with both teams having won seven times, lost seven, and tied seven. Incredibly, the overall point total was nearly the same, with Kenosha outscoring Park, 157–154, in the 21-game series.

It is likely that the Red Devils were more worried about the 11-game conference losing streak, dating back three seasons. With Pauloni and McMullen expected to return to the lineup after missing a collective five games, this could be the night they would break it.

Not only would it be Kenosha's night, the Red Devils would take out two years of Big Eight frustrations on the visitors from Racine. Ameche scored on an 84-yard kickoff return and short plunge as Kenosha handed Park a 40–6 loss, the Racine school's worst defeat in 173 games, since the school began playing football in 1928.

More important to the Red Devils and the large Lakefront Stadium crowd that supported them, it was Kenosha's first Big Eight Conference victory since October 31, 1947, when it defeated Janesville. Still, McKenna, covering the contest, didn't seem convinced in his report in the October 15, 1949, edition of the *Kenosha Evening News*.

He described the crowd the night before as "bewildered" by Kenosha's dominating performance. "The law of averages finally swung to the Reds' side. They are justly jubilant after having entered the winner's circle for league affiliates after such a long trial on the detour of heartbreaks.

"Coach Chuck Jaskwhich had his charges keyed up like a janitor in a 22 story apartment building. They unreeled alert, aggressive, 'know how' ball all the route, forcing the breaks and outclassing a Park foe that was stampeded into confusion and then became completely demoralized under the second half scoring scourge."

McKenna went on to say, "Everybody was a hero in Friday night's rampant march goalward," but he singled out Ameche "whose speedy hulk struck terror in the Park team every time he lugged the oval." Ameche carried nine times for 66 yards in the contest.

Bonofiglio, who McKenna said "was tossing passes with the deadliness of a Bogart pistol," completed two of three pass attempts for 41 yards, including a 31-yard strike to Fitch. Bonofiglio also converted three point-after touchdown kicks and ran for a two-point conversion on a botched snap.

Ameche's two touchdowns against Park vaulted him into a three-way tie for the conference scoring title four weeks into the season. Ameche, Charles Scheid of Janesville, and Joe Castagna of Madison East all had 30 points on five touchdowns through four games.

"It seems like old times to have names of Kenosha players included in the scoring column, especially after last season's offensive drought," wrote McKenna, almost wistfully.

The Red Devils demonstrated again the following week that they were a legitimately improved squad when they shut out Horlick, 26–0, scoring in every quarter in a steady rain on Racine's north side. Jaskwhich unveiled a new pass play in this contest in which Bonofiglio would fake a run right then pass back to his left. The play worked to perfection for a 29-yard touchdown on a fourth-down play in the third quarter.

Ameche had one touchdown in the contest, a 2-yard plunge in the second period, as Kenosha evened its record at 3–3, 2–3 in the Big Eight. With third-place Madison Central (3–1–1) next on the agenda, the Red Devils would have another chance to prove themselves.

That night belonged to the emerging star Ameche, who scored on runs of 67 yards in the first period and 37 yards in the third period. Fullback Frank Conley, who was becoming a reliable counter to Ameche in the backfield, scored the third touchdown as Kenosha registered a 19–0 victory at Breese Stevens Field in Madison while evening its league record at 3–3.

Ameche, who doubled as a part-time linebacker for the Red Devils, set up both of Kenosha's third-period touchdowns. He set up Conley's touchdown when he returned the opening kickoff of the second half to midfield. Then, with Ameche pounding the ball inside, the Red Devils racked up four first downs, and Conley carried in from the 3.

The final touchdown was set up by Ameche's interception at the Kenosha 46. After a 9-yard first-down run, Ameche blasted through the right side of his line for the 37-yard score. Coincidentally, the head official in Madison that night was George Lanphear, Wisconsin's freshman football coach and the man generally credited with dubbing Ameche "the Horse."

Kenosha's third straight victory and second consecutive shutout made a huge impression on Madison *Capital Times* sports writer, Lew Cornelius, who had this to say about the Red Devils and Ameche after the Central game:

> Quite a ball carrier—we got a glimpse of Alan Ameche, Kenosha's 16-year-old left halfback Saturday night in Kenosha's 19–0 victory over Central. All Ameche did was tear the Downtowners' defense apart for an average of 16.7 yards for each of his 10 tries. His total of 167 yards was 46 more than the entire Central back field could rack up.
>
> Ameche is a junior, stands over six feet tall and weighs close to 190 pounds [. . .] and brother is he fast. Once into the secondary there won't be many times he's dragged down. He explodes when he hits the scrimmage line—at least Saturday night. For my vote he's the best back in the conference.
>
> The Kenosha Squad is a gang of well built, good balanced lads and they are going to be hard to hold down from here on out.
>
> The Kenosha dressing room Saturday night sounded as though the Red Raiders had won a championship instead of just another ball game. The club is loaded with juniors and sophomores and with its big manpower advantage should cut the capers almost every campaign in the Big Eight football title chase.
>
> Coach "Gus" Pollack of Central thinks Kenosha is the best team in the Big Eight right now. His two assistants, Bob Alwin and Harold Rooney were agreeing with him Saturday night.

Ameche's two touchdowns against Central gave him 48 points for the season and the league's individual scoring lead heading into the season's final week. Kenosha's final game of the season would be Dad's Night at Lakefront Stadium against Madison West.

As if the Red Devils didn't have enough emotion on their side, there was also the little matter of what the Regents had done to them the previous season: West had piled the points on the hapless Kenoshans, 52–0. There were 17 Kenosha lettermen—James Le Sota, John Fox, Aldo Gentile, Fred Pauloni, Ed Ronzia, Keith Lindstedt, Bill Bowman, Bob Carbone, Mario Bonofiglio, John Schmitz, Bill Girman, Gene Fitch, Glen Thompson, Frank Conley, Ruel McMullen, Neal Rusecki, and Alan Ameche—all of whom harbored ill will toward the Regents for the prior beating.

On a miserably cold, windy, early November Wednesday night, the Red Devils would not only avenge that loss, they would use it as a stepping off point for the incredible season that would follow. With their fathers sitting on sideline benches and displaying large cardboard cutouts with their sons' numbers, the Red Devils pounded the Regents 21–0 in a game that was much more lopsided than the final score would indicate.

Ameche would nail down the conference's individual scoring title with touchdown runs of 49 yards and 1 yard. He would finish the season with 60 points on 10 touchdowns, 6 points better than Beloit's Shelvy Bandy, who leapfrogged into second place with four touchdowns against Janesville in his season finale.

For the night, Ameche would grind out 68 yards in 16 carries, slipping and sliding on the fresh snow that blanketed the Lakefront turf.

Senior captain Bob Carbone, the forgotten man after losing the quarterback job to Bonofiglio midway through the season, would provide the feel-good story of the night, scoring the game's first touchdown on a short quarterback sneak. Jaskwhich saw to it that Carbone saw plenty of time at quarterback, and he led the team in passing, completing three of six for 53 yards in his final high school game.

Kenosha outgained its visitors from Madison in total yardage, 229–82, and in first downs, 9–5. The game ended on an Ameche run to the Regents' 1-yard line.

McKenna, the team's chronicler for at least the home portion of its season, summed up the finale this way:

> The win achieved on a field left slippery by a light covering of snow that made the going risky and fumbles numerous due to the numbing effect of the arctic blasts, was the fourth in succession.

So the large swarm of loyal Kenosha cohorts were justified as they emitted loud hosannas in the victory celebration. They were jubilant over the season just closed but gleeful in their anticipation of further improved things to come in 1950.

Coach Chuck Jaskwhich has rounded out his first campaign at the helm with an overall record of five victories against three rebukes. He fashioned a lineup that settled for a third place tied in the Big Eight Conference with Janesville.

That accomplishment goes into the books as tremendous; last season the Reds failed to win a game in eight starts—seven in the circuit—for the cellar berth.

As expected, Kenosha was well rewarded for its late-season push when it came to handing out postseason honors. A panel of writers including McKenna, Cornelius, and Monte McCormick of Madison, George Raubacher of Janesville, Keith Brehm of Racine, and Frank Reichstein of Beloit chose Jaskwhich the league's coach of the year in his rookie season. They also chose Ameche as the league's top back and recommended him as one of four players for the Associated Press's all-state squad.

Ameche and guard Aldo Gentile were named first-team all conference while Lindstedt, Ronzia, McMullen, and Conley all earned honorable mention. Regarding Ameche, McKenna wrote: "With durable legs that churned, Ameche operated with the abandon of a light tank in open country. A rugged player, he was the type who absorbed punishment without succumbing to injuries. The rougher the milling, the harder he could pour it on. He was a marked man early in the season, but he was equal to the rock and sock battle the opposition threw his way."

Regarding Jaskwhich, McKenna was equally effusive in his praise: "With most of the same talent that failed to win a league game here over a stretch of 11 covering 1947 and 1948 and three games this season, he maneuvered the Reds into a third place tie with Janesville on four wins and three defeats; his overall rating was five and three. The amazing way he converted several of last year's players on the bottom place team into outstanding performers this fall reflects his ability and teaching technique.

"Always with a winner during his prep and college days as a player and a coach, Jaskwhich instilled plenty of spirit and 'know how' into the Reds, and the results vividly portray his 1949 success story."

Apparently, McKenna changed his mind about the team as well. He seemed very skeptical of their progress during the course of the season.

Coaches and writers freely admitted that Kenosha was the "hottest" ball game [sic] of them all as the campaign closed. Well grounded in fundamentals,

Kenosha rated as one of the best coached teams here in recent campaigns. Gaining experience with each succeeding game, the Reds gained poise and class, smartness and the respect of all coaches and rivals.

The irony was in the schedule making that sent the inexperienced Reds—at the outset—against the three pre-season favorites, Janesville, Beloit and Madison East. As it turned out, Kenosha tied Janesville for third place, while East took the crown and Beloit was runner-up.

Had these teams been sprinkled along the schedule with the other contenders, Kenosha could very well have been champion. As it was, the Reds gave East their hardest battle, losing only, 14–7, at Madison. That was the turning point for Jaskwhich's charges as they swept to successive wins over Racine Park, Racine Horlick, Madison Central and Madison West, previous to the East loss. Kenosha yielded to Janesville and Beloit after checking Waukegan in a non-conference opener.

At the team banquet, for which Lloyd Larson, the *Milwaukee Sentinel* sports editor, was the guest speaker, Ameche was announced as the team's most valuable player, and Bonofiglio was named the team captain for 1950. It was also announced that Ameche had somehow barely missed being named to Associated Press's all-state squad.

Perhaps Nicolazzi summed up the 1949 season best: "I wish for those seniors [in 1949] that Chuck had come a year earlier. I think if he had had two years to work with them, they would have a pretty darn good team."

6

The Best There Ever Was?

EVERYBODY LOVES A WINNER and Kenosha High School had itself a winner of epic proportions in the fall of 1950. They didn't just beat the other teams in the Big Eight, Wisconsin's toughest football conference—they annihilated them. Kenosha had one competitive game all season, an 18–13 victory over Madison East, and won its other seven games by a combined total of 343–48.

Undefeated Kenosha (8–0) averaged 45.1 points per game to its opponents' 7.6 points. The only reason the disparity wasn't wider was because Jaskwich refused to run up scores on his opponents, limiting his starters to action in the first and third quarters in all but the Madison East contest.

"We would never play in the second half," said Bonofiglio, the team's captain and quarterback of Kenosha's starters. "That's the way Chuck wanted it. We could have scored points all night, but that's not the way Chuck was."

Not only did the team draw standing-room-only crowds in excess of 5,000 for the home games with Horlick, Madison Central, Madison East, and Janesville, but a loyal cadre of 2,000–3,000 Kenoshans followed their team in road games to Fond du Lac, Beloit, Racine Park, and Madison West.

The players on the team were rock stars in Kenosha before there was such a thing as rock stars. The team's fullback, Bobby Hinds, remembers what it was like.

"After the games, I'd walk downtown near Walgreens where there was a shoe store, and every time I'd walk by, there was this guy, I guess he was the owner, and he'd say, 'Hey, what a great game.'

"After one of the games I walk by and he says, 'Come on in. I want you to pick out any pair of shoes in the store.' Mind you, I was a poor kid. If I

55

changed socks once a month that would have been usual. I just walked quick to keep the snow away.

"So he says, 'Walk over and pick out the best pair of shoes in the place.' So I go over to the rack and pick out some nice pigskin shoes. He said, 'Oh, my God. You have great taste. Those are the best shoes in the place. That is the most expensive pair I have in my store.'

"So I said, 'Well, thank you very much. That's very nice of you, but I have a question. Why do you keep calling me Al?'

"He said, 'You're Alan Ameche, right?' I said, 'Well no, I'm Bobby Hinds' and he said, 'Holy Christ, I thought you were Alan Ameche.'

"So I said to him, 'Do you want the shoes back?' because I had them on already with my dirty socks and everything.

"He said, 'No. You keep them.' So I got a new pair of shoes. But I'll never forget the look on his face when I told him I wasn't Alan Ameche. But that's the way it was that year, Kenosha couldn't do enough for us. It was an amazing time."

There aren't many high school teams that send almost its entire starting squad to play Division I college football, but the 1950 Kenosha High School team did just that. In addition to the seven players who went to Wisconsin, and Braatz, who went to Marquette, there were three juniors who matriculated to college the following year. End Paul Shwaiko, a midterm graduate, followed the group that went to Wisconsin, and juniors Bob Girman and Ron Rudy eventually followed Braatz to Marquette.

"I don't know if we were the best ever in Wisconsin, but we certainly could have been," said Braatz. "I don't know that much about rating teams. I can rate players better than teams.

"But I do know we had a very deep squad and by that I mean the second-team players were very good. If a starter got hurt, somebody else could step in and play at a high level. I think the depth of that team was something that was never really recognized.

"The other thing was the closeness of the team. I believe that's the reason the team was so successful. The only speed we had was Ameche, but everybody pulled his weight and played as a team."

Through six weeks of the seven-week Big Eight schedule, the Red Devils had surpassed the league's all-time scoring mark of 252 points, set by a Kenosha team in 1930, by 7 points. In their final game of the season, they added another 57 against Madison West to finish with 316 league points (361 including the season opening nonconference victory over Fond du Lac). In conference games, Kenosha averaged 45.1 points while allowing just 6.7 points.

If the 1950 Kenosha Red Devils aren't the greatest Wisconsin schoolboy football team of all time, they are certainly near the top of the list. Certainly the sports writers of that era thought that to be true. The strongest endorsement of the Kenosha team was written by *Wisconsin State Journal* sports writer Monte McCormick:

There are logical reasons why [the Kenosha High School football team] should be rated the best in the 26-year history of the Big Eight. It amassed 316 points in its seven conference games which is some 63 points more than any other member school ever accumulated.

The previous record was set by a Kenosha club that did not win the title but must be claimed with the fine elevens of the circuit. Kenosha's star back, Alan Ameche, set an all-time individual record of 108 points by scoring four touchdowns in his team's 57–7 trouncing of Madison West Thursday night. Those 108 points are 11 more than the previous high of 97 that was accumulated by another great running back, Jack Gilmore of Beloit in 1936.

Kenosha was forced to the limit in only one game this fall that was its 18–13 victory over East. It scored at least 45 points on every other opponent, including Fond du Lac of the Fox Valley conference, except Racine Park and ran up only 37 in that tussle.

It was the first Kenosha eleven to complete a perfect record season since the start of the conference in 1925. There have been other Red Devils clubs that have been undefeated in the Big Eight but their records either were marred by ties in the conference or defeats outside the league. When this Kenosha club is placed alongside of the finest clubs ever to parade in the Big Eight, it means that it is sitting in elite company.

There was the East team of 1949 and the West 11 of 1946 that were rugged. There was the 1936 Beloit club that could have run up almost any number of points on opponents; the league was weak that year and Beloit with two Negro backs in Gilmore and Eddie May were terrific.

There was the East team of 1935 that lost its opener in Rockford, then raced through the Big Eight undefeated and untied. There is a question whether that was as powerful a club as the East club of 1934; this was a club with tremendous power and size that beat Rockford and lost only to Kenosha, 6–3, that year when many passes were dropped in the end zone and in the clear and when it ran into troubles not of its own making.

There were Kenosha teams of 1930 through 1932 that were big strong laden with power and there were Howard Johnson's wonder teams at Central in the late 1920s.

Just placing Kenosha alongside the best in the past is abundant praise. The 1950 Kenosha team was sound, it had a strong running game, built around the tremendous power of Ameche and his ever present threat, and a sharp aerial attack with Mario Bonofiglio as the master technician. Bonofiglio threw accurately either short or long and he was hard to put a press on because of his running ability and agility.

The only statistical honor that evaded Kenosha was on defense. East took that by allowing only 39 points; Kenosha allowed 47 for second place.

A story that appeared in the Madison *Capital Times* also attempted to put the 1950 Red Devils in their proper historical perspective:

"Champions of champions!" That is the super-tag attached by football fanatics to Kenosha High's rough-riding Red Devils. And the reason is quite obvious. When the Red Devils captured the Big Eight Conference championship with a 57–7 rout of West at Madison Thursday night, they became the first in the 26-year span of the loop to achieve a perfect record for their school. Kenosha chalked up eight straight victories.

Four other Kenosha contingents have gained conference crowns and a co-championship. But as great as they are, none could escape at least a tie to dim its accomplishments.

The current Red Devils are acclaimed to one of the state's greatest scoring units in history. They accumulated 361 points and are claiming this as a Badger mark until somebody comes along with evidence to disprove the honors.

Coach Chuck Jaskwhich, the former Notre Dame quarterback, fielded a line averaging 190 pounds with the backs going 180. Generator of the bulk of the offensive power was left halfback Alan Ameche, a 200-pounder, 10-second speedster in grid gear. A smart durable runner, he rolled up 120 points, 108 in the conference, to topple the previous standard of 97 set by Beloit's Jack Gilmore in 1936. He also mowed down Gilmore's touchdown production output of 16 with a record 18.

Two of Kenosha's best ball carriers are Ronald Rudy, right half, and Bob Girman, fullback, the only juniors in the starting cast.

While Ameche is the player who catches the eye, most college coaches who have watched the Redmen would take quarterback and captain Mario Bonofiglio as their number one choice. Their second man would be Tom Braatz, left end. Frank Aiello on the right flank and Ruel McMullen, center, also rated as definitely big time caliber. Tackles are Dick Nicolazzi and Ed Ronzia with Stan Demske and Vic Borowsky at the guards.

Bonofiglio passes, kicks off, punts and converts points after touchdowns. In 89 pitches, he has hit the target 47 times, gaining nearly a half mile with his yardage and connecting for a touchdown aerial at least once in every game. He had several runs of 75, 70 and 60 yards for touchdowns on a "keeper" play, ghosting the end on a naked reverse.

As well as things turned out for the Red Devils, there was a shadow of doubt hanging over the squad before the season began, despite its strong finish to the 1949 season. Paul Shwaiko, a 175-pound junior speedster who was being counted on to play right halfback opposite Ameche, suffered a slight concussion of the brain in the team's intrasquad game at Lakefront Stadium, a week before the team's season opener at Fond du Lac.

Shwaiko was taken by ambulance to Saint Catherine's Hospital in Kenosha, where he was examined. Jaskwhich pronounced him out for the season after hearing the diagnosis. Shwaiko sustained the injury on the first play of the second half when he was kicked in the forehead while executing what the *Kenosha Evening News* reported was "a perfect block."

Fortunately for the Red Devils, there was always Ameche, and he scored two touchdowns in the scrimmage to lead his side to victory. Frank Aiello scored the other touchdown for Ameche's squad in the 19–13 victory. Rudy and Braatz scored for the losing side.

Jaskwhich also complained of uncertainty in the offensive line, where he had lost his starting guards, the Gentile twins—Aldo and Tony. Demske and Borowsky would eventually emerge at those key positions.

Before the Red Devils could take the field for the regular season, there was more bad news. The oft-injured Hinds suffered a bruised shoulder in practice the Wednesday before the Fond du Lac game, and it was revealed that Ameche was nursing a broken toe, which was handicapping his running in practice. Bob Girman, who was just settling in as right halfback in place of Shwaiko, was shifted to fullback, and Rudy moved into the right halfback slot.

As it turned out, all of Jaskwhich's concerns were for naught. The Red Devils rolled up 394 total yards (196 passing and 198 rushing) while holding Fond du Lac to 178 total yards and posting a 45–14 victory. Ameche, who saw limited action because of his sore toe, scored on runs of 2 and 31 yards, and Bonofiglio ran for two touchdowns, including an 85-yarder. But the surprising star was Rudy, who scored three touchdowns, rushing for 104 yards in just four attempts.

After the opening week of nonconference games, the Big Eight's pool of sports writers were polled. They determined that defending champion

Madison East would battle Kenosha for the top spot, with Janesville and Beloit as the top challengers. First up in the conference for Kenosha was Racine Horlick, which had won its nonconference opener, 13–6, over Arlington Heights (Illinois).

Before a crowd of "nearly 5,000" spectators at Lakefront Stadium, Kenosha pounded "an inadequate, undermanned, but spirited" Racine Horlick squad, 45–6. Kenosha's regulars were barely needed, according to Eddie McKenna's account of the game.

"With victory apparent after the first few minutes of skirmishing, Coach Chuck Jaskwhich played his second and third string boys for more than a half, keeping his vaunted regulars under wraps from the prying eyes of a heavy scouting delegation peering down from the press box."

Ameche was limited to seven carries, but he produced 86 yards and two touchdowns. According to McKenna he appeared headed to two more touchdowns when "his interference stumbled and tripped up his goalward tours."

Kenosha rolled for 348 yards, 205 rushing and 143 passing, while holding Horlick to 105 total yards.

"While Horlick's material is down this year, the game failed to serve as a gauge of Kenosha's true ability," McKenna concluded. "It proved, however, that there is plenty of potential, and if Jaskwhich can steer free of further injuries and the replacements develop at an even tempo, the Reds should be a rugged contender all the way. Hurts for a key man here or there could change the outlook to the gloomy side."

Next up for the Red Devils was undefeated Beloit, a team that had shellacked them, 34–13, in 1949. The Purple Knights were led by halfback Leon Bandy and fullback Tarzan Honor in opening victories over Rockford (Illinois) and Madison Central, and it was, as McKenna stated in the *Kenosha Evening News*, time to "get down to serious business."

Particularly galling to the Kenoshans was the way Beloit had piled on in the second half of that game. The Knights scored 27 of their 34 points in the second half and allowed Kenosha just six plays in the final two quarters.

As reported in an un-bylined article in the *Kenosha Evening News*, "Retribution was gained in full measure!" Before a Dads' Night crowd in Beloit, Kenosha handed the Purple Knights their worst defeat in Big Eight history, 60–0. The Red Devils scored touchdowns on 9 of their 13 possessions and forced Beloit into eight fumbles.

Ameche and Bonofiglio led the scoring with two touchdowns apiece, while Rudy, Aiello, Girman, Fred Bistrick, and John Iovine scored one apiece. Bonofiglio added six extra-point kicks.

Even bad plays had happy endings for the Red Devils on this night. In one of the few punting situations faced by Kenosha, Bonofiglio converted a bad snap into a 70-yard touchdown run in the third quarter. Rudy made perhaps the run of the night, racing 73 yards for a touchdown.

The score undoubtedly sent shock waves throughout the conference when the teams perused their Saturday papers. But there was a downside as well. Hinds, the hard-driving fullback, was injured yet again, this time sustaining a fractured ankle.

"I ran off left tackle and some guy twisted my leg and busted my tibia," Hinds recalled. "That was it. My high school football career was over."

But with five games remaining on the 1950 schedule, it was far from over for the rest of the Red Devils. With Madison Central up next, Kenosha was determined to build upon the momentum it had taken away from the Beloit drubbing, and it did just that. Ameche provided one of the best performances of his high school career, carrying 14 times for 198 yards as the Red Devils won, 53–7, in their homecoming game.

Witnessed by a Lakefront crowd McKenna estimated at 6,000, it was Kenosha's first homecoming victory in four seasons. As McKenna put it, the fans were there to see "Jaskwhich's fabulous football Vesuvius erupt," and the Red Devils didn't disappoint. The Kenoshans racked up 587 total yards, including 480 rushing yards, while holding their visitors from Madison to 41 total yards, including -9 yards rushing.

A total of seven players scored touchdowns for Kenosha, with Rudy crashing into the end zone twice. McKenna summed up Ameche's part in the victory: "Spearhead of Kenosha's platoon was 200 pound, fast-charging Alan Ameche, left halfback, who moved with the speed and devastation of a cannon shot. He scored the first marker of the game on a 30-yard run, and then set up other scores with his thunderbolt thrusts. A potential All-American, Ameche's swift blasts and hard jolting lunges made him an indomitable figure on the field. Hailed as one of the state's outstanding schoolboy stars and one of the greatest players ever produced in the Big Eight, Ameche is classed with the all-time immortals at Kenosha High School."

At the halfway point of the season, with Racine Park (1–2 in the Big Eight) up next, things couldn't have seemed rosier for the Red Devils. The Panthers' only conference victory had been an upset of Janesville, but they looked terrible the following week against Madison East.

Keith Brehm, the *Racine Journal-Times* sports editor, brought up an interesting issue in his preview of the Park-Kenosha contest. He credited Jaskwhich with being a sympathetic man for playing his starters just two quarters per game when it was clear the outcomes were well in hand. But Brehm wondered how many points Ameche and Bonofiglio would score if they were ever turned loose to play an entire game.

At the halfway point of the season, Ameche had five touchdowns (30 points) while Bonofiglio had 32 points (14 one-point conversions and three touchdowns). Brehm opined that the records of Beloit's Jack Gilmore had nothing to fear from any Kenosha player.

"At the present rate it doesn't seem likely that any of the Kenosha players will approach Gilmore's record," Brehm wrote.

> Jaskwhich has used his reserves much of the time to hold the scores down and so it is that seven of the Kenoshans have scored 12 points or more.
>
> Ironically, it is Coach Jaskwhich's attempts to hold down the score which have brought "beefs" from the Kenosha fans. It isn't that they want Jaskwhich to pour it on opponents but they complain that they get to see the "regulars" during a relatively small portion of the game.
>
> I know that Jaskwhich will hold back all he can but if they are able to do so, the starting players are likely to go for scores against teams like Janesville and Madison West. West in particular, pulled no punches (running up scores), when Kenosha was "down" a couple of years ago.

Apparently, the Racine Park coach, John Prasch, was on Jaskwhich's good side, because Kenosha kept the scoring in Racine to a relatively mild 37–7. Ameche and Braatz both scored a pair of touchdowns, but the 37 points was the Red Devils' lowest output of the season to that point.

Apparently paying no heed to Brehm's piece prior to the game, Jaskwhich played his starters just 14 minutes of the game's total of 48, according to McKenna's account. The veteran Kenosha sports writer provided this reasoning: "The flaws that cropped up in spots will be among the important items coming in for correction and polish in strenuous drills this week for the 'game of games' Friday night against Madison East, defending champion and a 1950 pillar of power.

"With an East scout peering down from the press box charting every Kenosha maneuver, Jaskwhich had Bonofiglio under orders to play this one close to the vest, using only simple plays and straight football routines so as not to tip Kenosha's hand for the East assignment."

Although the Red Devils accrued a relatively modest 253 yards from scrimmage on the night, Ameche, in particular, was a terror on special teams. He had punt returns of 57, 39, 32, and 23 yards and a kickoff return of 60 yards—

a total of 211 yards in five returns. Also, Bonofiglio kept his record of passing for at least one touchdown in each game intact, tossing two scoring passes to Braatz.

As good as Kenosha was in the first five weeks of the season, as dominant as the Red Devils were, and as spectacularly as Ameche and Bonofiglio had performed, none of it meant a thing with Madison East coming to town in week six of the Big Eight season. All the hype and hyperbole leading up to the contest—and there were reams written about the upcoming game—was deserved.

Unlike so many overhyped sports contests, this game actually lived up to its advance billing. All the components of a classic game were there. It was a late-season showdown in the state's best conference featuring two undefeated teams, the defense-minded defending champions versus the high-scoring challengers. The Purgolders brought a two-year, 12-game winning streak into the contest; the Red Devils' late resurgence in 1949 put their consecutive victory total at 9.

The game had superstars—East's center, Gary Messner, versus Ameche and Bonofiglio, all of whom would later team up at the University of Wisconsin. An overflow crowd estimated at more than 7,000 filled the bleachers and lined the fence at Lakefront Stadium. What they would witness was perhaps the greatest high school game ever played in Wisconsin. It was beyond competitive, and it was very losable.

Although it might seem totally illogical, the Red Devils played perhaps their worst and best halves of football on the same evening. Fortunately for them, they—in particular Bonofiglio and Ameche—saved their best for last.

There were no highlights for the Red Devils in the first half. The Purgolders scored on a 3-yard Ronnie Schara plunge in the first period and added a second touchdown on a 9-yard pass from Bob Wutzeler to rangy Leo Schlict. Wutzeler converted after the second touchdown, the only successful conversion of the game. The score at halftime was a dismal 13–0.

"Trudging wearily to the dressing room at halftime, the Reds, expecting a verbal lashing for their shortcomings by Coach Jaskwhich, sat in awed silence as the tutor calmly gathered his players around him, took chalk and went to the board and put down correct strategic moves," wrote McKenna, who assigned his assistant Jim Barnhill to cover the game also.

The *Kenosha Evening News* had also assigned a photographer to the game for a page exclusively of photos for Saturday's paper. Perhaps the anonymous shooter's best effort was a halftime shot of Jaskwhich, who appeared very dapper in a trench coat with every jet black strand of hair on his head slick and in place. Despite the gravity of the situation, Jaskwhich gave the appearance of inner serenity and self-control.

"I'll be very honest, I was afraid we were going to lose that game," remembered Nicolazzi. "When you are down, 13–0, at halftime you think that. I knew we were going to score [in the second half], I just didn't know if we could hold them from scoring any more. I didn't think we could. . . . I thought we were looking at something like a 21–19 loss."

What Nicolazzi hadn't counted on was the leadership of Jaskwhich. Anyone can lead when his team is overpowering the opposition, but this was the first time anyone in Kenosha had seen Jaskwhich put in this situation. Nobody came away disappointed.

"We got to the locker room [at halftime] and Chuck didn't say a word," Nicolazzi said. "There was no blasting, no taking anybody down. . . . It was all very calm. 'Here's what they are doing. This is what we're going to do in the second half. Don't worry. We'll be all right.'

"I had heard Chuck blister the walls when we were up 35 [points], but not that game. That night he was cool, calm, collected. He told us what he wanted to tell us and got his point across.

"Chuck knew how to coach. You don't have to holler all the time. There is a time to holler and a time to teach and pat on the back, and good coaches know when each is appropriate. Chuck knew the difference."

Like the others, Nicolazzi's running mate at offensive tackle, Ed Ronzia, had expected Jaskwhich to blow the doors off the humble Lakefront dressing room with halftime bluster. It never came.

"We expected to be chewed out because Chuck was known to chew us out even when we were winning games 24–0 or 28–0 at halftime," Ronzia said. "That game he was very quiet. He just told us these fellows from Madison East were using a slant defense.

"The linemen were slanting one way and the linebackers would slant the other way. So when it came to running plays, our blocking was really hampered. You'd go to block the guy across from you, and he'd taken off into the hole you were trying to take him out of. So we passed more in the second half to Alan and Tom Braatz and that was it."

Jim Barnhill's sidebar story on the game in the *Kenosha Evening News* focused on the Purgolders' strategy and Jaskwhich's halftime adjustments to counter East's plan for slanting its six-man defensive line in the same direction. According to Barnhill's story, Kenosha gained just 71 total yards in the first half, 58 by rushing.

"There is no question that East was a very good team," Nicolazzi said. "Whatever they did was right and whatever we did was wrong. If we ran to the right, that's where they were slanting their line and linebackers. If we ran left, that's the way they were going."

Indeed, the Purgolders' coach, Butch Mueller, had apparently picked up something in scouting the Red Devils that tipped off which direction their plays would follow. Jaskwhich had a counterplan, fortunately.

"To combat this defense alignment, Jaskwhich instructed quarterback Mario Bonofiglio to concentrate his attack up the middle and the results were quite apparent immediately after the second half started when the Reds rolled up four straight first downs in marching to their first score," recorded Barnhill. "In this drive they used their air lanes only once. Ameche's TD tour accompanied by a beautiful fake on the defense was also up the alley."

McKenna enlarged on Jaskwhich's halftime corrections: "Jaskwhich pointed out that East was using a six-man line for slant charging, a maneuver somewhat puzzling to the Reds. This style was hampering the wide attempts of the backs, except Ameche, who knew when to cut in sharply."

On its first possession of the second half, Kenosha marched 60 yards in 10 plays for its first touchdown. Bonofiglio attempted just one pass in the drive, which ended with a 15-yard Ameche touchdown run. Bonofiglio missed the first of three point-after touchdown conversion attempts.

The Kenosha defense stiffened on East's next possession, and a 10-yard Ameche punt return gave the Red Devils possession at their own 45. Two plays later, Bonofiglio spotted Ameche open across the middle, 17 yards downfield. Ameche added 22 yards after the catch for a 39-yard potential game-tying touchdown. But Bonofiglio missed the extra-point conversion again, and Kenosha trailed, 13–12, late in the third quarter.

In the fourth quarter, Bonofiglio more than redeemed himself for his shoddy kicking. Rudy set up the Bonofiglio-Ameche hero scenario when he intercepted a Wutzeler pass at the Kenosha 45 and returned it 14 yards to the East 41. Kenosha failed to score on this possession as the third quarter ended, but its defense pinned down the Purgolders on their next possession.

Bonofiglio then fielded a quick kick and returned it 4 yards to the East 41 again. On the next play, Bonofiglio passed 41 yards to Ameche for the winning touchdown.

"Big Alan barged all the way for the touchdown, leaving East tacklers strewn in his path, laid low by his ability to shake them off and take advantage of the deadly blocking offered by his mates," wrote McKenna. "Bonofiglio missed his third kick."

"We kid Mario about that to this day," Nicolazzi said. "18 to 13 doesn't sound that impressive. 21 to 13 would sound a lot better."

East had one last chance for victory, recovering a Kenosha fumble at the Red Devils' 22 with about a minute left in the game. The Purgolders gained 9 yards in two plays before time ran out on them and Kenosha laid claim to the 18–13 victory.

Despite his shortcomings with his foot, Bonofiglio played a strong defensive game and was the game's statistical star on offense, completing 6 of 19 pass attempts for 144 yards and two touchdowns. He also ran for 29 yards in 4 carries while Ameche led all ball carriers with 15 carries for 70 yards plus all three of his team's touchdowns.

"Sure, we worried, but we never even thought about losing," remembered Bonofiglio. "I missed three extra points, so that wasn't good. We had to play defense to win and some plays in the second half and we were able to do it."

McKenna was at the top of his game in describing the Kenosha comeback victory in his game story:

> Outplayed and outfoxed in the first half when they dropped to a "vanishing vermillion" the Reds regained their poise and confidence, exploded with the fury of a blazing forest fire and completely dominated the opposition in the last two quarters of the super-charged struggle.
>
> The back-breaker of the stubborn East challenger was 200 pound Alan Ameche, labeled as All-American potential. He blasted loose like a bull with a hot-foot for three TDs. The touchdown terror reeled off two scores in the third quarter, and produced the payoff trip in the fourth quarter. The last two encounters were set up on pitches down the middle by Capt. Mario Bonofiglio. His scoring excursions were for 15, 39 and 41 yards.
>
> A 10 second man in his grid gear Ameche, who can shift to high instantly, showed the speed and stamina of a "Citation" going down the stretch. He showed how he won the Big Eight scoring title last season and why he is the current leader with tremendous punch in his powerful escapades.

In that era of sports writing, the reporters would interview coaches after a game, but for some reason, it was taboo to use direct quotes from those interviews in their game stories. Players interviews weren't even considered, so we will never know how Ameche or Bonofiglio felt on that night of October 20, 1950.

In all the stories written about the undefeated Red Devils, there was just one direct quote included in their coverage in the *Kenosha Evening News*. It appeared in Barnhill's story, and it wasn't from his question but from a conversation overheard between Jaskwhich and Mueller after the game.

"Evidence of the successful diagnosis of East's play was contained in Coach Mueller's comments to Jaskwhich after the game," reported Barnhill. "'If we could have played the game without the halftime intermission, we would have beaten you. I knew that when your club came out for the second half you were going to give our defense trouble.'"

Kenosha's quest for a perfect season took a giant step forward with its comeback victory over Madison East, but with two games remaining with Janesville and at Madison West, nothing was assured. Janesville would enter the Dad's Day game at Lakefront Stadium with a 2–3 conference mark, but the Bluebirds were competitive with every opponent and presented a potential "trap" game for the Red Devils.

Pregame reports of a confident Janesville squad were quickly dismissed, however, as the Red Devils jumped out to a 27–0 early second-quarter lead and coasted to a 46–7 pounding. The 46 points enabled Kenosha to set a new Big Eight season scoring record of 259 points, 7 better than the Kenosha championship team of 1930. On the same night in Madison, East handed West its first conference loss, assuring the Red Devils of at least a share of the conference title.

Ameche, Bonofiglio, and Braatz were unleashed by Jaskwhich and rewarded the coach with their best efforts of the season. Ameche scored four touchdowns (two on runs, two on pass receptions) while carrying 13 times for 103 yards; Bonofiglio threw five touchdown passes, completing 11 of 18 for 162 yards; and Braatz gathered three touchdown passes, on 30-, 6-, and 7-yard efforts.

Ameche's scoring outburst gave him 84 points for the season and a fighting chance of breaking the scoring record of 97 set by Jack Gilmore from Beloit in 1936. The only thing standing between Ameche and the record and between the Red Devils and a perfect season was Madison West in the season finale. As it turned out, the Regents provided only token resistance.

West stayed within hailing distance at halftime, trailing by just two touchdowns, 12–0. But for the first time all season, Jaskwhich poured it on an opponent in the second half. Maybe it was the memory of the 52–0 pounding West's coach, Willis Jones, laid on the winless Red Devils in 1948, the year before Jaskwhich's arrival, but more likely it was the individual and team Big Eight scoring records that motivated the Kenosha coach.

Ameche added four more touchdowns to his cache, and his late-season surge (13 touchdowns in four games) gave him a total of 108 points for the season, destroying Gimore's mark.

The Red Devils padded their league scoring record, getting to 316 points in conference games. Also, McKenna claimed in his story that night that Kenosha's 361 points in eight games represented a Wisconsin high school record "until someone comes along with concrete evidence to disprove the mark."

"Alan Ameche, who functioned like a robot monster, spilled into touch-down paradise four times to wipe out the all-time Kenosha and Big Eight individual records," McKenna added. "Sagging the scales at 200 and a 10-second man in grid gear, Ameche in 20 trips mounted up 111 yards for an average of 5.5. Only an act of congress or a strait-jacket could subdue the bone-crushing, Gilda Gray hip twisting escapades of the 'all time' grid immortals in the red weskit."

Barnhill, who again was assigned a sidebar story to supplement the *Evening News*'s coverage of the event, unearthed a couple of newsy tidbits for his piece. Apparently, before the game he had spent some time in the very subdued Red Devils' dressing room, where he overheard Ameche say, "I'm a little nervous."

As a portent of things to come, Barnhill also reported seeing the Wisconsin head football coach, Ivy Williamson, at Breese Stevens Stadium that night, in a crowd estimated at 9,000. Ameche gave his future coach an eyeful, scoring on touchdowns of 1, 3, 8, and 2 yards.

Girman had a big night also, rushing six times for 87 yards, including a 66-yard touchdown run on the game's first play from scrimmage. Bonofiglio also had a great game, running for 48 yards and passing for 135 yards (5 completions in 10 attempts) and one touchdown.

Kenosha outgained West, 564–127. The Red Devils' offensive ledger balanced, with 303 rushing yards and 261 passing yards.

Ameche never was really asked to comment about his high school team for publication, but it is clear that although he left Kenosha, never to return after his senior year of high school, Kenosha never left him. Ameche especially relished the role he and his teammates played in turning around the fortunes of the Kenosha football program.

"One of the good things too, and this goes all the way back to high school," Ameche told Tom Butler of the *Wisconsin State Journal* in 1975, "was starting at the bottom and going to the top. Our sophomore team in high school scored one touchdown all year. We won the championship and were undefeated as seniors."

As expected, Kenosha cleaned up the postseason honors. Ameche, the repeat winner of the conference scoring title, also repeated as the league's

MVP. He was joined on the first-team All–Big Eight squad by teammates Braatz, Borowsky, Ronzia, McMullen, and Bonofiglio. Aiello, Demske, and Nicolazzi were named to the second team, and Girman, Rudy, Hinds, and defensive tackle Ray DeLaat were all given honorable mentions. Inexplicably, Jaskwhich didn't repeat as coach of the year. That honor went to Madison East's Mueller, whose Purgolders finished second in the league.

Ameche and Bonofiglio were all named to the Associated Press's first-team all-Wisconsin squad. Braatz and McMullen made second team, while Borowsky made the third team.

The AP story noted Ameche's 20 touchdowns and 120 points and said that Bonofiglio "who weighs 163, had a completion average of 52.8 percent, gaining over 1,000 yards while converting 47 successful passes in 89 attempts." It was also reported that Ameche averaged 7.8 yards per carry in his senior year at Kenosha.

Not surprisingly, most of the members of that team feel they had earned the right to call themselves the greatest high school team in Wisconsin history. Bonofiglio and Hinds are emphatic about that, whereas Nicolazzi isn't as sure about his squad's place in history.

"I think, at the least, we were the best team in the nation that year," Hinds said. "*Saturday Evening Post* magazine said we were number one in the nation and I don't think there is any doubt about it.

"As far as Wisconsin goes, we were the best team I've ever seen. How do you get two all-Americans like Ameche and Bonofiglio and not be the greatest? Then you've got Tom Braatz and guys like Ed Ronzia, Dick Nicolazzi, and Ruel McMullen."

Bonofiglio is even more emphatic in his viewpoint.

"In our senior year, we knew we were going to be a very good team, but we didn't know we were going to be that good," he said. "We were the best ever in Wisconsin, no doubt about it.

"You can't compare anybody to what we did. We played in the toughest conference in the state, and we had seven guys from the class get scholarships to Wisconsin. They haven't had seven guys from Kenosha go to Wisconsin in thirty years.

"We [the starters] played half the game and still averaged almost 50 points a game. Our opponents scored like 40 points all season and that was mostly against our third team.

"We knew we were going to win every game, no doubt about it. It was just a question of how long an opponent would last and would they leave us in or take us out right away?

"No way did we run up scores. Chuck would never allow that. Except for the Madison East game, our games were over at halftime."

Based on the size of some of today's high school players, Nicolazzi, who coached football and for years was the athletic director at West Allis (Wisconsin) Central High School, isn't so sure his own team would have stacked up well.

"We were very good, but I don't think we could compete with the kids they have out there now," Nicolazzi said. "Some of these teams have 235-pound tight ends and 275-pound tackles.

"I was the biggest kid on our team and I was six feet tall and weighed 215 pounds. We were all around six feet. These teams nowadays are so fast, so big, so strong . . .

"In our day we were great, but today we wouldn't stand a chance. I don't care who we had at running back. Al would have still scored, but there is no way we could have stood up to the size some of these teams today have."

It's a debate that, in Kenosha at least, will never be settled. But Hinds is sure of this much.

"It was a phenomenal experience, something I'll never forget," Hinds said. "Everybody pulled together, there was no jealousy on anybody's part. I just feel so fortunate that I was a part of that team."

7

❧ ❧

The Millers Tale

THERE HAVE BEEN BITTERLY CONTESTED college football recruiting wars. There have been recruiting battles that have divided families and cities and even states. There have been recruitments that have ended in NCAA investigations and even in courts of law. But the recruitment of Alan Ameche had something probably no other college football recruiting battle has ever had. Since the fight was for the greatest football player Wisconsin has ever produced, Ameche's recruitment could be said to have been a beer war.

Although practically every major college program in the Midwest, and others like Kentucky and North Carolina, offered scholarships to Ameche, the endgame came down to two schools—Wisconsin and Notre Dame.

The University of Wisconsin, ninety miles northwest of Kenosha in Madison, had plenty going for it in Ameche's eyes. It was the school where his brother, Lynn, had preceded him; six of his high school teammates were heading there to play football; there was state pride; there was proximity; and there was "On Wisconsin."

"I remember when we were in high school, Alan went out to Madison to visit Lynn," Yvonne said. "When he came back he was wearing this cute red tie and he was singing 'On, Wisconsin.'

"Lynn introduced Alan to classical music at that point and took him to the music library on campus. Alan couldn't stop talking about it. I think he just liked everything Wisconsin had to offer."

Yvonne had plenty more to say about Ameche's college choice in Booton Herndon's *Sports Illustrated* piece. She denied that his reason for picking Wisconsin was because six of his Kenosha teammates had received scholarships from the Badgers. She elaborated on her husband's high school visit to Madison.

"When we were sophomores in high school Lino spent a weekend in Madison, visiting his brother. He came straight to my house as soon as he got back to Kenosha. He had on a white shirt and a red tie and he looked awful cute. He told me that the Wisconsin campus was the most beautiful place he had ever seen and that the Wisconsin song was the most beautiful he had ever heard. He sang it for me, from beginning to end. But what really got him was the music room. He said they had every phonograph record in the world there, and you could play them as loud as you wanted to. Lino was sold on Wisconsin from that day on."

Ironically, Yvonne leaves no doubt where she had hoped Alan would go.

"I wanted him to go to Notre Dame," she recalled. "There were no girls there."

Yvonne had plenty of allies in high places, and Notre Dame had no shortage of selling points either. There was the whole Notre Dame aura, initiated by Knute Rockne and at that time in the very competent hands of Frank Leahy. There was the religious aspect—Ameche was a man of strong faith and belief in the Catholic Church. And there was Coach Jaskwhich, a man whom Ameche respected greatly and who happened to be a Notre Dame alumnus.

And last, Notre Dame had some very rich, important, and persistent alumni who had made it their mission in life to adorn Ameche's head with a golden helmet. One in particular, Fred Miller, the owner of the Miller Brewing Company, may have even crossed the line into that dreaded gray area that separates legal and illegal.

Miller was not only a Notre Dame alumnus, but he had been an All-American offensive tackle there under the legendary Rockne. He also was a man who was used to getting his way and didn't easily take no for an answer.

His dogged pursuit of Ameche became a statewide issue in the spring of 1951. It pitted Miller against University of Wisconsin alumni, and since there were more than a few beer drinkers in that crowd, it became a spirited battle. It was even written about in later University of Wisconsin football media guides under the heading "Facts, Figures and Legends of Badger Football," which stated: "During his college recruitment, [Ameche] was being heavily pressured to attend Notre Dame by Fred Miller, philanthropic owner of Milwaukee's Miller Brewing Co. Wisconsin patrons, however, threatened a boycott against the buying and consumption of Miller beer if Ameche attended

Notre Dame. Under threat of boycott, Miller backed off and Ameche signed with Wisconsin."

John Steadman, a *Baltimore Sun* sports writer, went into more detail on Ameche's recruitment by Notre Dame in his newspaper's coverage of Ameche's untimely death in 1988.

The death of Ameche at age 55, following heart surgery, recalls the intriguing and amusing scenario of how he was recruited from Kenosha High School in 1951. He laughed about it, but it was the only time in history that a major brewery was going to face a boycott against its product if the player that was pursued, Ameche, went to Notre Dame instead of Wisconsin.

Notre Dame was so determined to have Ameche enroll that coach Frank Leahy suggested he "go home and make a novena," believing that nine days of prayer and reflection would change his mind. Pulling out all stops, Notre Dame had a distant cousin, actor Don Ameche call on its behalf.

"But I still wanted to go to Wisconsin," [Ameche] explained. "I respected Notre Dame but I figured it would be better if I stayed home and went to my state university with a lot of the boys I played with at Kenosha High."

When he was in the throes of arriving at a decision, added pressure was put on him to attend Notre Dame by Fred Miller, the Irish captain of 1928, who was the philanthropic owner of the Miller Brewing Co.

Finally, Wisconsin partisans organized a committee to keep Ameche on home turf. The threat was made that if the promising fullback went to Notre Dame, as had previously happened with another running back, Neil Worden, from Milwaukee, that a statewide demonstration would be made against the buying and consumption of Miller beer.

The "game plan" worked. Miller backed off, and Ameche went to Wisconsin and became a Heisman Trophy winner after gaining 3,212 yards in four years, an NCAA record at the time.

That's not exactly the way Bobby Hinds remembers the situation, and he claims to have been in the living room at the Ameche home on 16th Avenue that spring day in 1951 when Miller, Leahy, and the Mount Carmel parish priest came to visit. The Ameche family had taken Hinds in because he had no other place to live at the time.

Hinds agrees that Miller was certainly applying a full-court press on Ameche to commit to Notre Dame, but the beer baron didn't exactly back off voluntarily.

"Fred Miller, Frank Leahy, the great Notre Dame coach, and the parish priest all came over to the house," Hinds recalled. "They even had Don Ameche, who was a friend of Leahy's, call Alan and tell him to consider Notre Dame and everything would be taken care of."

Don Ameche, who was a famous movie star, was Ameche's second cousin, but according to Yvonne, that was the first time the two had ever spoken. Apparently Don Ameche's father and Augusto were first cousins.

"Don Ameche was from Kenosha, of course, but Alan didn't even know him," she said. "I think they were second cousins, but Alan never spoke to him before or after that. Don Ameche didn't even like Kenosha, and he really wanted nothing to do with it."

The call from Don Ameche didn't impress Alan and neither did what happened next, according to Hinds.

"Fred Miller wrote out a check for $1,500, which of course was totally illegal," Hinds said. "Remember, $1,500 was a lot of money back then. It was about what Al's dad made at Simmons in one year.

"So, Miller hands the check to Mrs. Ameche and says, 'This is for you Mrs. Ameche and all I am asking is for Al to say verbally that he is going to Notre Dame.'

"Just to show you how sophisticated Alan was, he walks over to Fred Miller and said 'Don't you ever do that again.' He was genuinely pissed that Fred Miller had used that sort of bribery on his mother.

"Obviously she didn't take the check and Al went to Wisconsin. I was there when it happened. Wisconsin was so fortunate to get a man like Alan Ameche."

It was not the first time Hinds has related the story. In 1988, days after Ameche's death, he was interviewed by Dave Zweifel of the Madison *Capital Times*.

"Alan was furious that someone would put his mother, who was extremely poor, under that kind of pressure," Zweifel quoted Hinds as saying. "You gotta remember this was 1951 and $1,500 was an awful lot of money. So he said the hell with Notre Dame."

Yvonne won't confirm Hinds's allegations, but she wouldn't deny them either. She hints there might have been Wisconsin boosters who were also willing to provide Ameche with illegal perks for his services.

"I'm not aware of that story at all," she said, referring to the Hinds's Miller tale. "I do know that Notre Dame wanted him to go there and there was somebody pulling strings. They even offered to send me to Saint Mary's [then the sister school of Notre Dame].

"But there were no cars offered. It was a scholarship.

"They offered his dad something. It was a pittance every month, but I don't remember how much. It's like this kid [Cam Newton] last year with people saying that his father wanted money. I think there should be money for the kids to play for a college. But at this point I'm not going to say somebody said they would give Alan's dad $100 a month. . . . I don't want to go there.

"I heard there were people who wanted him to go to Wisconsin that made monetary offers. What they were, I don't know. Who said they would help, I don't know, and I don't want to go there. I think it's controversial.

"I was at a party not too long ago and there was a man there who played for Notre Dame. He said, 'What about that guy [Newton] whose dad was trying to get all that money?'

"I said, 'Well, you know Alan got a little help.' He said, 'I don't think you should tell anybody that,' but I said, 'Why not? It wasn't a lot. We never got a car. We got a little place to live [when they were married and living in Madison].'"

Yvonne said the most they ever got was dinner and a small stipend from Bob Leske's Supper Club, a popular Madison restaurant at the time they lived there. "We would go there after the games, and Bob would pay him to shake hands and greet people. It was no big deal.

"After he greeted people, we'd have big steak dinners. It wasn't like here is a big car or anything like that."

According to a story written by Tom Flaherty of the *Milwaukee Journal* prior to the 1989 Heisman Trophy award, the year after Ameche's death, many considered Wisconsin's victory over Notre Dame in the recruiting sweepstakes an upset. Flaherty's assumption was based on his interview with Milt Bruhn, who was Williamson's top assistant and successor.

When Ameche was drawing attention as a star running back at Kenosha Bradford High School, a lot of people didn't expect Alan to become a legend at Wisconsin. His high school coach, Chuck Jaskwhich, had played quarterback at Notre Dame. Everyone expected Ameche to end up at Notre Dame.

Badgers coach Ivy Williamson pulled a recruiting coup.

"We knew that his coach was a Notre Dame graduate," Bruhn said. "We felt he was probably leaning toward Notre Dame.

"When Ivy recruited him, he brought in four or five of his high school classmates. If it hadn't been for that, he probably would have gone to Notre Dame. He wanted to stick with his friends."

Whether it was wanted or not by Ameche, both Notre Dame and Wisconsin sought to curry favor with him by bundling offers to his high school teammates. Notre Dame made offers to Bonofiglio and Ronzia, while Wisconsin made them to Bonofiglio, Ronzia, Nicolazzi, Aiello, McMullen, Hinds, and Braatz. All, except Braatz, who went to Marquette, accepted the Wisconsin offers.

"My sister was in nursing at Marquette and she sold me on the place," said Braatz of his decision to attend Marquette. "She kind of looked after me after my father died. Plus, Lisle Blackbourn was the coach at Marquette at the time and he was a strong-minded person. I had offers from Wisconsin, Northwestern, and Indiana, but I chose Marquette."

Bonofiglio and Ronzia both rode with Ameche in Miller's private plane to South Bend to see the sights of Notre Dame and meet the players and coaches. Ronzia recalled the flight to South Bend and the surprise the trio received when they got there.

"Chuck [Jaskwhich] told us to have a nice talk with [Notre Dame athletic director Moose] Krause and Leahy," Ronzia said. "So lo and behold, we get there and next thing we know they suit us up with football uniforms.

"Notre Dame was having its spring practice, but we didn't do any contact drills. They had us doing wind sprints, hitting the dummies, and conditioning stuff. Basically I would say it was like a tryout. They wanted to see what we had.

"The plane dropped us back off in Kenosha and Mario and I got out. Miller took Alan off to the side and talked to him, but I wasn't privy to what the conversation was about.

"When we got home, we told Chuck what happened, and he said, 'I didn't think they would have done that.' So don't ask me if it was legal or not."

While there is no record of Ameche or any of the Kenosha crew suiting up for a tryout in their visits to the University of Wisconsin, Ameche's official visit to Madison was anything but low key. Apparently his reputation as the state's premier high school football was well known in Madison.

Flaherty's story included an interview with Ameche's four-year teammate at Wisconsin, Jim Temp, who happened to be in Madison on a recruiting trip the same weekend as Ameche. Temp recalled how the world seemed to stop when Ameche and his Badger recruiters entered the restaurant.

"He was so highly recruited," Temp said. "I remember they brought my mom and dad and me down to Madison to show us the campus. We were at one of the hotels in Madison having lunch or dinner with one of the assistant coaches.

"All of a sudden, there is a big hush and in came Alan Ameche. Remember how it was with Bart Starr when he was playing [for the Green Bay Packers]? People would see him, and it was almost, 'Shhhhh. There's Bart.' This was, 'Shhhhh, there's Alan.' And he hadn't played a down yet. He was being recruited to come to Madison.'"

Bonofiglio claims the trip to South Bend was actually his and Ameche's second outing with the beer baron. There had been plans to make the trip earlier, but it was cancelled because of foul weather.

"Fred Miller was a big Notre Dame alum, and he wanted Alan and I to go there," Bonofiglio said. "I'm sure he figured if he got me to go there, he could get Alan to go there, too. We were always best of friends. There was never any jealousy between us.

"So, we took the train to his office, and we were going to fly to South Bend from there. We went to his office and what an office he had! He had a lounge chair in there that could seat ten people.

"He said, 'Boys, the weather is a little bad out there today. It's raining so I don't think it's a good day to fly.' He asked how we were going to get back to Kenosha and we said, 'the train.' He gave us fifty dollars for the train, and it was like a dollar to ride the train back then.

"Fifty dollars, wow! He called us again and we actually saw Notre Dame. It was very beautiful with the Golden Dome and all."

Bonofiglio claims that he and Ameche actually decided on Wisconsin when they were riding home on the train after their first meeting with Miller.

"We were coming back on the train from Milwaukee and talking about going to Madison," he said. "Everybody was going to Madison, so we just wanted to go there. It's 100 miles away and our families and friends could watch us play."

Bonofiglio claims the decision was as simple as that. If there were any underhanded offers made to Ameche, he wasn't privy to them.

"There was nothing really that Notre Dame offered, at least not that I know of," he said. "We just figured it was the best place for us to go. There were no offers of giving us this or that. Nope, I would have known about it."

The general consensus among those who knew him best was that Ameche picked Wisconsin because of his friends, his general comfort level with Madison, and the university.

"Alan was recruited all over, there were so many teams after him," Ronzia recalled. "I don't know for sure why he picked Wisconsin, but I think it was because of the proximity and the fact that his friends were all going there.

"I know this much though. He didn't go to Wisconsin because it was a package deal to help the rest of us. I read a rumor once that said Alan wouldn't go to Wisconsin unless Frank Aiello, Mario, Bobby Hinds, Dick [Nicolazzi], McMullen, and myself got scholarships.

"I'm sure in my case, Chuck pushed for me, but I don't think it was in any way tied to Alan. Ameche didn't go to Wisconsin because he was part of any deal. It really ticked me off when I read that. I'd like to think I made it on my own."

Surprisingly, Jaskwhich apparently never intervened on Notre Dame's behalf with any of his players, despite his strong ties to the South Bend university. Because of their unanimous respect for their coach, his recommendations would have certainly carried a lot of weight with all of them.

"As far as I know Chuck never tried to influence any of us to go to Notre Dame," Ronzia said. "He was there if we had questions, but I think he wanted us to do what was best for us."

Bonofiglio confirmed that Jaskwhich never talked to him or Ameche on Notre Dame's behalf.

"No way did Chuck get involved," Bonofiglio said. "He didn't want to influence anybody's decision because if things didn't work out the way they planned, he didn't want them mad at him. He never tried to influence anybody's decision or tell them where they should go."

Hinds is in basic agreement with the others regarding Ameche's decision but added a twist of his own.

"All of us were going to Wisconsin. Mario was going to Wisconsin. I was going to Wisconsin. Ruel McMullen was going to Wisconsin. Everyone was there and we were all treated well."

Hinds believes Vern Woodward, his boxing coach at Wisconsin, was more influential than Ivy Williamson on Ameche choosing Wisconsin. Hinds took Ameche with him on a boxing recruiting trip when they were sophomores, and both formed a very favorable impression of Woodward.

"Vern Woodward was the guy, just a real good person, and he gave us a great reception. They didn't know who Alan Ameche was at that point, but Alan got the feeling that they weren't out to exploit anybody."

Hinds told the story of the recruiting trip to Zweifel in the *Capital Times* interview.

"One day when we were sophomores and our football record was so bad no one ever heard of Alan Ameche, we hitchhiked to Madison because I wanted to look at the boxing set-up," Hinds said. "Woodward showed us around and when he found out we hitchhiked all the way from Kenosha, he figured no way was he going to let us hitchhike back.

"He put us in his personal car and took us back himself. Alan never forgot that. He figured if Wisconsin had guys like Vern Woodward, it must be one heckuva place to go."

After the blowup with Miller at the Ameche home, it was pretty much a fait accompli that the recruiting war was over and Ameche would take his game to Madison. But it wasn't official until the news appeared in the *Kenosha Evening News* on June 2, 1951, under the byline of Jim Barnhill, who had taken over as sports editor after McKenna's sudden death.

There was no February letter-of-intent signing event like there is now. Barnhill simply reported that Ameche and Bonofiglio had announced they would be attending the University of Wisconsin in the fall. Notre Dame, Northwestern, Michigan, Tennessee, Drake, Kentucky, Marquette, Wyoming, North Carolina, and "many others" were mentioned as having been possible suitors of Ameche.

"The South Bend school was particularly interested in the talents of Ameche, a 200 pound halfback whose broken field and power running established a Big Eight conference scoring mark last fall with 18 touchdowns," Barnhill wrote. "Frank Leahy watched him perform in workouts and spoke with Ameche Tuesday. Ameche celebrated his eighteenth birthday yesterday."

Williamson didn't talk much to the media, let alone talk about incoming freshmen, but it was reported that he didn't expect Ameche to contribute much as a freshman. Perhaps that is because the Western Conference, which was the original name of the Big Ten Conference, had just voted to waive the rule banning freshmen from varsity competition.

But according to one report, a scout for the Chicago Bears declared that Ameche was good enough to transition from high school directly to the NFL. The Bill Furlong piece in *Sport* magazine is a bit fuzzy on details but concludes with this statement about Ameche: "One head-hunter for the Chicago Bears had reported that he thought Ameche was 'the only boy I've ever seen who could step right from high school up to the Bears.'"

Nobody seems to know who this anonymous "Bears" scout was, but Ronzia has one theory. He thought the source might have been the former Kenosha and Drake University star Tom Bienneman, who played from 1951 through 1956 for the Chicago Cardinals.

"That's the only thing I can think of," Ronzia said. "I remember Tom coming to our workouts in the summer and helping out. He wasn't a scout, but he certainly knew a good player when he saw one."

Maybe it was because of his stocky, muscular build, but when Alan got to

Madison, Williamson decided that the 6–0, 200 pound Ameche was a full-back and not a halfback.

Much has been made of Ameche's running style, however, because it was anything but that of a classic fullback. He ran erect, his head up, with the ball tucked under his right arm. His left arm flailed in the wind as he used it for balance, not unlike how a tight-rope walker uses a long rod. Ameche ran with his knees high, even in short-yardage situations. The only time he would lower his upper torso in classic fullback style was in the case of imminent collision with a would-be tackler. Perhaps Furlong's flowery description captures Ameche's running style best:

> He has been known to accumulate tacklers like a Bikini-clad bathing beauty attracting stares, then shuck them off like a puppy quivering and shaking water from his body after a bath. That he is able to canter through the line with several human barnacles attached to his shell is a tribute to his extraordinary power, for Ameche runs with his head up and his back straight instead of crouched over like a plunging fullback. It is the most vulnerable of running back positions, one which gives the tackler an opportunity to perform a subtle bit of mayhem in the normal course of duty. "He'll get killed if he tries that in pro ball," one professional player has commented.
>
> Indisputably, the technique is as hazardous for the ball-carrier as it is for the tackler. "Alan is too hard to tackle low," observes Jim Barnhill, the sports editor of the *Kenosha Evening News*, "so most guys go after him high, usually with necktie tackles."
>
> Despite the dangers involved in Ameche's stand-up style of running, Ivy Williamson, head coach at Wisconsin, has prudently refrained from changing it. "Apparently, he knows where he is going," Williamson has said, "and wants to see everything on the way."
>
> Williamson is not greatly upset by Ameche's style. "He's a halfback-fullback type of runner," explains the long, lean coach of the Badgers. "In high school he played left half rather than full." Undoubtedly Ameche's dual assets, his ability to sweep the ends like a buck deer in flight and then erupt through the line like a live charge from a bazooka, have provided the foundation for his success.

Herndon's 1954 *Sports Illustrated* piece described the Ameche style thus: "Williamson gives The Horse his head completely. Al runs for daylight, cutting in or sweeping wide, wherever an opponent is not. It is the instinctive coordination of eye and foot, the incredible maneuverability, which makes the Horse a constant touchdown threat in addition to a battering-ram."

Ronzia describes Ameche's rampaging running style in simpler terms. "Al ran with his knees so high, you didn't know where to tackle the guy," Ronzia said. "He ran straight up but then when they would close in on him, he'd lower his shoulder and barrel into the linebacker."

As a former director of scouting, Braatz takes a more clinical approach in his analysis of Ameche's style. But he also was in the unique position of having first-hand knowledge on the difficulty of wrangling Ameche because he had played against him four times, since Marquette versus Wisconsin was an annual affair in those days.

"I played against him, so I know how hard he was tackle," Braatz said. "He kept his pads low and he hit you hard. I once said that in high school Alan used to hit like truck; in college he hit like a train.

"The thing is, he didn't present a big target. You had to tackle him low."

When he puts on his general manager's cap, Braatz still gives Ameche glowing reviews.

"He was the number-one draft choice [in the 1954 NFL draft], and I think Lino would be a first-round pick even today," Braatz said. "He was big, strong and he was fast. Remember, he was the state shot put champ and he was a sprinter. You don't see that combination too often."

Braatz goes so far as to compare Ameche favorably with Jim Brown and Jim Taylor, who were considered the NFL's premier fullbacks while Ameche was still playing.

"I would say Jim Brown was a more elusive back. Lino was more of a straightforward runner and Brown was more of a darter. Speedwise, they were about the same.

"As far as Taylor goes, he was a different kind of back than Lino. He was a very hard inside runner, a very tough guy to bring down. He was short and squatty."

8

The Year of the Horse

L UCKILY FOR ALAN AMECHE, HIS REPUTATION as a program-changing running back preceded him. Otherwise people in Madison might have gotten the wrong idea about the young man.

Maybe it was a case of youthful exuberance, or the thrill of being away from home for the first time in his life. Or perhaps it was a celebration of the brilliant future that he knew awaited him in Madison. Whatever possessed him isn't known. What is known is that Alan Ameche arrived in Madison in the late summer of 1951 for the opening of the University of Wisconsin football camp sporting a hideous shock of orange hair.

As a lark while they prepared for the annual Wisconsin North-South High School All-Star game a few weeks earlier, he, Braatz, and Mario Bonofiglio, as well as future Badger captain and former Madison East rival, Gary Messner, had dyed their hair what they thought would be a shade of red. Something went wrong, very wrong, and Ameche in particular was left with a tonsorial conversation piece that defied explanation.

"His most spectacular stunt as a teenager was dyeing his hair bright orange—'the color of an overripe cheddar cheese'—by way of celebrating his appearance in an all-star game in high school," stated the Furlong article.

The Wisconsin Sports News Service called the color of his botched bleaching a "sickening orange hue," that eventually morphed into a "taffy-brown shade."

"We were up in Green Bay for the all-star game and we were just monkeying around," Bonofiglio said. "You know, just kid stuff. It didn't turn out too good but it grew out after a while."

Their future Badger teammate Jim Temp, from La Crosse, Wisconsin, played on the North Squad while all the hair dyers were on the South team, but he remembers the incident well.

"Alan and Bonofiglio and a couple other nutballs, and all I can tell you was that it was not good," said Temp, who would go on to play four seasons for the Green Bay Packers after a fine career in Madison. "They were a bunch of characters just having fun, but they really looked terrible.

"The important thing is the country hicks from up north beat the city boys pretty good. It seemed like half their team was from Kenosha and the other half was Milwaukee Washington."

If the hair caper wasn't enough to catch the collective eye of the Badgers' coaching staff, Ameche's freshman publicity questionnaire for the university's sports news service might have raised an eyebrow or two. From the looks of it, Ameche didn't take a lot of time filling it out, but what he had to say was revealing.

Ameche's most detailed answer was in response to high school honors received. He wrote that he was "captain, all-state, all-conference, most. Val. Player and high scorer." But he saved his two shortest answers for later. In a fifty-one-word question asking him to "give full details," Ameche was asked to describe the greatest obstacle he faced in achieving success in sports.

His answer: "Financial difficulties."

But his shortest answer, and the one that probably got the biggest laugh in the football office, was to the question "What is your hobby?" His answer: "Yvonne."

That's it, just Yvonne. Apparently he felt no further embellishment was necessary.

If the coaching staff needed more proof that they had a certified free spirit on their hands, not exactly a cherished quality in a sport that requires almost military-like discipline, it was provided early in the team's training camp. Bobby Hinds loves to tell the story of their first training camp in Madison.

"I actually came to Madison a week prior to football starting and I bought myself a Victrola," Hinds related. "God only knows where I came up with the money for a Victrola, but I got it.

"Alan and I both loved classical music. When I lived at his house, we didn't have any money, so we'd go over to Simmons Library and rent out some LP albums, then go over to Allendale where we knew a girl who would let us use her Victrola.

"So we're at camp, it was 100-some degrees out, a real heat wave. I told Alan I had a Victrola and some music so come down to my room and listen before bedcheck.

"Well, it was so hot out that we were both nude and didn't think anything of it. You couldn't even wear any clothes it was so hot. So we were listening to music and laying in bed together.

"Well, they had the manager of the football team going from room to room to check and see that everybody was in their beds at curfew. So he gets to Alan's room and sees he is not in his bed, so he comes walking down the corridor to check my room.

"He opens the door and there was Alan and me laying together nude, listening to classical music. I still remember the kid's face turning crimson red. We were in the same bed but never gave it a second thought.

"The guy started stuttering and mumbling his words and Alan picked up on it right away. The guy said, 'You gotttttta ggggoooo to yyyyour room immediately,' he said.

"Well, Alan had a terrific sense of humor. He just leaned over to me and kissed me on the forehead. I don't think the guy could get out of there fast enough."

In all honesty, Ameche's "quirkiness" probably didn't draw a lot of attention in the offices of the football staff. After thirteen seasons of mediocrity that was the Harry Stuhldreher era, Ivy Williamson had the Wisconsin football program turned around and pointed in the right direction.

In 1949, his first season at Wisconsin, Williamson had posted a 5–3–1 record, and things got even better in 1950, when the Badgers went 6–3 and a very promising 5–2 in the Big Ten. With the leading defense in the nation in 1950, nicknamed the Hard Rocks, even bigger things were expected of the 1951 squad.

It was also the first year that the NCAA relaxed its rule against freshmen playing at the varsity level, but every preseason report filed on the Badgers that fall indicated that Williamson had no intention of playing any freshman, even one so highly touted as Ameche. With captain Jim Hammond the Badgers were set at the fullback position. Hammond was good and would be drafted the following spring in the tenth round of the NFL draft. But then along came Ameche.

In Wisconsin's intrasquad scrimmage before the season began, Ameche gave the Wisconsin loyalists a taste of what was to come. According to a report in the *Kenosha Evening News*, Ameche "was singled out for praise by Coach Ivy Williamson after ripping off steady gains from his fullback spot and piling up a big individual yardage aggregate."

Ameche's red team won, 20–12, over Bonofiglio's white team. Bonofiglio and Jim Temp hooked up for one of the white touchdowns.

It wasn't until his first game against an outside opponent, a junior-varsity contest against Iowa on the Friday afternoon before the varsity's season was to start, that Ameche showed his true colors. Ameche scored two second-half touchdowns on runs of 1 and 74 yards. Legend has it that Ameche was pulled out of that game and received a "battlefield promotion" to the varsity for the next day's game against Marquette.

By the time he would take the field for that game, he would already have a nickname. Freshman coach George Lanphear, whose own nickname was Muscles, loved to hang nicknames on his players, and his choice of monikers for Ameche was a natural . . . the Horse.

There are as many versions of the legend of how "the Horse" came into being as there are storytellers. But all agree that it was Lanphear who did the dubbing.

There are two schools of thought about Lanphear's thought process. One is that Ameche's high-kneed gait reminded Lanphear of a horse. The other is that Lanphear appreciated Ameche's work ethic to the point where he thought he worked like a horse. Even Ameche, in subsequent interviews, went both ways on Lanphear's reasoning.

Ronzia and Nicolazzi both claim to have been on the scene when Lanphear first called Ameche the Horse.

"Lanphear, that's who it was," Ronzia said. "I'm glad you asked me that because some people have gotten it wrong.

"The young guys were scrimmaging the varsity and we ran a simple play up the middle. 'God, he runs like a horse,' Lanphear said. Alan did run straight up and down with his knees high, then he'd turn his shoulder and barrel into the linebacker."

Nicolazzi is pretty much in agreement.

"Lanphear was our freshman coach and at an early practice, he started calling Alan, Horse. That was it, from then on he was the Horse. None of us ever called him that, it was for the press. But Alan 'the Horse' Ameche sounds better than Lino 'the Horse' Ameche. Right?"

Hinds, who was also on the scene freshman year, has a little different take than his high school teammates.

"Coach Lanphear called him the Horse because he was working so hard. They were hitting the sled—you'd hit it, then push it—and Al just worked so hard when he was training. Lanphear said 'You work like a horse' and it just kind of stuck."

The official press release of the Wisconsin Sports News Service embraced the high-stepper theory.

"They hung the tag 'The Horse' on the 18-year-old Alan Ameche, fresh-man fullback from Kenosha, the first time practice field sideliners saw him bolt through the tough varsity line, highstepping and sunfishing like a mean rodeo bronco."

Furlong's article in *Sport* magazine embraced a hybrid version of how "the Horse" came to be.

"But it wasn't his statistical prowess which first attracted attention to Alan Ameche. It was his manner of running with his knees high and his arms flail-ing, much in the manner of a drum majorette proudly prancing down the field between the halves. It is for that reason that Ameche is so difficult to tackle low. Most of his followers believe that he acquired the nickname 'The Horse' because of the similarity between his running style and the precise stepping of a show horse. Alan himself believes the nickname derives from a comment made by one of the coaches during a practice session at Wisconsin. 'There goes Ameche again, working like a horse.'

"'The funny thing,' Alan says thoughtfully, 'is that I didn't feel I was work-ing hard at all.'"

It's doubtful that anyone in the announced crowd of 45,450 for the Marquette-Wisconsin game in Madison on September 29, 1951, had any idea what or who the Horse was. Ameche's performance that afternoon—one carry on the second-to-last play of the game for one yard, barely caused a ripple. But his day was to come.

The hero that day in the Badgers' 22–6 victory was Roger Dornburg, who scored the game's first touchdown, returning an interception 53 yards.

"After that first game, Alan came over to my room to listen to some music," Hinds said. "He got in the game against Marquette for about five minutes and you know what he said to me? He said, 'If I keep this up, I'm going to get my letter this season.' That's all he wanted, to get his letter."

Ameche's comment turned out to be a classic understatement. He earned his membership in the Lettermen's Club the following week, when the Bad-gers opened their Big Ten season under a threatening gray sky against the University of Illinois.

The Badgers had arrived in Champaign Friday afternoon, and Ameche and several others were able to catch some of the jayvee game from the side-lines. With Bonofiglio at quarterback, the Badger youngsters were able to grind out a 24–14 victory over their hosts. But Bonofiglio was zero for four in extra-point conversions, a fact not lost on his good friend from home.

"That's the way to boot that leather, M-A-R-I-O," Ameche good-naturedly ribbed Bonofiglio from the sidelines.

The next day, the Badgers lost a heartbreaker to the number-eight-ranked Illini, but Ameche, in relief of Hammond, rushed 10 times for 40 yards. The game was billed as a showdown between potential Rose Bowl contenders, and it didn't disappoint.

Poised to expand on a 10–7 lead in the third quarter, Wisconsin pushed the ball to the Illinois 1-yard line but couldn't punch it into the end zone in four tries. Wisconsin had controlled the ball 9½ minutes to open the second half, but the Badgers' failure to put points on the board at the end of the drive led to their 14–10 defeat.

The legendary Illinois coach Ray Eliot, famous for his spellbinding oratory, recounted the story of Illinois' stand many times in his motivational speech, "The proper state of mind."

"Wisconsin is at our 1-yard line and we had this little 185-pound linebacker named Chuck Boerio, who's yelling at Wisconsin's quarterback Johnny Coatta 'Hey Johnny, send Ameche at me.' Can you imagine the audacity of such a thing? Most of us would pray that Ameche went north somewhere, but here he was telling them to bring him on.

"Well Ameche came at him and Boerio threw him for a three-yard loss. The game, the Big Ten championship, the Rose Bowl . . . it all came down to one yard."

In a game that Loren Tate, the long-time *Champaign News-Gazette* sports editor, described as Illinois' "Babe Ruth's called shot against the Cubs" game, the Illini prevailed and went on to win the Big Ten title. Reserve quarterback Don Engels led the winning drive, which included a leaping catch by Rex Smith on a deflection off teammate Steve Nosek. John Karrs dove in for the game-winning touchdown.

Ameche's longest run that afternoon was 7 yards, but Ameche made a huge impression on the Illini and Eliot. In what would be the first of countless superlatives to be laid at the young fullback's feet, Eliot called him "the best freshman fullback" he had ever seen.

Even Williamson, a man who carefully chose every word, gave Ameche what from Williamson was great praise.

"He has a wonderful attitude," Williamson told the *Wisconsin State Journal*, apparently applying extreme caution so as to not cause swelling of his young freshman's head. "He works hard, he's industrious and he's sincere. He's a very much improved ballplayer."

But in this case, Williamson's actions spoke much louder than his words. By game three, at Camp Randall against ninth-ranked Ohio State, Williamson installed Ameche as his starting fullback, a role he would maintain, with one exception, for the next three and a half seasons. Hammond permanently was moved to defensive halfback to bolster the Hard Rocks defense, which would go on to lead the nation in 1951.

Williamson went into the season thinking that he probably wouldn't take advantage of the freshman eligibility rule, which incidentally lasted just one year before the NCAA reversed itself and made freshmen ineligible again in 1952. But he never second-guessed himself when it came to Ameche.

Ameche had a breakout game against the Buckeyes, gaining a net 79 yards in 18 carries. Unfortunately, the Badgers and Ohio State battled to a 6–6 tie, casting a negative pall on Wisconsin's chances of a first-ever Rose Bowl invitation.

The Badgers clearly outplayed their guests, outgaining the Buckeyes 346–106 in total yards. Ameche outgained Ohio State on the ground by himself, 79–61 yards.

Ameche set up Wisconsin's touchdown, reeling off runs of 16 and 11 yards and putting the Badgers deep in Ohio State territory in the second period. Quarterback Johnny Coatta completed three consecutive passes to give Wisconsin a 6–0 lead. Both Williamson and Ohio State's young coach, Woody Hayes, had praise for Ameche.

"It was just a matter of too much defense, and of course, the guy who really ate us up was Ameche," Hayes said graciously after the game.

"I guess Big Al carried most of the offensive burden," said Williamson, giving his freshman fullback a verbal pat on the back.

The Badgers weren't particularly upset by their slow start in the Big Ten because they realized it was at least partially due to some unfortunate scheduling. They weren't about to let it derail their season. The following week, the Badgers unloaded on unranked Purdue at West Lafayette, Indiana, and it can be accurately described as Ameche's coming-out party.

He plowed through the Boilermakers for 148 net yards on 25 carries. Ameche's longest run of the day, and of his college career as it turned out, covered 64 yards but didn't result in a touchdown because he was dragged down at the Purdue 1-yard line. He did score on the next play, however, the first touchdown of his collegiate career.

Wisconsin beat Purdue, 31–7, and benefited from two safeties in the contest. It was becoming apparent that Williamson, despite having a seasoned quarterback in Coatta, was going to give his Horse free rein. After the game, Williamson was asked about Ameche's unorthodox upright running style.

"Yes, I guess so," Williamson said dryly. "But I don't think I'll change him."

By now, Ameche was already gathering national attention and was even written about in a brief *New York Times* article.

"Nobody paid much attention to Alan at the outset but when in a practice session, he went through the varsity line with the ease of a trained dog through a paper hoop, he was elected to the 'club.'

"They call him 'The Horse' and the tag can't be disputed. It can be backed up with figures. One minute he's the equivalent of a brewery wagon horse, pulling along everything in sight. In another minute he might be carefree galloper. Anyway he has lugged the ball 268 yards in 54 attempts for almost a 5 yard average and except for 1 yard and one play against Marquette, all of it was jarred off the Illinois, Ohio State and Purdue defenses on successive Saturdays."

The article went on to compare Ameche to Pat Harder and Ed Jankowski, perhaps the two finest fullbacks in Wisconsin history up to that time. It was quite a statement to make about an eighteen-year-old freshman who was only four games into his college career.

"He can smash as did Jankowski and take off on end runs after Harder's fashion. You might say that for a 200 pounder he really gets around."

Ameche showed no signs of a letdown in Wisconsin's next two victories: an easy, 41–0 victory over the thirteenth-ranked Northwestern Wildcats in Evanston, Illinois, and a 6–0 win over visiting Indiana. Against the Wildcats, Ameche rushed for 124 net yards in 23 carries and didn't play the last 25 minutes of the game. The hero that day was Jerry Witt, who scored four touchdowns, including a 60-yard reception from Coatta and a 69-yard run from scrimmage.

Against the Hoosiers in a game played in a November 3 blizzard in Madison, Ameche covered 57 yards in 15 carries, all in the first quarter. Wisconsin won the game with 58 seconds left to play when Coatta connected with Bill Hutchinson on a 35-yard touchdown pass.

By now the University of Wisconsin Sports News Service was touting Ameche by saying "in some parts, qualified football observers figure he's the outstanding frosh back in the nation.

"Ameche is big, fast, strong and willing. While a highly touted all-stater on a Kenosha team which made shambles out of the tough Big Eight conference in Wisconsin in his prep days, Alan wasn't figured on to come along as fast in the stepped-up action of Big Ten competition."

Through the Indiana game, Ameche had carried 92 times for 449 yards, all but 1 yard of which came in Big Ten games. That amounted to an average of almost 5 yards per carry.

Prior to the Northwestern game, the Wisconsin publicity people felt good enough to trot Ameche out in front of the media for what was believed to be his first interview.

"I'll never be sorry I came to Wisconsin," Ameche told Jack Burke of the Associated Press. "The coaches are wonderful and have helped me tremendously. One reason I came here was because of Badger offensive patterns, much like I had in high school and it hasn't been too much of a job to switch from left half to fullback.

"It feels great to be able to play on the varsity. It's a marvelous opportunity for a freshman and I'm grateful.

"Right now, we're concentrating on the Wildcats. We have a lot of respect for them. We look for a close game."

Williamson, quoted in the same article, was still his usual reserved self.

"He is coming along pretty good," the Wisconsin coach said of his star freshman. "The fellow lacks experience of course, like all freshmen. He has worked hard to improve his blocking."

The reason Ameche played just one quarter in the tight Indiana contest was because he had suffered a broken left wrist in the first quarter. Although it was severe enough for him to leave the game, he refused to have it x-rayed because he was afraid of what the result might be. The wrist would bother him for the rest of his life.

"I don't think this has ever been written about, but Alan broke his wrist in a game his freshman year," recounted his widow Yvonne. "He never told anyone because he thought he would lose his starting position if they knew he had a broken wrist.

"All his life that wrist would bother him. He couldn't even wear a wrist watch at times because it hurt him so much. He was drafted after his senior year and he was supposed to go in the Army, but they turned him down because they said he couldn't cock a gun with that wrist.

"By that time he knew he was going to play professional football, so he didn't want to go in the Army. Nobody could believe they wouldn't take him. Everybody thought the Colts paid somebody off so he wouldn't have to go in."

Hinds, who was also classified 4-F because of a similar injury to his right wrist, remembers the story a bit differently.

"I got drafted before Al and went to the Milwaukee draft board for my physical. The guy asks about the wrist injury and I told him, 'It's OK, I can box with it.' But he says, 'No, you're 4-F.'

"So I come back to Madison and Al says, 'Bob, what happened?' I said, 'You won't believe this, but I'm 4-F because of my wrist.' So he said, 'Jesus, I've got the same injury with my left wrist and I don't want to go in either.'

"So he gets there and tells them about his wrist and how much it hurts him and how he can't carry a rifle. The guy recognizes him as Alan Ameche and says, 'Don't worry, you'll be an officer. They carry pistols, not rifles.'

"Somehow, they didn't take him. I think Al finally told them, 'Look, I have this broken wrist and it really hurts me.'"

Despite the pain, Ameche didn't let it slow him down. He led the way as the Badgers won their final three games of his freshman season, scoring victories over the nonconference University of Pennsylvania (16–7) as well as Big Ten opponents Iowa (34–7) and Minnesota (30–6).

The Badgers' season-ending six-game winning streak gave them an impressive 7–1–1 record and a number-eight ranking in both the AP and UPI final polls. The loss to Illinois in the second week of the season was Wisconsin's only loss, but it did come back to hurt the Badgers because Illinois ended up winning the Big Ten title and the berth to the Rose Bowl.

As for Ameche, he only got stronger in the season's closing weeks. Playing just the first quarter against Penn, he carried nine times for 49 yards. The Hard Rocks defense was the story in this contest, scoring all 16 points on a blocked punt recovered in the end zone, an interception return for touchdown, and a safety.

Williamson turned him loose in the final two weeks, as he carried 25 times for 126 yards against Iowa. Coatta provided the big play of the game against Iowa, connecting on a 53-yard touchdown pass to Rollie Strehlow. Ameche carried 31 times for 200 yards against Minnesota. He had a touchdown against Iowa and two versus Minnesota, bringing his season total to four.

The Minnesota game was played in snowy conditions and temperatures that were near zero. The foul weather must have agreed with Ameche because his 200 net yards against the Gophers would set the Wisconsin single-game rushing record.

More importantly, Ameche set Big Ten records for carries (147) and yards rushing (774) and school records for carries (157) and rushing yards (824). The previous Big Ten rushing record of 732 yards had been set by Johnny Karras of Illinois in 1949. Ameche accounted for almost two-thirds of Wisconsin's ground gained in 1951.

For some reason, Williamson didn't bother to use Ameche as a pass receiver out of the backfield, although Ameche had proved in high school that he was more than ready to accept that extra assignment. In his freshman year he caught just one pass for 13 yards, and inexplicably that would be his only reception in four seasons at Wisconsin.

Even with the paltry receiving total, he was able to finish third in the Big Ten in total yardage gained, behind Minnesota's quarterback, Paul Giel, and Coatta. Ameche averaged 5.2 yards per carry and was named honorable mention in several all-Midwest and all-conference teams.

Ameche was a bona fide star as a freshman, but he had to share the spotlight with the Hard Rocks defense, which is still recognized as perhaps the greatest defense in Wisconsin history. The 1951 defense still holds Wisconsin season records for total defense (1,393 yards allowed; 154.8 average per game), rushing defense (601 yards; 66.8 average per game); scoring defense (53 points; average 5.9 per game), most safeties (4), most punt returns (51), and lowest yield per play (2.58 yards).

Wisconsin's yield of 154.8 yards per game was tops in the nation in 1951, and the 66.8 rushing yards allowed was second best. The Wisconsin defense was so dominant that it actually outscored their opponents' offenses, 58–53, for the season. According to a note in the Wisconsin media guide, a Wisconsin fan wrote a letter to Williamson and his staff to "punt on first down, so he could see more of the defense."

As for Ameche, sportswriters weren't the only ones noticing the freshman fullback. Apparently leading-man good looks ran in the Ameche family, but Alan's appeal to the opposite sex was more of a rugged, macho kind than that of his well-polished and suave second cousin, Don Ameche.

"He had a lot of girls chasing after him," Hinds recalled. "True then, true today. Girls like athletes."

Herndon's *Sports Illustrated* piece featured a great story about Yvonne's visit to Madison and her eye-opening experience in Ameche's Kronshage Hall dormitory lobby.

"Yvonne visited Madison one weekend late in his first season after Al had become The Horse. Waiting for him in the dormitory parlor she heard the phone ring eleven different times, and eleven different coeds wanted to speak to Al-an [sic]. Ameche never had a chance after that. Yvonne and Lino were married in his sophomore year, when both were nineteen."

There were even reports of young coeds camping out on the steps of Kronshage Hall, just to catch his eye or perhaps exchange a few pleasantries.

"Alan was a fun-loving guy before he got married," Temp said. "There was no question he liked the girls and they liked him. We were all surprised that he got married so soon.

"I remember he would stand in front of the mirror in the training room. He'd look at himself, with his hair slicked back and he'd put his arms back and start pumping his arms.

"We'd walk by him and say, 'Come on, you don't need to look at yourself so much.' But it's no wonder the girls liked him. Alan was really built. He had a great sense of humor and every guy on the team liked him.

"I remember we were riding the bus to the Ohio State game and I was across the aisle from Alan. I wanted to get his attention, so I tapped him on the thigh. I remember thinking it was like hitting a concrete block. The guy was nothing but muscle."

Furlong wrote a very apt description of Ameche. "In appearance, Ameche has the well-muscled, tapered form of a 'halfback-fullback type.' He stands just under six feet tall and weighs about 208 pounds. He is deep-chested and thick-necked—his collar size swells from 17 to 17½ during the season—but he carries his weight along lines much smoother than those of the traditionally squat, square frame of a fullback.

"He is very dark complexioned, has brown eyes and wavy, slightly bristly dark brown hair. He has what he delicately describes as a 'prominent' nose, a feature which has thus far left him without any neurosis."

Yvonne claims she would have loved to go to Madison as a coed rather than a young wife, but said it just wasn't in the cards for her to go to any college.

"It's funny," she said, "but when my kids were growing up, people wouldn't ask them, '*Are* you going to college?' It was, '*Where* are you going to college?' I grew up in Kenosha in an era where it was, 'Are you able to afford college?' and not many were at the time. Remember my father died and I was raised on Social Security, so when I reached eighteen, the checks stopped coming in.

"You grow up with the idea you were going to get married, not grow up and be a lawyer or a doctor."

After graduating from high school, Yvonne went to work in the office of a Kenosha dentist.

"There was a lot going on in my life at that time," she explained. "My family was shifting. My sister got married and my father's death was very traumatic. My mother was a very young widow. She didn't drive so we didn't own a car. I remember pulling a wagon to go to the grocery store."

Benedetta and Augusto Amici. (Ameche family photo)

Baby Lino Dante Amici.
(Ameche family photo)

When Benedetta returned to Italy with little Lindo and Lino in tow, there was no guarantee she would return to Kenosha. (Ameche family photo)

Ameche celebrates his First Communion at Mount Carmel Catholic Church in Kenosha. (Ameche family photo)

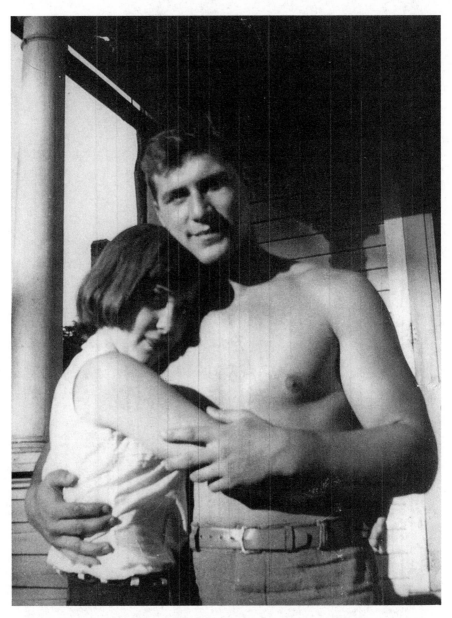
High school sweethearts Yvonne Molinaro and Alan Ameche share a tender moment in front of the Ameche home. (Ameche family photo)

Ameche and Bobby Hinds (*right*) trained for the Kenosha Golden Gloves with local boxing promoter Tommy Dorff (*center*). (courtesy of Bobby Hinds)

Ameche (*left*) and Bobby Hinds (*wearing helmet*) clown around with City of Kenosha workers before departing for the University of Wisconsin. (Ameche family photo)

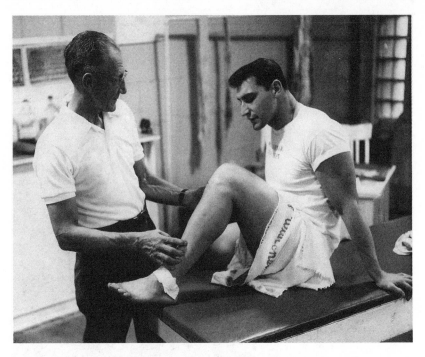

A University of Wisconsin trainer examines Ameche's tender left ankle.
(Ameche family photo)

Ameche's weight seemed to be a constant issue and Ivy Williamson peers around the
corner to check the status of his star fullback. (Ameche family photo)

The smile says it all as Ameche makes weight at Wisconsin. (Ameche family photo)

Ameche takes a breather from practice at Wisconsin. (Ameche family photo)

Despite demands on his time from his young family and intercollegiate football, Ameche was a serious student and eventually returned to Madison to earn his degree. (Ameche family photo)

Ameche and Ivy Williamson share a light moment before the Badgers practice. (Ameche family photo)

Ameche admires the statue of Abraham Lincoln outside the University of Wisconsin's Bascom Hall. (Ameche family photo)

9

Coming Up Roses

ALAN AMECHE PROBABLY WOULDN'T HAVE been able to give a precise answer if asked how many weekends he hitchhiked between Madison and Kenosha his freshman year. It was that many. But by his sophomore year, Ameche's hitchhiking days were over. Somehow he managed to throw together enough cash from his summer jobs to buy a small used Ford to get himself back and forth. Despite all the conventional wisdom, hitchhiking might have been a safer way to go.

Bonofiglio's favorite Ameche story involves the car and one of those trips between Madison and Kenosha.

"We were coming home from Madison on Highway 12, and it was a really foggy day," Bonofiglio recalled. "Just so foggy. You couldn't see anything.

"So Alan tells me to go sit on the fender on the car and direct us. So, all the way home, I'm on the fender telling him, 'left, right, left.' Normally it's a two-hour trip, but it took us four hours to get home that night.

"We were nuts. We were crazy. I always tell that story."

Hopefully, he never told that story to Williamson. After Wisconsin's 7-1-1 record in 1951, a season that saw the Badgers come within a touchdown of a Big Ten title, hopes were understandably high heading into 1952.

Gone was John Coatta, the aerial half of Wisconsin's potent two-pronged offense, but back were many of the key players of the Hard Rocks defense. More important, Ameche also was back.

Strong-armed Jim Haluska was penciled in to replace the graduated Coatta at quarterback, and the sophomore from Racine would need to be at his best. Coatta's 1,154 passing yards (eight touchdowns) placed him second in the

Big Ten in total offense in 1951, but more significantly, he kept opposing defenses from ganging up to stop Ameche.

Voters in the Associated Press poll were impressed enough to install the Badgers as the number-seven team in the nation in its preseason poll. A 42–19 drubbing of Marquette in the season opener figured to boost their standing. Haluska had a huge game in his first college start, completing 14 of 21 attempts for 237 yards and three touchdowns. Harland Carl scored touchdowns on runs of 11 and 51 yards and a pass reception of 54 yards. But for some reason, known only to the poll's voters, Wisconsin instead slipped a notch to number eight.

As with the Marquette game his freshman year, in which Ameche had one carry on the second to the last play of the game in a mop-up role, he again saw very limited action his sophomore year, despite being the focal point of the Wisconsin offense. He rushed for a net 78 yards in 22 carries, but all of them were in the first half.

It's hard to disagree with Williamson's decision to rest his star player in a game like the one against Marquette, which wasn't in the same class as the Badgers. But many observers, including some of Ameche's high school teammates, didn't feel that he was being used in a manner that maximized his talents.

"If you look at what Al did in high school and what he did for the Colts, it makes you wonder why they never threw him the ball at Wisconsin," observed Dick Nicolazzi. "He got a lot of yards out of the backfield, catching that little swing pass from Unitas with the Colts.

"One on one, you just weren't going to stop Al. I suppose he had enough carries, he didn't have the carries that teams give their best back now. But at that time, he was in the backfield with three other guys so I guess they had to divide it up.

"If they had given him 30 carries a game I don't know how much he would have had left by the sixth game of the season. He had a bruising style. He dished it out pretty good, but he took a pounding, too."

Bonofiglio is even more critical of the way his good friend was employed in Madison.

"I don't think they ever used Alan the right way in Madison," the quarterback said. "They would give him the ball when it was third and one, third and two. Why not give him the ball on first down? He was clearly their best back but they treated him like he was just a short yardage guy.

"Ameche could do it all. He blocked, he caught passes, and he even played defense. Somebody asked me once how he compared to Ron Dayne

[Wisconsin's only other Heisman Trophy winner] and there is really no comparison.

"Ron Dayne ran behind a line that was 6–6, 350 pounds. Ameche would have had 10,000 yards if he had a line like that. Ron Dayne never threw a block at Wisconsin and he always ran wide [to the outside]. Ameche got his yards running up the middle.

"I said Ron Dayne was never going to make it in pro football because he didn't know how to block. Ameche led the league in rushing his first year in pro football and Dayne never amounted to anything."

The Badgers needed a full dose of Ameche in the second week of the 1952 season, because next up was number-two-ranked Illinois, the team that handed the Badgers their only defeat the previous season. Ameche would carry a career-high 32 times for a net 116 yards and a touchdown as Wisconsin avenged the loss, 20–6, in Madison.

Illinois used what amounted to an eight-man line, designed specifically to thwart Ameche, but he still managed 3.6 yards per carry. Ameche was at his best when he was needed most. Of Wisconsin's 22 first downs on the afternoon, eight of them came on Ameche carries.

Ameche's longest run of the game was just 13 yards, but perhaps his best run was the one that kept alive Wisconsin's first touchdown drive. Facing a fourth-and-3 situation at the Illini 35 and both sides expecting Ameche to get the call, he pounded straight ahead for 4 yards and the first down. Ameche accounted for 23 of Wisconsin's 73 yards in the touchdown drive.

Wisconsin's dominating victory not only established the Badgers as the team to beat in the Big Ten, it catapulted them to the number-one ranking in the nation, the first time that had ever happened since the inception of polls. The Badgers replaced Michigan State, not yet a member of the Big Ten, even though the Spartans escaped with a slim 17–14 victory over Oregon State in Portland that same day.

But as in 1951, Wisconsin's early-season schedule was a killer, and week three of the season was a trip to unranked, yet always dangerous, Ohio State.

Unfortunately for the Badgers, their stay on top was a short one. Williamson would get seven shots at Ohio State in his seven-year stint as Wisconsin's head coach, and the best he could manage would be the 6–6 tie in 1951. In 1952, the Buckeyes would hand the Badgers their only regular season Big Ten loss, 23–14, before a mammoth crowd of 80,345. Ameche had a good game, rushing for 105 yards in 25 carries, but it wasn't enough as fumbles hurt the Badgers that afternoon.

The loss dropped the Badgers all the way to number twelve in the rankings, but it elevated their play. In a game in which Ameche sat out the second half, Wisconsin trounced Iowa, 42–13; Ameche had 54 yards in 13 carries with just his second touchdown of the season. Noteworthy were Hutchinson's 54-yard run from scrimmage and captain George O'Brien's record 96-yard punt.

With the Badgers struggling to gain momentum for their Rose Bowl stretch drive, they were stymied by their own quirky schedule. Wisconsin faced mid-season games against high-quality nonconference opponents. Number-ten-ranked UCLA visited Madison on October 25, and the Badgers traveled to Houston to play Rice and their all-American running back, Dick Moegle.

Both games took a toll on the Badgers, but in different ways. The UCLA contest was bad for team morale because the Bruins made the tough overland trip into Madison and dominated the Badgers, 20–7.

The worst thing about the game for the Badgers was how UCLA manhandled the Wisconsin offensive line and kept a lid on Ameche. He was held to 31 yards in 14 carries, his lowest output since his first college game against Marquette.

Perhaps the only positive that came out of the game was UCLA's unabashed respect for Ameche. The Bruins' coach, Red Sanders, freely admitted that his defense was geared to stop Ameche and afterward he explained why.

Sanders paid Ameche perhaps the biggest compliment he was ever paid, comparing him favorably with the great Bronko Nagurski. "Ameche is the strongest runner in football history, not even excepting Bronko Nagurski," Sanders gushed after the game.

Williamson, asked to comment on Sanders's statement, fumbled his response. "Ameche is a real football player," was the best he could offer.

The UCLA loss dropped Wisconsin all the way to number eighteen in the rankings and apparently frayed some nerves inside the Badger camp. Despite Sanders's superlatives regarding Ameche, Williamson decided not to start his best player in steamy Houston in a game that had enjoyed advance billing as "Ameche versus Moegle."

The official reason for Ameche's benching in favor of Johnny Dixon was that Ameche was undergoing a mid-season slump. Another report blamed a weight gain for Ameche's benching. An Associated Press story claimed Ameche's weight had "soared" to 217 pounds before the Rice game, which if true, would have been about nine pounds over his ideal weight.

But apparently there was more to Ameche's benching than a weight gain or midseason slump, as was reported at the time.

Although by all accounts Haluska was doing a good job of balancing the Badger attack, apparently Ameche thought that his pal Bonofiglio, who had been performing well in practice, should be given an opportunity to show what he could do in a real game. Although neither Ameche nor Williamson ever confirmed that they ever met to discuss it, such a meeting was later reported in several places.

Bonofiglio won't confirm the reports, but doesn't deny them either.

"Some people say that because Alan and I were friends since the seventh grade and he knew I wasn't happy there," Bonofiglio said. "Maybe he did go to Ivy, I don't know.

"They never gave me a chance. They had me playing on a squad that was playing against the varsity in practice all week. We would run the plays that the opponent that week would run, so the varsity would be ready in the games."

At any rate, Ameche wasn't in the lineup when the Wisconsin offense took the field for the first time that afternoon. When Dixon fumbled the ball away on the Badgers' first possession, Williamson figured he'd made his point and played Ameche the rest of the way.

The official Wisconsin press release on the subject claimed Ameche was in the "coaches' doghouse for a mid-season slump," but Dixon's fumble might have saved the situation from escalating. It seems that Ameche's brother, Lynn, had made the trip to Houston to see the game, and Alan wasn't happy that he was unable to start the game.

"But the stunt almost backfired," wrote Furlong in his piece in *Sport* magazine. "For Williamson wasn't aware that Alan's brother Lynn had traveled all the way to Houston to watch Alan against Rice and Alan had quietly resolved to leave the team if his brother was disappointed. The turn of events not only insured [sic] his tenure with the team, but helped pave the way for a three-touchdown performance against Indiana and two more scores against Minnesota."

Apparently Furlong believed the line about Williamson benching Ameche because of a slump. "When Alan experienced a mid-season slump, Williamson exercised a bit of psychology by announcing that Johnny Dixon, second string fullback, would start against Rice. The psychology worked."

It's doubtful that it had anything to do with Williamson's ploy, but Ameche did have a great game in Houston. He rushed for 116 yards in 23 carries as the Badgers beat the tough Owls, 21–7. Haluska connected with Jerry Witt on a 42-yard touchdown pass with nine seconds left in the first half. (Coincidentally, the game was played in Rice Stadium, which is a short walk from the Texas Medical Center, where Ameche would die thirty-six years later.)

Although it seems that none of Ameche's teammates knew the drama behind the scenes in Houston that day, the trip remained embedded in their memories for years for other reasons.

"I'll tell you what I remember about that trip," Jim Temp recalled. "When our plane was landing it was bumpier than the dickens and so hot in that plane.

"I looked back and saw [assistant coach] Bob O'Dell and one of the players throwing up into a bag. I kept swallowing and swallowing, but I never did [throw up]."

Defensive tackle Mark Hoegh, who was a junior at the time, remembers Houston's terrible heat and humidity, and the toll it took on him and the rest of his team.

"I missed some games with pneumonia that season and the first game I came back for was the Rice game," Hoegh recalled. "I damn near died down there, it was so hot and miserable.

"The thing I remember was that after the game I was so dehydrated that I walked into the shower with my full uniform on and turned on the cold water, full blast."

The Badgers would return to cooler climes for the final three weeks of the regular season. With home games remaining against three unranked opponents, the Badgers, ranked number eighteen after the Rice victory, still had a shot at a first-ever Rose Bowl berth. But first, Wisconsin needed to get past Northwestern and Minnesota at home and Indiana in Bloomington.

The Wildcats were up first and put up a surprisingly stout fight. Whatever the problem had been between Williamson and Ameche, it was in the past because Ameche had one of his best games of the season. He carried 31 times for a net of 159 yards.

Next up was Indiana on the road, and Ameche, who had scored just two touchdowns on the season, found the end zone three times in Bloomington. Ameche carried 20 times for 162 yards with touchdown runs of 1, 43, and 31 yards.

Ameche was so good, he even coaxed some superlatives out of Williamson. "He was terrific," Williamson said. "The best I've ever seen him."

Perhaps the 31-yard run in the fourth quarter was Ameche's best effort. According to the AP report, he shook off "two or three" Hoosiers on his way to the end zone.

Ameche almost tied the existing Big Ten record for touchdowns in a game but fumbled on the 2-yard line in the game's waning minutes.

Despite the fumble, the Indiana coach, Bernie Crimmins, was favorably impressed with Ameche.

"Ameche is one of the truly great football players I've ever seen," said Crimmins, a former backfield coach at Notre Dame. "He was the difference in the whole game. Our tackling was one of the weak spots, but I think Ameche was the main reason for that."

Indiana had lost to number-one-ranked Michigan State, 41–14, the previous Saturday and Crimmins thought that Wisconsin was on a par with the undefeated Spartans.

"I think it would be a real battle," said Crimmins of a hypothetical matchup between the Spartans and Badgers.

Wisconsin was more focused on winning the Big Ten, and that Saturday provided a huge step in that direction. Not only did the Badgers beat Indiana, but Michigan handed Purdue its first conference loss of the season.

According to the *Wisconsin State Journal* report: "The third quarter ended and as the teams exchanged goals, the field announcer gave the third quarter score at Ann Arbor—Michigan 21, Purdue 10. The Badgers howled with glee, jumped up and down and fairly flew out of their huddle."

There was no scoring in fourth quarter of the Michigan-Purdue game, and the game ended at 21–10. Purdue had led the Big Ten most of the season with an unblemished record, but the Boilermakers, who had tied Minnesota, 14–14, the previous week, were stumbling to the finish line.

The Purdue loss at Michigan meant that the Badgers held their Rose Bowl chances in their own hands. A victory over Minnesota in the regular season finale would give the Badgers the berth no matter what the result achieved by Purdue at Indiana the same day. With victories by both teams, the Badgers would finish at 5–1 to Purdue's 4–1–1 Big Ten record.

Minnesota entered the final week of the season as a factor in the Rose Bowl race as well. With a victory, the Gophers could knock the Badgers out of the top spot and tie or finish ahead of Purdue with a 4–1–1 record.

Despite the fact that Haluska was upholding his part of the bargain and having a strong season throwing the football for the Badgers, the Wisconsin-Minnesota contest figured to be a showdown between Ameche and the Gophers' fine back, Paul Giel.

Ameche entered the final week successfully defending his conference rushing title with 596 yards in 121 carries. Giel entered in sixth place, rushing for 344 yards in 96 carries.

It figured to be a wild finish to the closest Big Ten race of all time, but it was wilder than anyone could have imagined. When the final tallies were in that Saturday, no less than five of the Big Ten's nine members (the University of Chicago had already left the conference in 1946 and Michigan State didn't join until 1953) were within a half game of the top spot.

The lynchpin of all the craziness was a 21–21 Wisconsin-Minnesota tie that saw the ball trade hands an incredible five times in the game's final 65 seconds of play. The tie was fine with the Badgers, who found themselves in a tie for the top spot with Purdue at 4–1–1. The Badgers were chosen by the league's athletic directors to represent the conference in the Rose Bowl on the following Monday by virtue of the fact that they had never been there before.

Ohio State (5–2), Michigan (4–2), and Minnesota (3–1–2)were clustered within a half game of the top in the final league standings. The Buckeyes' 27–7 victory over the Wolverines in the final week added to the pile-up.

The five turnovers in the final minute were the result of both teams apparently feeling they needed a victory to get to Pasadena, and thus they were playing fast and loose with the football. Wisconsin, which hadn't won a Big Ten title, shared or outright, in forty years was perhaps the more desperate team. But it was Minnesota, which had to come from behind twice in the contest, that blinked first.

The parade of turnovers began when Burt Hable, who was Haluska's backup at quarterback, intercepted a halfback pass from Giel at the Wisconsin 28 with 65 seconds left. The Badgers, who had no intention of settling for a tie, came out passing, and Haluska completed passes to Harland Carl for 27 yards and 5 yards to Jerry Witt to get to the Minnesota 47.

Then Gino Cappelletti intercepted Haluska and brought it back to the Wisconsin 48, but Giel, who had played spectacularly most of the day, committed his second turnover within seconds. Don Voss jarred the ball loose from the Minnesota halfback and recovered it himself at the Wisconsin 45 with 31 seconds left in the game.

Amazingly, Haluska gave the ball back on the next play when it was intercepted by Clinton Andrus, who returned it to the Wisconsin 28. With time for just one play remaining, Giel again tried a long pass and this time it was intercepted, again by Hable, in the end zone.

The veteran *Wisconsin State Journal* sports editor Henry J. McCormick was so moved by what he saw that he broke the golden rule of journalism to interject himself into his game story: "Those final 65 seconds were the wildest ever seen at Camp Randall within the writer's memory." What should have been remembered as an epic battle between Ameche and Giel will always be noted for the last-minute craziness.

Even before the late-game turnoverfest, it was one of the most dramatic games ever played at the historic venue. As McCormick wrote, "a capacity crowd of 52,131 witnessed as wild a finish as any football game ever has produced on that historic field." Before his three turnovers, Giel was the whole show for the Gophers, running for one touchdown and passing for the other two. With his running and passing he accounted for 252 of Minnesota's 322 total yards.

Ameche was almost Giel's equal on that day, rushing for 125 yards in 25 carries with two touchdowns. But the Wisconsin fullback had a huge helping hand from the speedy Carl, who rushed for 102 yards, including a 55-yard touchdown, and 41 yards in pass receiving. Carl's touchdown was the first of the game and spotted Wisconsin to 7–0 lead with the extra-point kick of Paul Shwaiko.

Minnesota scored the game's next two touchdowns to take a 14–7 lead. The Gophers tied the score late in the first period on Giel's 31-yard pass to McNamara and took the lead early in the second quarter on Giel's two-yard plunge.

Ameche tied the score late in the second period on a 5-yard run to cap a 13-play, 75-yard drive. The lead photo of the *State Journal*'s sports section the next day shows the Ameche touchdown, but he is totally blocked out of the photo by three Minnesota tacklers as he barely crosses the goal line.

Despite the sloppiness of the game—Wisconsin had six turnovers (three lost fumbles, three interceptions) and Minnesota had eight turnovers (three lost fumbles and five interceptions)—it will go down as one of the most memorable games ever played at Camp Randall.

Despite the game's imperfect nature, it was a thing of beauty to Wisconsin fans because two days later, the Big Ten athletic directors would vote to send Wisconsin to the January 1, 1953, Rose Bowl. That meant an extension of the 1952 season, and it would certainly be an eventful thirty-nine days between the Minnesota game and the Rose Bowl.

Within minutes of the Rose Bowl announcement, an estimated 2,000 students left class to celebrate the news. The roving celebration, which included an impromptu band, roamed the campus and eventually moved up State Street to the state capitol. The revelers brought traffic to a standstill, and when they approached the capitol building, they were greeted by Governor Walter Kohler, who appeared on a balcony and led a chorus of "Varsity."

The subhead on the *Wisconsin State Journal* on the Sunday after the Wisconsin-Minnesota tie proclaimed Southern California's 14–12 victory over UCLA, thus earning the Trojans the berth opposite Wisconsin in the

Rose Bowl. But before the Badgers could focus on USC, there was still business to be taken care of in Madison.

Williamson had a disgruntled sophomore on his hands in Mario Bonofiglio. When the young quarterback from Kenosha learned he would not be on the squad traveling to Pasadena, he confronted Williamson with his resignation.

"They picked two seniors [backup quarterbacks] to go to Rose Bowl instead of me because they were seniors," Bonofiglio explained. He was referring to Gus Vergetis and Hable, fresh off an outstanding game as a defensive back against Minnesota.

"I'm better than those two guys. They were terrible. They couldn't make a high school team, but Ivy took them to the Rose Rowl because they were seniors and I got very upset about that. I went to his office and told him I was going to leave.

"He said, 'Come back next year and we'll give you a chance at quarterback.' I said, 'No, it's too late, Ivy. I'm leaving.'

"He said, 'Where are you going?' And I told him I didn't know. Honestly, I didn't know. I don't even remember how I got home from Madison that time.

"Why should I stay and waste my time? I hated to leave Madison and I hated to leave Alan, but I had to go. I talked to Ivy and I left. I think Ivy wanted me to stay, but I also think he was worried Alan might come with me actually."

There was no indication that Ameche had any inclination to leave Wisconsin, but that didn't stop Bonofiglio. Most of Williamson's players had nothing but praise for the coach, but not Bonofiglio, who even made an allusion to Williamson's alleged drinking problem.

"Ivy was a nice guy, but he wasn't a football coach," Bonofiglio said. "He was no coach. He wasn't really liked. He had a few other problems, too."

Bonofiglio claims he really had no idea what he would do next, but then an opportunity to play at the University of Miami fell into his lap.

"I went home and two guys from Waukegan called me and they wanted me to go to Miami," he said. "They sent the coach up to Kenosha to talk to me and my mom and dad. I was an all-American my first year there, so obviously it worked out for me. We ran the option there and I loved it."

The NCAA transfer rules required that Bonofiglio sit out a year, but as he said, he returned to the playing field for the Hurricanes for the 1954 season. Bonofiglio, who was known for his slick ballhandling, received honorable mention all-American honors as he rushed for 226 yards in 32 carries while completing 14 of 32 pass attempts for 232 yards.

At least one of his former teammates, Bobby Hinds, wishes that Bonofiglio had stayed in Madison.

"Mario was sensational in the scrimmages. . . . He had no equal," Hinds said. "If they had played him, they never would have lost a game. Wisconsin hasn't had a quarterback before or since who was as good as Mario."

Bonofiglio claims that Ameche told him Williamson always regretted his departure.

"Alan was the best. He said Ivy used to ask how I was doing in Miami. Alan would tell me Ivy would check the newspapers every game, and he would know exactly what I did at Miami."

10

Here Comes the Bride

For Yvonne Ameche, the night her future husband Alan proposed marriage to her is frozen in time.

"I remember it well," she said. "We were at the Valley Restaurant [just north of Kenosha] having dinner when he proposed.

"No, he didn't get on his hands and knees. That's just in the movies. But it was very sweet."

And what about the timing? With the responsibility of leading his team to the Rose Bowl resting squarely on his broad shoulders, Ameche would seem to have had enough on his mind at the time.

"I don't know, it just seemed like the right time," Yvonne reminisced. "There was a lot of going back and forth between Madison and Kenosha, and I know we missed each other quite a bit."

So a date was set—November 27, 1952—Thanksgiving Day. Now all that needed to be done was the planning and the promises.

One big promise in particular needed to be made. Furlong's article in *Sport* detailed Ameche's mother's concerns about the marriage of her nineteen-year-old son and how he convinced her everything would be fine.

"[Ameche] hasn't forgotten that he's going to school to acquire an education. Last semester he earned two A's, a B and two C's.

"'He promised me to get good grades,' says his mother.

"Alan's promise came when he announced his intention of marrying his high school sweetheart, Yvonne Molinaro, whom he first met at Washington Junior High. His mother, quite naturally distressed, not only at losing her youngest son but also by the possibility that the responsibility of marriage, combined with the pressures of football, might cause his school-work to deteriorate.

"Alan made good his promise after marrying Yvonne, an attractive blue-eyed girl with light brown hair."

The *Kenosha Evening News* society page offered a fairly detailed account of the Ameche-Molinaro wedding.

Miss Yvonne Katherine Molinaro was the bride of football star Alan Dante Ameche in Thanksgiving Day nuptials at Holy Rosary Catholic Church. The wedding aroused great interest throughout the state since the University of Wisconsin football team on which Ameche is fullback, was chosen to play in the Rose Bowl game on New Year's Day.

White mums decorated the altar for the 9 o'clock mass. The Rev. Oswald Malzer officiated and Miss Jill Molinaro, Madison, cousin of the bride, was vocal soloist.

The bride's ice-blue gown featured a lace bodice with a Peter Pan collar and long sleeves. The satin ballerina-length skirt was covered with a nylon tulle accordion pleated overskirt. A poke bonnet of ice-blue lace held her fingertip veil. An orchid topped her prayer book. John Brunner, uncle of the bride, gave her in marriage. She is the daughter of Mrs. Katherine Molinaro, 4822 20th Avenue.

Mrs. Robert Flatley, sister of the bride, was matron of honor. Her beige lace, ballerina length gown was designed with a portrait neckline and three-quarter sleeves. Brown Fuji mums made up her headpiece and bouquet.

Lynn Ameche was best man for his brother and Mario Bonofiglio and Robert Hinds served as ushers. The bridegroom's parents are Mr. and Mrs. Augusto Ameche, 5523 16th Avenue.

Breakfast was served at the bride's home by the wedding party, followed later by dinner at Ray Radigan's. Open house was held from 4 to 7 o'clock at the Molinaro home.

The newlywed pair will honeymoon in Georgia, after which Mrs. Ameche will return to Kenosha to live until mid-term. Then she will join her husband in Madison where he is a sophomore student. The bride is employed as dental assistant to Dr. S. M. Lapp.

"It was a nice wedding," Yvonne would later say. "It was what my mother could afford."

Some of Ameche's Wisconsin teammates were somewhat surprised that he would get married at such a young age, but his best friends from Kenosha saw it coming.

"I wasn't surprised at all," said Hinds, who by the time of the wedding had given up football, because of a wrist injury, to concentrate on boxing, which was still an NCAA-sanctioned sport at that time. "They had been together for years and they had been planning on getting married for a long time.

"I knew it was coming. He was living in Madison and she was in Kenosha, so it was kind of a natural thing to do."

Dick Nicolazzi, who was friends with both the bride and the groom, also was not surprised.

"I think they had been going together for so long, they just finally said, 'Let's do this,'" he surmised. "I think it was a good thing for Alan. They lived off campus and getting married and having kids gave him stability.

"They were young, but they knew what they were doing. Alan grew up to be a wonderful man, a great man, and Yvonne is a great person, too."

With limited time for a honeymoon, the newlyweds decided to fly to Atlanta to spend what amounted to a long weekend with Lynn, who was also married by this time. Ameche was an old hand at flying, having survived the nightmarish flight to Houston for the Rice game earlier that month, but Yvonne had never set foot on a plane before.

"We didn't have any money, but we wanted a honeymoon. Alan was such a tease," Yvonne recalled. "There was a bad smell on the plane and I asked him what it was.

"He said, 'Oh, it's the burnt bodies from the last crash the plane was in.' He knew I was scared, so I could have killed him, but that was his sense of humor."

There was little time for romance because Ameche was expected back in Madison for classes and football practice. For the first time in Wisconsin football history, the season wasn't over before Thanksgiving arrived. Not coincidentally, there was a Rose Bowl to be played and a month of preparation leading up to the game.

It was decided Yvonne would remain in Kenosha with her mother for the month of December and then move to Madison after the New Year and semester break. It turned out that the spring semester was anything but glamorous for the young wife of the football star.

The young couple had applied for and received married-student housing, but Ameche must have longed for the good old days at Kronshage Hall when he saw his new accommodations.

"They gave us housing and we shared the bathroom with seven other people," Yvonne remembered. "Our place was two rooms in a house.

"I remember there was this long hallway and our bedroom was on one end of it and the bathroom was on the other end. You had to get dressed to go the bathroom. There were so many people living in this house.

"We had a tiny living room and the kitchen was a closet. This is what they gave us. Oh, and I had to carry water from the bathroom for cooking or to wash dishes.

"Our refrigerator was on the first floor and we had to go through somebody else's apartment to get to it. I got two shelves with the refrigerator and to get to it, we had to go through this other apartment. Oh, and the washing machine was in the basement.

"It was terrible."

If Ameche felt cheated by getting married at such a young age, he never said that to Yvonne.

"I don't think he was the type who would have ever joined a fraternity or anything like that," she said. "He just wasn't that type.

"His friends were always welcome at our house, and a lot of guys were always there to play cards. He loved cards, poker and pinochle.

"If he felt he was missing out on something, he never vocalized it to me. I missed out on a lot, too. But we missed out together."

The young lovers got a quick dose on the harsh realities of married life, but the cramped house was just the beginning. Yvonne was by now pregnant with Brian, the couple's first of six children, and there was a near tragedy. Driving to Madison from Kenosha late that winter, the couple was in a very bad accident that left Yvonne with serious facial injuries.

"I was pregnant with Brian and we were on our way to Madison," she recalled. "By now Alan had a car. I don't know what kind it was, but it was a small little coupe.

"Alan went to pass on hill on Highway 50 [between Kenosha and Lake Geneva] and he hit a patch of ice. The car skidded out of control and we hit a telephone pole.

"There was a friend of Alan's in the car in the backseat, but I can't remember his name. Well, when we hit the pole, he came forward and pushed me, and I went forward and went right through the windshield and then came back through it.

"My face was a mess. Alan asked me if I was all right and when I turned to look at him, blood was just pouring from my face. All I could think of was my mother's coat. She had let me borrow her nice cashmere coat."

Ameche and the passenger weren't seriously hurt, but Yvonne needed to be taken back to Kenosha for surgery.

"They didn't have a plastic surgeon on staff back then, so when they put me back together, my eyebrow was crooked and my eye was deformed," Yvonne said. "I had five plastic surgeries on the side of my face, so those weren't real happy years.

"Here I was, the wife of a big football star, and I was going around like this [she covers her face] the winter after we married."

Yvonne was convinced that Ameche would abandon her when he saw what her face looked like after the accident. But she grossly underestimated her new husband.

"I was convinced when he saw me he wouldn't like me anymore," she said. "I thought this is it. My one eye was all up and I couldn't close it.

"When they took the bandages off and I saw my face for the first time, my mother said, 'Vonnie, it was the saddest thing I ever saw because you didn't make a sound. There were just big tears in yours eyes.'

"I stayed with mother after the accident, and when [Ameche] came home and saw me the first time, I cried so hard. He said 'Don't worry, we'll get your face fixed.' I had my first plastic surgery when I was pregnant with Alan, our second son, and I had the last one when we were in Baltimore. There were five in all. If you look closely, you can still see where I had the surgeries."

Obviously it was a trying time for all concerned, but through the whole ordeal, Ameche stuck with her.

"He said 'We'll get you fixed. We have no money, but we'll get you fixed.'"

It took some slick maneuvering on the part of the Ameches, but Yvonne did get her plastic surgeries.

"I sued Alan," she explained. "In Wisconsin at that time, a wife could sue her husband if he was at fault in an accident, and he was clearly at fault.

"So I sued his insurance company and I won. We had to replace the telephone pole, but we got money to get the car fixed and for the plastic surgery.

"Those were difficult years for me," she said. "Not only didn't I look right, but I had three kids in diapers. I was at home with three kids and a beat up face, but I couldn't worry about it. I'm sure they were tough times for Alan as well."

Brian was born on June 19, 1953, and Alan came along a year after that, and Cathy the following year. Having three children in rapid fire succession certainly couldn't have helped things at home.

"Honestly, I don't know why," Yvonne said when asked why she had so many babies so early. "It just happened."

The stress of the young children was manageable, but when Ameche's parents came to live with the young couple in Alan's junior year, the situation

almost became unbearable. At that time, Augusto, now sixty-six, was ill, suffering from high blood pressure, and he hadn't been able to work for about
two years. Elizabeth didn't feel she could take care of him alone.

So in the autumn of 1953, Ameche invited his parents to move in with
him and his growing family in Madison. Ostensibly, Ameche could help his
mother with Augusto, while she would help Yvonne with Brian (and soon-
to-be-born Alan), while Yvonne supported the family. Yvonne was less than
thrilled with the plan.

"Alan's mother and father came to live with us and I went to work,"
Yvonne said. "They took care of Brian, and I found a job as a receptionist for
a doctor. I also learned how to take blood and give shots.

"By this point they were retired. They saw I could make money, so I went
to work."

Ameche was such a celebrity by now that the *Wisconsin State Journal*
published a big story about the Ameche parents moving to Madison in early
October 1953. A two-line banner headline breathlessly reported the coming of the Ameches: "Ameche's parents to come here to live with Badger
football star."

"Madison's population will increase by two today with the move here of
a couple of proud parents and grandparents from Kenosha—Mr. and Mrs.
Augusto Ameche," began the article, written by Lew Roberts.

Mr. and Mrs. Augusto Ameche are sorry to leave friends of 26 years standing
in Kenosha, but they're both pleased and excited with the prospect of living in
Madison with their son and his family.

The Badger fullback, his wife Yvonne and the couple's 3½ month old son
Brian have just moved from 2010 Vilas Avenue to a bungalow at 311 Craig
Avenue, Blackhawk Park. The elder Ameches will join them there today.

A moving van will bring the furniture from the Ameche home in Kenosha
this morning. Mr. and Mrs. Ameche will come by auto this afternoon.

The story went on to quote Elizabeth: "It will be two years in February that
the doctor told him he must not work anymore. It's been kind of a worry to
me. Just two of us alone here and my husband sick.

"Then our son asked us to come and live with him. It will be so nice."
Unfortunately, it didn't work out that way.

"It wasn't good," Yvonne said. "She was very difficult. It just didn't work."
Nonetheless, Augusto was excited about the move as well.

"Yes, tomorrow afternoon we will all be together in Nino's [sic] house," the elder Ameche said. "My wife, me, my son Nino and his wife Yvonne and my grandson, Brian Augusto Ameche. Augusto, that's my name."

The *State Journal* article told how the Ameches became football fans when Alan "rewrote Big Eight Conference records while playing with Kenosha high school."

The article said that the Ameches saw their son play two home games in 1951 and two more games in 1952. Augusto attended both Dad's Day celebrations and "got a tremendous ovation as he waved an enthusiastic hand in filled Camp Randall when introduced with fathers of other Badger gridders."

They planned to see more Badger games now that they were in Madison, but they were unable to see the 1953 season opener, a 20–0 nonconference victory over Penn State, because they were in Kenosha packing.

"We listened on the radio though," Mrs. Ameche said. "It was such a good game.

"We like Madison very much. We will miss so many friends, here in Kenosha. But then it's not very far and we can come back once in a while. And we hope they will come and see us in Madison."

The story ended with these prophetic words: "Augusto Ameche would like to visit his native Italy someday. No definite plans or anything, just sort of a dream that's pleasant to run through over and over again in his mind."

It was prophetic because the elder Ameches stayed in Madison for less than a year. They moved back to Italy for about a year and then returned to Kenosha. Augusto died of complications from his high blood pressure in January 1956.

Elizabeth later moved in with Alan and Yvonne again after he retired from professional football and had moved permanently to the Philadelphia area. She died of a heart attack in 1984 at the age of eighty-two.

"She lived in a home for the elderly but would come and stay with us on the weekends," Yvonne recalled. "I remember her saying that the watch she was wearing hurt her arm, and I told her she should go to the hospital. But it was too late, she had a heart attack."

11

Pasadena Dreaming

IT WAS JUST A FLEETING MOMENT WHEN measured in the totality of Alan Ameche's life, but the two weeks he spent in Southern California for the 1953 Rose Bowl seemed so natural.

Ameche was perfect fodder for the West Coast newspapers, and not just the sports pages, but the Hollywood beat as well. The nineteen-year-old newly-wed was big, strong, ruggedly handsome, and the star of the visiting team from Wisconsin. And yes, the Ameche name carried more than a little weight in Tinseltown as well.

Don Ameche, Alan's second cousin, was forty-four years old by this time and past his leading-man days in such motion pictures as *Alexander's Rag-time Band* and *The Story of Alexander Graham Bell*. (His best performance, the one for which he would win his only Academy Award, was in *Cocoon*, and that would be in 1985, thirty-two years later.)

So it was only natural that when the West Coast media was allowed access to the Wisconsin players, the first question was for Alan Ameche and in-volved his relationship with Don Ameche.

Writing for the *Milwaukee Sentinel*, Tony Ingrassia penned: "The coast papers have been having a rough time getting straightened out on Al (The Horse) Ameche's relationship to Don (the movie star) Ameche.

"Some say they are related, some say they aren't. For the record, in Al's own words, 'My father and Don's father were cousins.' That ought to settle that. . . . One paper carried this item in a story about Ameche. 'Unlike his famous kinsman, the perfect profile Don, the Badger back owns more rugged features including a nose that is somewhat long and pointed.'"

The story continued: "'Why do you run straight up?' a teammate taunted. 'Why not lower your head and barrel into 'em?'

"'Because I'm afraid I might spear somebody, that's why,' he retorted. Al, who sort of likes his rugged features, failed to see the humor."

Given the star status of both men, it was probably the most-asked question of Alan Ameche during his football career.

Bill Furlong asked it in his story for *Sport* magazine. Ameche's answer: "'We're related, sure,' he says, 'but it's not what you would call a close relationship.'"

As mentioned earlier, the only conversation between the two Ameches occurred when Don had called Alan at the behest of Notre Dame football coach Frank Leahy. The irony there is that Don Ameche graduated from the University of Wisconsin after attending Marquette and Loras College. However, Don Ameche apparently had no loyalty to the University of Wisconsin, which wouldn't surprise anyone in Kenosha. He had little use for Kenosha after achieving fame and fortune in Hollywood.

"Alan always liked Kenosha, not like Don Ameche," Yvonne said. "They wanted to give Don Ameche some Italian award in Kenosha and he said, 'Why would I come back there? I thought it was a terrible place to live. I thought it was ugly.'"

A column by Jim Barnhill in the *Kenosha Evening News* surmised that Alan Ameche was the most photographed Badger leading up to the big game.

"Ameche was pictured with Lana Turner, Doris Day, Bob Hope, Dolly [Polly?] Bergen, Leah Feland, Tournament of Roses queen, and many others. One L.A. paper [the *Examiner*] ran nearly a half-page picture of the Kenosha fullback."

The Badgers had arrived in Pasadena on December 18, and Williamson was relentless in his preparation for the game. The Badgers had two practices each day they were in California, right up until the day before the game.

The day he arrived in California, Ameche sent a jumbo-sized postcard of the Rose Bowl to his parents, who were still living at 5523 16th Avenue. The postcard had a return address of Room 307, the Huntington Hotel, Pasadena, California.

Hello Mom and Dad.

   Here I am 2,500 miles away and I did it all in about 7 hours. I feel very well and hope all at home feel the same. It's warm here and very beautiful. We start practice right away tomorrow morning and continue until January 1. Twice a day.

I'll write you soon.

Love, Alan

Ameche also missed his new bride Yvonne and his good friend Mario Bonofiglio, who left the team after the regular season ended. Ameche had a fake newspaper printed up with a two-line banner headline that read "Bonofiglio and Ameche crash Hollywood!" The phony newspaper, the *Hollywood Star News*, ended up in Ameche's scrapbook along with the postcard to his parents.

Although his family and friends in Kenosha would have to watch the game on television sets, they would have a good view of the game. NBC, which televised the game nationally, boasted that it would employ six cameras at the game and would have a seventh camera in backup in case there was an unfortunate break in the transmission, as there had been several weeks earlier during the USC-UCLA telecast.

It was good that Ameche and his teammates were allowed to squeeze in a little fun in California, because Williamson, with his two-a-day mentality, drove the team relentlessly.

According to a story by the *Milwaukee Journal* sports editor, Oliver Kuechle, "police on motorcycles patrolled the area around the practice field." Williamson chose a secret location for the team's practices because, as Kuechle stated, "Williamson deemed it necessary for truly secret practices."

The pressure on Williamson was not from the home front. In its December 28, 1952, issue, the Sunday *Milwaukee Journal* magazine featured a smiling Williamson on its cover with the title "Wisconsin's Man of the Year."

In one of his stories, Kuechle referred to Williamson as "The big guy, who has given Wisconsin the four greatest years of football in the school's history." So Williamson's feelings of pressure to beat Southern Cal were probably self-imposed and probably more akin to peer pressure than anything else.

In 1947 the Pacific Coast Conference had entered into an exclusive relationship with the Big Ten, in which both conferences' champions would meet each January 1 in the Rose Bowl. In the six years that preceded the 1953 game, the Big Ten was a perfect 6–0. Williamson didn't want to be the first Big Ten coach to lose at the Rose Bowl, even though he was taking Wisconsin to its first bowl game of any sort.

Covering the Badgers for two straight weeks without a game must have been somewhat daunting for the small press contingent that sought refuge from the Wisconsin winter in sunny Southern California. Williamson seemed to struggle with quotable material, perhaps because he wanted to keep a tight lid on any news that might aid USC in its game planning.

Here are some typical snippets from Williamson as recorded by Kuechle: "I think we're coming along. The only thing we're worried about now is the condition of some of the boys and specifically Chuck Berndt (tackle), who is still about 10 pounds overweight, and Bob Kennedy (guard) and Alan Ameche, who are about five pounds over. We've got to run them. They got a half mile of extra work Friday and they'll continue to get it until they're in shape."

While Williamson might have had an issue with Ameche's fluctuating weight, he apparently had no problems with his star's work ethic.

"[Ameche] is the last man to leave the practice field and the first to report," Williamson told reporters in California. "The whole team's attitude is good but Ameche is definitely the most eager and the hardest worker."

Williamson said that scrimmaging would be kept to a minimum while in California because he didn't want any injuries. Despite Williamson's best efforts, Harland Carl suffered an injury in practice that week, an injury that might have determined the outcome of the game. Williamson's close-to-the-vest dealings with the press and his penchant for secrecy, however, kept Carl's injury under wraps until game day.

"We want to avoid real scrimmage as much as we can," Williamson told the press. "We just don't want to take a chance of hurting anybody. If we can get through the next 10 days without any scrimmage at all—fine. That's the way we'd really like it."

Kuechle apparently was so hard up for story ideas that he actually printed a story in which Williamson lectured him on the importance of luck in football. A cynic might surmise that Williamson's quotes in the story were almost deliberately simple, for example:

"Luck. With it we could win. Without it, I'm afraid we could lose."

Perhaps the most laughable thing about this Williamson quote is that Kuechle included it in his story for the *Milwaukee Journal*.

"In the Ohio State game of 1949, everything we did was wrong," Williamson continued his lecture. "We'd loop one way in the line and Ohio would go the other way. We'd shoot our linebackers on another play and Ohio State would come up with something that made us look like suckers. Invariably we'd guess wrong."

Ohio State won that game, 21–0, in Williamson's first season at Wisconsin. He chose the Northwestern game of 1951 (41–0, Wisconsin) as a case of good luck.

"A year ago against Northwestern though, just the opposite was true. Everything we did was right, everything Northwestern did was wrong. It was strictly luck—a combination of good guessing on our part and wrong guessing on theirs. Except for the luck, we weren't 41–0 better than Northwestern at all."

Kuechle concluded his story with these Williamson pearls. When asked if he could control the luck, Williamson replied, "Only to a small extent.

"Sure we can have some broad general patterns or assignments, but beyond them it is still a matter of luck, a matter of guessing right and doing the right thing on every play.

"That game on New Year's Day can be determined entirely by luck—by the little things that a lot of spectators probably never see."

After reading that story, it's surprising Rose Bowl officials didn't cancel the game and just flip a coin to determine the winner. But as Williamson surely was aware, the outcome of the game would be decided by preparation, perspiration, and execution.

Both Southern Cal and Wisconsin were run-first, pass-second teams. The Trojans featured all-American quarterback Jimmy Sears, while Wisconsin featured Ameche. Harland Carl, who drew comparisons with Badger great Elroy Hirsch because of his superior speed, gave Wisconsin an outside threat.

For the second consecutive year, Ameche led the Big Ten in rushing, an achievement made more remarkable by the fact that, as a fullback, his primary duty was supposedly to block for the speedier halfbacks. Ameche was a great blocker, but it was his rushing totals that got him first team all-American honors and first-team Big Ten honors as a sophomore.

In 1952 conference play Ameche ground out 721 yards in one less game than he had played in as a freshman, when he rushed for 774 yards. Also, for the second straight season, Ameche broke the Wisconsin single-season rushing record, going for 946 yards (before the Rose Bowl game). Ameche's 205 carries during the regular season was also a new Wisconsin record.

Carl had impressive numbers as well, but the junior from Greenwood, Wisconsin, never reached his full potential because of injuries. He missed the entire 1950 season because of a wrist injury but carried 24 times in 1951 for a team-high 6.7 yards per carry. He missed two games with injuries in 1952 but still rushed for 414 yards and had 214 yards in 12 pass receptions and 149 yards in kickoff returns. One of the games he missed in 1952 was the UCLA contest, and many observers felt Carl's absence had allowed UCLA to gear its defense toward stopping Ameche.

The UCLA coach, Red Sanders, had devised the only defense that effectively shut down Ameche in 1952. Believing that Wisconsin didn't have the speed to get outside of the UCLA defense without Carl, Sanders bunched his defense in the middle, holding Ameche, primarily an inside runner, to 31 yards in 14 carries.

Ironically, Carl had missed that UCLA game because he had been accidentally knocked cold by an Ameche knee in the previous week's game against Iowa.

"Harlan was supposed to get inside and make a block on the Iowa linebacker," recalled Hoegh. "Alan got the ball and the defender bumped Harlan into Alan's knee. It knocked him cold and he ended up spending the night in a hospital in Iowa and wasn't able to play the following week."

In the Rose Bowl Wisconsin needed Carl at his best to prevent a repeat of the UCLA strategy. Unfortunately for the Badgers, that wasn't to be the case.

It seems that Carl had injured his leg during practice earlier in the week and didn't enter the contest until the waning minutes, when it was effectively over. What made matters worse was that Carl's backup, Bill Hutchinson, was injured and forced to leave the game early. Williamson was forced to improvise with Roy Burks, the third-string right halfback, who was hampered by chronic knee problems.

So the burden placed on Ameche's shoulders to carry the team was immense. Whether it was high school, college, or the NFL, Ameche never let down his team, but never would he be as valuable to his team as he was on the first day of 1953.

Battling against the number-one-ranked defense in the nation that was stacked to stop him, Ameche would turn in the second-greatest rushing performance in Rose Bowl history up to that time. Ameche launched his body into the teeth of the Trojan defense 28 times and netted 133 yards.

The rest of the Badger runners combined for just 77 yards, and Southern Cal had just 48 total rushing yards as a team. Only Bobby Grayson of Stanford, who had rushed for 158 yards in the 1936 Rose Bowl, could claim more yardage than Ameche gained on that day.

Unfortunately for the Badgers, Ameche's heroic effort wasn't enough. As Ameche sparkled, the rest of the Wisconsin offense sputtered, and USC eked out a 7–0 victory. The Wisconsin defeat, the first ever for a Big Ten team since the coupling of that conference and the Pacific Coast Conference in 1947, was not for lack of opportunity. No less than five times the crowd of 101,500 in Pasadena's sun-baked Arroyo Seco watched as Wisconsin approached or penetrated the Trojans' red zone. And five times they saw the Badgers turned away empty-handed. Wisconsin had drives end on the Southern Cal 14-, 21-, 7-, 17- and 20-yard lines.

Ameche talked with *Kenosha Evening News* sports editor Jim Barnhill after the game and summed up his frustration quite well.

"We just couldn't put it over," Ameche said. "We could move the ball from 20 to 20 but something always seemed to pop up when it looked like we could go all the way."

The first half could have been described as a war of attrition with very little to contribute to the highlight reel. Carl spent the half on the bench with a sore leg, then his replacement at halfback, Hutchinson, was knocked out of the game on a jarring tackle. Defensive end Bill Voss, the Badgers' best pass rusher, also was sent to the sidelines for the day with a second-period knee injury.

The Trojans weren't exempt from the injury epidemic either. Sears, arguably Southern Cal's best player, was knocked out of the game three minutes into the first period with what doctors later described as a broken fibula.

Sears's replacement at quarterback was backup halfback Rudy Bukich, who went on to be a journeyman NFL quarterback. With an untested quarterback in the game, the Trojans' coach, Jess Hill, took a very conservative approach, and it got them nowhere in the first half.

With neither team able to generate much offense in the scoreless first half, it turned into a battle for field position on the part of the teams' punters, who were in the unfamiliar role of leading men. Although gaining fewer yards than the Badgers, Southern Cal stayed in the game on the strength of superior punting by Des Koch. He averaged over 51 yards per punt, including a 73-yarder from his own end zone, which shattered a Rose Bowl record.

Although the Badgers held the advantage in yardage in the first half, it took two key interceptions late in the second period to keep the Trojans off the scoreboard. Roger Dornburg and Paul Shwaiko both had key interceptions deep in Wisconsin territory late in the half.

Apparently, a change in direction was what was needed because both teams came out in the third quarter ready to play. For Wisconsin, it was left to Ameche to make the big play, and he did just that.

After a short kick return to the Wisconsin 13 to start the second half, Haluska handed to Ameche, who banged off the left tackle and galloped down the sideline for 54 yards. Ameche was caught from behind and shoved out of bounds at the USC 33-yard line, but it appeared that Wisconsin finally had something going.

"We saw Alan break loose for a long gain and we thought he was going all the way," said Badgers defensive end Jerry Wuhrman. "Unfortunately, somebody caught him from behind."

Haluska, who had a good game himself (11 for 26, 142 yards) did his best to keep the drive alive. On the next play, he flipped a 9-yard pass to Erv Andrykowski, and then Gerald Witt took a pitchout 2 yards to the USC 22.

But then disaster struck. Burks fumbled the football, and USC's Bob Hooks recovered it at his own 27. The Badgers probably figured it was no big deal at the time. Southern Cal was still deep in its own territory and hadn't shown the ability to score all day.

But it *was* a big deal. With no rushing first downs in the game until late in the third period, Hill apparently figured that the only way to win the game was to show his confidence in Bukich and let him pass the football.

The young signal caller from Saint Louis repaid his coach by marching his team 73 yards in nine plays for the game's only touchdown. Bukich completed five of six passes in the drive with the game winner being a 22-yard strike to his wide-open halfback, Al Carmichael, at the goal line.

"Oh boy am I happy," Carmichael gushed to an Associated Press reporter after the game. "That was really a beautiful pass."

Despite Bukich's inexperience, Hill's change in strategy made perfect sense. The Badgers completely throttled the USC running game in the first half, and with Voss out, the Trojans stood a good chance of protecting Bukich, who would finish 12 completions in 20 attempts for 137 yards.

"That was the first time we've used that pattern," Hill told the AP after the game. "Rudy Bukich really threw a strike. This undoubtedly was the best game of his career."

Said Bukich of the winning play: "I had just the right feel when it left my hand."

Sam Tsagalakis tacked on the extra point, making the score a seemingly surmountable 7–0. In the fourth quarter, Tsagalakis would attempt a 22-yard field goal that would hit the upright of the goal post and fall harmlessly to the Rose Bowl turf.

"When we lost Voss, we not only lost a great defensive lineman, but our principal pass rusher," said Williamson, who was never one to make excuses. "After that, Bukich of the Trojans had plenty of time (to pass the football)."

To their credit, the Badgers battled to the final gun. Effectively using screen passes, Wisconsin picked up a first down at the USC 15-yard line on a 33-yard pass from Haluska to Witt. The drive stalled when Ameche was thrown for a 2-yard loss and Witt was ruled out of bounds on a reception at the USC 3.

Ironically, the Badgers' best chance to score came in the waning minutes of the contest, when Carl mysteriously appeared for the first time. He seemed to be running fine as he got open in the end zone. Unfortunately, Carl juggled the perfectly thrown pass from Haluska, and his momentum carried him out of bounds before he was able to secure it. No outsiders will ever know what Williamson truly thought about Carl's performance that day, but Barnhill, who gathered some of the best quotes from the day, left no doubt how he felt. He tracked down Carl in the locker room after the game and left no ambiguity in reporting how he felt:

> We also talked to Harland Carl after the game. The Badger star who always seems to come up with some injury when he is needed most was a controversial figure in the West Coast papers.
>
> There were those who opined that Carl isn't a tough competitor while many felt Carl, in good physical shape, would have been the difference if he had been able to go the route.
>
> "My leg wasn't right. It wasn't in top shape," Carl said. "I told Coach when he asked me, that I was ready if he needed me. I wanted to play but Burks was doing a good job."
>
> The Badgers will probably do well to depend on Carl for only spot duty next fall. Carl is susceptible to injuries easily and they always seem to come at a time when he is needed most.

Despite Barnhill's uncomplimentary assessment of Carl, he returned to Madison in 1953 for his senior season and even played one season (1956) for the Chicago Bears. He would later be an assistant coach at Wisconsin.

If Williamson had any angst after the game, it was for a question posed by a reporter that seemed to puzzle him. The reporter asked the Badgers coach if he would like to "bring another team to the Rose Bowl."

> "That's not really a question for the coach," Williamson answered. "But we've been treated very well. It was a good, tough ball game and I certainly don't have any complaints—except of course that we lost.
>
> "We played up to our ability. We just didn't have enough to make the scores. They were too good for us today. Jess Hill the Trojan coach, certainly showed us a beautifully balanced defense that didn't have a real weakness.
>
> "But we did have opportunities and I imagine that in such games, the loser always feels that he could just as well have won."

Wisconsin's backfield coach, Bob O'Dell, made it clear that he was very proud of the effort given by the entire team.

"I'm so darn proud of our boys, I could kiss every one of them," O'Dell told the Associated Press. "They were wonderful, every one of them. They did everything we asked of them and more. I'm just sorry for their sakes that they couldn't win this game. They had it coming."

Wuhrman agreed with his coach. "It was a great Rose Bowl, except we didn't want to be the first team from the Big Ten to lose. We were a good team but so was Southern Cal and we just couldn't score on them that day."

Hill, as you might expect, was quite complimentary to Ameche, whom he called "the best fullback I've seen all year.

"He was awfully tough on those five- and six-yard plunges. But you can't tell me he weighs only 205 pounds."

The final statistics show a game dominated by Wisconsin. The Badgers had more net yards (353–233), rushing yards (211–48), first downs (19–16), and plays (84–74). Even with Bukich's second-half surge, the Trojans only outgained the Badgers through the air by a relatively modest difference of 185 to 142 yards. Bukich was 12 of 20 for 137 yards with two interceptions, while Haluska was 11 of 26 for 142 yards and two interceptions.

Nevertheless, Ameche thought that UCLA, which had shut him down earlier that season, was the better team from Los Angeles.

"Southern Cal is a good, hard-hitting team, but I felt UCLA was even tougher," he told Barnhill.

The Associated Press report may have unwittingly discovered one of Wisconsin's first-ever Fifth Quarter performances by the marching band:

> Out in the stadium, the Wisconsin band played and marched with the same enthusiasm and precision which it had displayed before the game. As thousands of Wisconsin alumni, students and other fans prepared to make the long trip back home, there were few complaints heard.
>
> Milt Gantenbein, former end at Wisconsin and with the Green Bay Packers, summed it up.
>
> "That's a real outfit—from the head man, Ivy, down to the last sub. I'm telling the world, I'm proud to be a Badger. They deserved to win that ball game."

Over in the Southern California locker room, Victor Schmidt, the commissioner of the Pacific Coast Conference, was a happy man after one of his member schools had broken the Big Ten's Rose Bowl stranglehold.

"This is the happiest day I've had in seven years," Schmidt said.

12

Ivy and the Boys

M IDWAY THROUGH THE 1954 FOOTBALL SEASON, Ivy Williamson was
asked to tender a request to the University of Wisconsin's Board of
Regents for a pay raise. The Regents must have been braced for the worst
because Williamson had leverage like no other coach in Wisconsin football
history. In six seasons Williamson had taken the program from moribund
under Harry Stuhldreher to vital, relevant, and beyond profitable for the first
time in the program's history.

In his first five seasons, Williamson had crafted a phenomenal 30–12–4
record, including the school's first conference championship (1952) in forty
years. He had a future Heisman Trophy winner in his backfield, the mood
was upbeat, and the turnstiles at Camp Randall were spinning. He had
turned down major offers to be the head coach at several colleges, most
notably USC.

At $14,600 per year, Williamson might have been the most underpaid
football coach in America, even by 1954 standards. According to *Sports Illustrated*, the University of Wisconsin's total athletic revenue in 1953 was
$720,921, of which $517,447.96 was taken in by the football program. Of
the thirteen other sports Wisconsin sponsored at the time, only basketball
paid for itself.

So with the leverage of negotiations tilting heavily in his favor, what did
Williamson ask the Regents to award him? Nothing. In his mind, $14,600
was quite ample.

An article, written at the time by Newspaper Enterprise Association sports
editor Harry Grayson attempted to explain Williamson's thought process. As
important as Williamson was in reviving Wisconsin's football fortunes—and

Grayson called him "the best defensive coach in the Big 10"—Williamson didn't feel his work was more important than what was happening in the classrooms at the university.

> Williamson is one football coach who knows when he is well off—at $14,600 a year. Besides being the best defensive coach in the Big 10, the Michigan alumnus is avoiding a pitfall that often starts a character builder on the downgrade.
>
> It's extremely hard for a botanical researcher, who for 20 years has been bent on finding a wilt-resistant strain of tomato, to understand just how important it is for a fellow professor to teach young monsters how to run around knocking guys down. This becomes even more difficult for the plant pundit to comprehend when the master mind is being paid so dearly for his unique services.
>
> As head football coach, Williamson has had the same tenure as a professor and definitely wants to get along with his colleagues.

According to Grayson, at their December meeting the Board of Regents "accepted Williamson's request and passed a resolution commending the head man for being so considerate."

Williamson was not a complicated man; in fact, he was quite the opposite. He was an advocate of hard work and modesty off the field and maximum effort on the field. It was a formula that worked for him growing up in Prairie Depot, Ohio, near Toledo, and later while earning three letters in football and two in basketball at the University of Michigan.

Michigan won three Western Conference championships and was 24–1–2 when Williamson played as an end there in 1930, 1931, and 1932, and he was all-conference and the team's captain in his senior season. Williamson was a college teammate and fellow Yale assistant with future president Gerald Ford.

After graduation from Michigan, Williamson coached Roseville (Michigan) High School to an undefeated season in 1934 before accepting the assistant coach position at Yale in 1934. He stayed there until 1942, when he enlisted in the U.S. Navy and served through the end of World War II.

After the war, Williamson had an epiphany of sorts. He returned to Yale to reclaim his old job, and he realized that being a football coach was what he was meant to do with his life. Here's what he told *Sports Illustrated* in 1954.

"I guess that's when I took a look at myself,' he says today, ducking and bobbing shyly behind his desk. 'I figured as long as I was going to be a football coach, I ought to try to be a good one."

This time around, Williamson stayed for only a year at Yale. He left for the head job at Lafayette College, where he was 13–5 overall for 1947 and 1948. He applied for the open job at his alma mater, but Bernie Osterbaan got the Michigan job. Then he got the call from Wisconsin to replace Stuhldreher, and he didn't hesitate.

Perhaps the best description of Williamson ever written was offered by the *Saturday Evening Post* writer Harry Paxton, under the title "That Gentlemanly Coach at Wisconsin."

"Ivy Williamson is a big, unruffled Midwesterner from a small Ohio farm town. He speaks mildly and calmly. He never dramatizes himself, but somehow everybody who comes in contact with him seems to get the feeling that here is a nice, honest fellow with a good head on his shoulders.

"He has a natural gift for winning and keeping the confidence of all sorts of people—alumni and other boosters, faculty and school officials, players and prospective players."

And there was this about Williamson, which the average football fan surely didn't realize. As witnessed by his acknowledgment that football wasn't as important as what was going on in the classrooms of Madison, Williamson put a very high premium on education and was a very intelligent man himself.

While he was coaching high school ball and while he was an assistant at Yale, Williamson continued to take courses at Michigan toward his master's degree, eventually receiving it in 1940, seven years after graduating from the Ann Arbor school. His coach at Michigan, Harry Kipke, said of Williamson, "Ivan Williamson is the smartest player I have ever had or hope to have."

In his *Sports Illustrated* piece, which chronicles the success story at Wisconsin under Williamson, Booton Herndon had this to say about the unlikely synergy that existed between Ameche and Williamson.

"(Wisconsin's) success is based on a winning combination of two incongruous elements. One is a tall, agonizingly shy head coach, Ivan B. Williamson, a living contradiction to Dale Carnegie. The other is a likable kid, born Lino Dante Amici, who receives mail addressed to 'The Horse, Wisconsin.'"

With few exceptions, Ameche, like the rest of the student-athletes who played for Williamson, respected him. They didn't always agree with him, but he had a reputation for being fair, even-handed, and a good strategist.

"Lino didn't talk much about football at home," said Yvonne Ameche. "We were raising a family together. Those are the things we talked about.

"But I do know that Alan liked Ivy and that was one of the main reasons he picked Wisconsin. They remained very good friends through the years.

"Ivy had a picture of Alan hanging in his office and when he died, [somebody] sent me the picture. I had copies made and gave them to all my children. It's Alan in his last game [at Wisconsin], sitting on the bench and looking up. It's just a fabulous picture, the expression on his face."

Jerry Wuhrman became one of Ameche's closest friends on the squad, especially after the Kenosha crew that came in with him as freshmen began to fall to the wayside.

"I think they had a very good relationship from what I could see," Wuhrman said. "Let's face it, they needed each other. But I never saw any complications in their relationship. I think Ivy was a very personable guy, a father figure to us."

Added Dick Nicolazzi: "He was just a nice man. A very nice guy to all of us."

If there is one thing that Williamson wasn't, it was a screamer. He believed that coaching involved keeping his head clear and not cluttering his thought waves with rage. He actually designated a member of his coaching staff, freshman coach George Lanphear, to be his designated screamer on game day.

"Ivy was not a leader in the sense of being a rah-rah kind of coach," recalled Jim Temp. "Ivy had the same pregame speech and halftime speech the whole four years I went to Madison. You could have put them on a tape recorder and you wouldn't need Ivy.

"We can lick'em, we can lick'em, we can lick'em," he'd say it over and over again.

"But again, he didn't have to yell because he had George Lanphear on the sidelines for that. He was the mouthy one. He would work on the officials the whole game and probably got us a few calls we shouldn't have gotten."

Mark Hoegh remembers Williamson's mannerisms much as Temp did.

"He wasn't a hollerer, not the kind of coach who motivated his players by hollering at them," Hoegh recalled. "He had some good signs in the locker though. The only one I can remember was 'Make good or make room.'

"But the night before a game all he would say was something like, 'They have a good quarterback, but we can beat this team.' He wasn't a rah-rah guy, but he was always very prepared. I like Ivy and I certainly respected him."

Wuhrman agrees about Williamson's low-key manners. "He just wasn't an outspoken type of coach with the fiery halftime pep talks, that sort of thing. He had pep talks; they just weren't with the real dynamic flair like some other guys. He was more interested in getting the team to pull together, that's why he was hired."

There is no questioning Williamson's credentials as a coach. When he decided to walk away from coaching after the 1955 season to accept the Wisconsin athletic director's post, he was undeniably the most effective Wisconsin football coach of the modern era up to that time.

Williamson finished with a 41–19–4 record in seven seasons at Wisconsin. He took Wisconsin to its first Rose Bowl, won its first conference title in forty years, and achieved a 66.7 winning percentage. To put that in perspective, Barry Alvarez was 3–0 in Rose Bowl games and in 16 seasons carved out a 118–73–4 record (61.5 percent).

Only the current coach, Bret Bielema, who unlike Williamson and Alvarez did not have to rebuild his program from scratch, has a better winning percentage among modern Wisconsin coaches. Through the 2011 season, Bielema was 60–19 with two Rose Bowl appearances for a 75.9 winning percentage.

Williamson had just one losing season in his head-coaching career—1955, when the Badgers went 4–5 in the aftermath of the Ameche era. It was the same year that the Wisconsin athletic director, Guy Sundt, died on the job.

Williamson was faced with a decision. Should he remain football coach and hope to build the program back to where he had it with Ameche? Or should he take the job security of being the athletic director and turn over the reins of the football program to his top assistant, Milt Bruhn?

It was a difficult decision for Williamson, but in retrospect, it was probably the correct decision. After one year on the job, a *Milwaukee Sentinel* reporter, Tony Ingrassia, asked Williamson if he had made the right decision.

"Definitely yes," Williamson said. "Like anyone who spent 25 years in coaching, I naturally miss it. But I'm happy to continue in the role of an administrator rather than a coach.

"There is less seasonal concentration involved than in coaching, and you don't have the association with the players. But you do have more dealings with faculty and other university officials."

According to Ingrassia, Williamson chose to make the move when he did for several reasons.

"Unlike coaching which is highly hazardous, Ivy could look for far greater security as athletic director. And, for that very reason he knew the position wouldn't be available again for some time . . . if ever. He also knew the Badgers were in a 'down' cycle as far as football talent was concerned and perhaps a couple of bad years would dim his popularity."

At least one sports writer was happy to see Williamson leave the coaching profession. The *Milwaukee Journal* sports editor, Russ Lynch, was upset that the Badgers lost five of their last six games after a 3–0 start to the 1955 season. But he was particularly angry about the 17–14 home loss to number-sixteen Illinois because Williamson chose to tie the game with a field goal in the waning seconds rather than trying to win it with a touchdown.

> Judging by Saturday's football game at Madison, the promotion of Ivy Williamson to athletic director at Wisconsin seems very timely.
>
> When a football coach reaches the point where he is willing to settle for a tie, it is just as well that he moves along from the battle field to the refuge of a desk in an office . . .
>
> Milt Bruhn, it is to be hoped, will bring to the job an uncompromising desire for victory, which Williamson apparently has lost.
>
> That's what Ivy gets, isn't it, for trying to avoid a loss by ordering his best percentage play? The only thing wrong—the field goal missed.

Bruhn wasn't exactly the "uncompromising" difference Lynch was hoping for. Bruhn stumbled his first season, going 1–5–3 in 1956, but he seemingly righted the ship after that. From 1957 through 1963, Bruhn fashioned a 43–21–1 record with just one losing season, 4–5 in 1960. Unfortunately, he was 8–19–2 in his last three seasons, forcing his long-time friend Williamson to show him the door after the 1966 season.

According to an Oliver B. Kuechle story in the *Milwaukee Journal*, the Wisconsin athletic board interviewed seven candidates to replace Bruhn and narrowed the field to two—Notre Dame assistant John Ray and Williamson's former quarterback, John Coatta, who had been an assistant under Bruhn for the last two seasons.

According to Kuechle, "Williamson recommended Ray for the job as Bruhn's successor and so told University President Fred Harrington.

"'Get him,' Harrington is supposed to have said. When Ray demanded $27,500, however, Harrington refused to go that high and Coatta was named. Coatta received $19,500."

Ray, who would be Ara Parseghian's long-time defensive coordinator at Notre Dame, went on to accept the head-coaching position at Kentucky, where he was 10–33 in four seasons. But as shabby as Ray's record was at Kentucky, it was much better than Coatta's record at Wisconsin.

Coatta was an unmitigated failure as Wisconsin's coach. He set an NCAA record for most consecutive games without a victory to begin a career—23. He did not win a game in his first two seasons and was mercifully fired after the 1969 season with a 3–26–1 record (winning only 11.7 percent).

To make matters worse for Williamson, apparently one of the men the search committee passed on was future Michigan coach Bo Schembechler, who was the head coach at Miami (Ohio) University at the time.

Williamson wasn't around to see Coatta's inevitable firing after the 1969 season. Williamson had been fired as Wisconsin's athletic director by the Board of Regents on January 10, 1969.

"The board felt that new leadership was needed," Charles D. Gelatt of La Crosse, then president of the board, told the Associated Press.

Williamson was allowed to stay on as a professor of athletics in the School of Education, but his salary was cut from $23,000 to $18,800. Williamson never got involved in his new assignment because on February 19, 1969, a little over a month after being ousted from the athletic department, Williamson, then fifty-eight, died of head injuries. He was pronounced dead of irreversible brain stem damage sustained in a mysterious fall down a flight of stairs leading to his basement at his home at 62 Fuller Drive in Madison.

According to reports, Williamson was returning a container of soup to a freezer compartment in the basement. His death report indicated that his wife Beulah was holding him when the ambulance arrived to take him to the hospital.

"The official word was that he tripped," Temp said.

Added Wuhrman: "Who knows the whole story? It could have happened to any of us, falling down the stairs like that. Who knows what happened?"

What is known is that Williamson deserved a better fate from the athletic board at that time. Not only had he given Wisconsin its best football of the modern era, but he had been an aggressive expansionist as athletic director.

Tom Butler wrote a great piece in the *Wisconsin State Journal* about the short-sightedness of the decision to fire Williamson. He listed all of Williamson's achievements as athletic director and football coach and concluded it with,

> So let's remember Ivan Williamson for what he did for us "yesterday."
>
> Another prevalent philosophy simply expresses a "hurray for me" attitude. . . . Don't tell what you did for me yesterday. How about today?
>
> Ivan Williamson got caught up in that whirl and it cost him his job as athletic director.
>
> Actually, he was more or less the victim of inflation, rising costs and dwindling football attendance.

During his thirteen-year reign as athletic director, Williamson oversaw two expansions of Camp Randall Stadium, he revived the hockey program, oversaw construction of the Camp Randall Memorial Building, built the UW Natatorium, and revitalized the track and field program.

With the 1958 stadium expansion, the field was lowered 10 feet and 12,000 seats were added, giving Camp Randall a capacity of 63,435. In 1966, the communications center and second deck were built, the latter increasing capacity to 77,280.

As Butler pointed out in his article, Williamson worked tirelessly for the athletic department despite being in great physical pain.

"Through all the troubles he was racked with pain, first because of a spinal injury that forced him to wear a special surgical collar for a long period, and later from a perforating ulcer that necessitated two major operations just two years (before his death)."

The greatest irony of Williamson's demise was that it was football, the sport he loved and understood and was so successful at, that eventually dragged him down. As the losses on the field mounted, the problems off the field increased as well.

After back-to-back winless seasons, Coatta faced a mutiny from his African American players, who complained that some of the program's coaches didn't understand them. The African American players boycotted the team's postseason banquet in 1968 and forced the resignation of assistant coach Gene Felker.

Financially, the entire Wisconsin athletic program was a mess because of the dwindling football revenues. The Regents estimated that the athletic department would lose $442,700 in 1968–69, with a loss of more than $700,000 in two years.

Therefore, it is not inaccurate to say that Williamson was a victim of his own success. It's probable that he paved the way for his dismissal by providing Wisconsin with its success in football in the early 1950s.

The *Milwaukee Sentinel* sports editor, Lloyd Larson, reached that exact conclusion soon after Williamson was ousted as athletic director.

The 1952 team tied for the Big Ten crown with Purdue to break a 40 year title drought for Wisconsin and was the first to represent the school in the Rose Bowl.

Two of Williamson's teams tied for second, two finished third and one (his first in 1949) took fourth. Now, after 20 years, Ivy is out of the Wisconsin sports picture mainly because as athletic director, he failed to find a solution for a football problem similar to the one he solved as a coach.

Talk about irony! . . .

The removal order of the athletic board, with the Regents concurring, came as no real surprise. Grumbling has increased steadily in the ranks of Wisconsin followers as football fortunes faded badly the last six years under Milt Bruhn and John Coatta.

Although the coaches, especially Bruhn, couldn't escape all the "heat," most of the criticism was heaped on Williamson for failing to assert himself and take the steps necessary to get the football situation straightened around.

The recent turn of events at Michigan, Williamson's alma mater, may have helped speed Ivy's departure from the Wisconsin athletic scene. Despite an 8–2 record, Bump Elliott was eased out of the head coaching job. Bo Schembechler already has taken over as his successor. The Wolverines' new athletic director, Don Canham, undoubtedly is the man mainly responsible for both moves.

Many a Wisconsin man has said, "We need a take-charge guy like Canham. He didn't stall around until things went to the dogs." And the athletic board and other higher authorities obviously went along with his suggestions and recommendations.

There was one more bit of irony in the story of Ivy Williamson's demise. The night Williamson died, February 19, 1969, there was a visitor in Madison. His name was Elroy "Crazylegs" Hirsch, and he was in town to meet with the university's athletic board and the board's search committee to replace Williamson. Hirsch would be chosen to replace Williamson as Wisconsin's athletic director.

13

The Iron Horse

FOR HIS FIRST TWO YEARS AT THE University of Wisconsin, Alan Ameche was "the Horse," plain and simple. For his final two years, thanks to the infinite wisdom of the NCAA rule-makers, he was "the Iron Horse."

In an effort to cut the skyrocketing costs of college football, the sport that paid most of the bills for all other college sports with the exception of basketball, the NCAA decided in 1953 to return to the dark ages and reinstitute ironman football. "Two-platoon" football, which had been invented by Michigan's Fritz Crisler after World War II and perfected by Army's Colonel Earl "Red" Blaik, was deemed a luxury that college football could no longer afford.

Blaik was first introduced to two-platoon football when Army defeated Michigan, 28–7, in 1945. In that game, Crisler employed eight defensive players, eight offensive players, and three players who played on both sides of the ball. Despite beating Michigan with ease, Blaik was impressed with Crisler's innovative system and decided to employ it with modifications at Army.

Digging into his military background for terminology, Blaik dubbed the different units "platoons." Between 1946 and 1950, Blaik's two-platoon teams twice finished second in the AP poll and never finished lower than eleventh. Consequently, almost every major football program in the country adopted two-platoon football.

This system of unlimited substitution brought an obvious improvement in the quality of play. To carry the military analogy a step further, there were always fresh troops on the field.

It all changed, however, before the 1953 season, when the NCAA instituted its new rule that stated that only one player could be substituted between plays. If the substitution was made in the first half, the player substituted for was not allowed back into the game until the second half. If a player was substituted for in the second half, he was finished for the day.

Needless to say, most players and coaches thought the new rule was a huge step backward. Some, however, like Tennessee head coach "General" Robert Neyland, were all for the change. Neyland rather crudely hailed it as the end of "chickenshit" football.

Like it or not, the rule remained in effect until the fall of 1965, when two-platoon football was welcomed back and even special teams—kicking and punting squads—were introduced to the game.

But the original rule change also meant big changes in Madison. Offensive players had to learn defense and defensive players had to learn offense. Players who had been starters suddenly found themselves on the bench because now, instead of 22 starters, there were 11.

Most of the players felt like Roger Dornburg did about the new rule.

"I was a linebacker for two years and then they came up with the new rule and we had to play both ways and all of a sudden I'm a defensive halfback," Dornburg said. "Beats the hell out of me, why they changed the rule. It was a God awful rule."

Even stars like Ameche were affected. With the rule change his job description changed from fullback to fullback/linebacker, his minutes increased, his carries decreased, and ultimately his offensive production declined.

"You bet it hurt [Ameche] playing both ways," said Dick Nicolazzi. "It was a stupid rule. I guess the idea was to cut down on the number of scholarships they were giving out, but it took a hell of a toll on a running back to play linebacker, too."

For his part, Ameche played the good soldier. He had played some in the defensive backfield in high school, but playing linebacker was totally foreign to him. More important, by this time in his career Ameche was well aware that NFL teams were anxiously awaiting him and that playing both ways did nothing but shorten his career and potentially end it. Still, he said publicly that he appreciated the challenge of learning the new position and even welcomed dishing out some hits.

"There are a lot of things to watch, where the end plays, how he shifts his feet, the movement of the tackle and I guess I have to learn it all at once," Ameche told Bill Furlong in the *Sport* magazine article of November 1953.

Talking of the abolition of the two-platoon system before the season, he spoke of it as a fait accompli, as something which no argument could change in 1953.

But he recognized it as a threat to his future, not because of the problem of playing defense as well as offense—"I've found that I enjoy playing defense"— but because of the possibility of injury. "In any game in which I've played both offense and defense," he said quietly, "I was dead tired at the end." It is fatigue, he knows which breeds injuries on the football field, and it is an injury that could end his football career most easily.

So he talks about his future not in terms of what honors his football feats in college may bring him, but in terms of "whether or not I'll be healthy" after two more football seasons. Although he has suffered only one injury of consequence in college—he hurt an arm against Indiana in 1951—he has a weak left wrist and is prone to injury in the area where his toes join his feet. "My feet get wedged and bent in some mighty peculiar positions in a pile up," he explains. "I don't know exactly how."

Thanks to the new rule, every football coach in the country entered the 1953 season with enough angst and trepidation for a career. Williamson seemed particularly overwrought in the preseason.

"We are bound to be off from last year," Williamson told the Associated Press, referring to the Rose Bowl season. "If we had not lost three of our best men through injuries, in addition to our normal losses by graduation, we might have just enough to be a bothersome team. Those extra losses hurt us too much."

Williamson was referring to quarterback Jim Haluska, Don Voss, an All-American defensive end in 1952, and Paul Shwaiko, a valuable two-way performer at halfback. Haluska broke his leg playing summer baseball and, like Voss, who had suffered a severe knee injury in the Rose Bowl, was ruled out for the entire 1953 season. Also out for the season, but for academic reasons, was Shwaiko, a valuable performer, especially in the defensive backfield.

Voss was probably the team's best pass rusher, but it would be even more difficult to replace Haluska, who was the star of spring practice. In 1952, his first season replacing John Coatta, Haluska had been surprisingly effective.

He completed 123 of 225 attempts for a school-record 1,552 yards and 12 touchdowns. Most importantly, his passing efficiency kept the defenses honest and took some pressure off Ameche.

The official University of Wisconsin prospectus for the 1953 football season had this to say about the Badgers' chances:

If two-platoon football still were in effect, Coach Ivy Williamson's football pro-gram at the University of Wisconsin simply would be one of replacements for the 1953 season.

His job then would be to replace six out of seven starters in the offensive line, none whatsoever in the backfield. Defensively he would have to replace four linemen, a right side linebacker, two defensive halfbacks, and a safety.

And, by and large, Ivy could muster replacements who by mid-season could approximate the level of efficiency attained in 1952.

But the new rules which virtually erase the two-platoon method of gridiron operation, propose the difficult change-over to a double-duty unit within a very much limited (by comparison) time period of preparation. . . .

Judging from the spring game, most writers concluded that Wisconsin appears to have a squad that will play hard, smart defensive football and one that can be pretty hard to handle on offense as long as Jim Haluska is healthy. It was doubted that any team could give Wisconsin a "plastering" for the Bad-gers seemed to have the confidence, poise and know-how that are essential components for sound defensive play. Now, with Haluska's status in doubt, the $64 question awaits the answer from the "right" quarterback.

In addition to the more serious injuries of Voss and Haluska, Jerry Wuhr-man and the oft-injured Harland Carl would also enter the fall season nursing knee injuries suffered in spring football. With all these injuries to key players, the abolition of the two-platoon system might actually have been a blessing for the Badgers because the limitation of substitutions could help dilute the depth-of-talent advantage that some teams enjoyed over Wisconsin.

For his part, Ameche was ready for the challenge. Married life apparently had been agreeing with him because he reported to preseason camp at 207 pounds on August 31, his lowest weight since freshman year and 5 pounds under what Williamson deemed to be his best playing weight. Ameche's prospects for relief also were enhanced by the progress of his understudy, Charlie Thomas, who Williamson said was showing "great improvement on both offense and defense."

But if Ameche didn't have enough to worry about with learning a whole new position, there was also the situation at home. His parents moved from Kenosha early in the football season, and his mother and Yvonne didn't get along. First son Brian had come along in June 1953, and soon after Yvonne became pregnant with the couple's second child, Alan. (He was the second of six children the couple would have.)

And with all of his buddies from Kenosha, except for Shwaiko who was a year behind, now gone from the Wisconsin football program, Ameche's circle of friends was changing as well. Like the Ameches, Jerry and Delores Wuhrman were married in 1952. Delores and Yvonne became good friends, and Wuhrman, who was a year ahead of Ameche and the cocaptain of the 1953 squad, became friends as well.

"We were the only two players who were married and had kids while we were still in college," said Wuhrman, who became a metallurgical engineer after his graduation from Wisconsin. "We used to steal milk from the training table and take it home for the kids.

"I wouldn't say Alan and I were close friends, but we did have a bond because of the kids. I didn't know Alan that much before he got married, but I would say he was a very mature guy . . . just a really solid guy.

"His wife Yvonne and Delores became really good friends though. They'd go to the games together and I don't think they'd watch the game. They'd just talk about the kids. I think Delores even typed some of Alan's term papers.

"I never got myself in situations where I had to depend on a friend as much as I might have, but I knew that Alan was the type of guy who was there if I needed him. Our relationship was getting together with the kids, not going to some of the wild parties that some of the other players might go to."

The 1953 season started at home with a nonconference contest against Penn State. The Badgers, unranked and sporting brand new all-cardinal-red home uniforms, dominated the Nittany Lions, 20–0.

Ameche had the best opening day of his Wisconsin career, rushing for 115 yards in 28 carries, including a 2-yard touchdown run in the second quarter. The toll of averaging 55 minutes on the field didn't seem to wear on Ameche on the warm September afternoon, but it would be a long season.

Penn State battled the injury-riddled Badgers on even terms in the first period, but Wisconsin started to assert itself when it took over at its 46-yard line in the second period. Jerry Witt's 24-yard sprint on a pitchout set up Ameche's first touchdown.

Wisconsin went up two touchdowns in the third period on an 86-yard drive engineered by Gust Vergetis (8 of 12 for 82 yards). Clary Bratt scored the touchdown on a 9-yard sweep.

The Badgers expanded their lead to three touchdowns when substitute halfback Bob Gingrass scored on a 4-yard run. Ameche's future backfield mate with the Baltimore Colts, Lenny Moore, scored what appeared to be a 64-yard touchdown for the Nittany Lions, but it was nullified by a holding penalty.

Ameche appeared to hold up his responsibilities at outside linebacker because the closest Penn State came to scoring was a penetration to the Wisconsin 15 early in the fourth quarter. Reviews of Ameche's linebacker play were mixed at best. Generally speaking, he was an adequate linebacker for someone who had to relearn defense in his junior year of college.

"My recollection is that Alan was not a real strong defensive player," Wuhrman said. "He played defense because it was essential. It wasn't platoon football anymore.

"I don't even recall why they did it, but it was a silly rule. It wasn't just the Big Ten, it was everybody. I guess their costs were getting out of hand.

"I would say it's enough of a challenge to play one way. You don't want to send somebody out on the field and have them ration their effort. That's probably the reason they did away with [the rule] eventually."

Dornburg agreed with Wuhrman regarding Ameche's play as a linebacker.

"Ameche had to play fullback and linebacker, and I can't say he was a great linebacker. But he certainly was a great fullback."

Mark Hoegh and Jim Temp disagreed with their former teammates, taking the position that Ameche was a good defensive player.

"I thought Alan was tough on defense," Hoegh said. "I thought he was a great linebacker. Heck, he was an all-American as a junior and he was playing both sides of the ball, so he couldn't have been too bad.

"The thing about Alan is he played hurt a lot. He didn't have a choice, he had to go both ways."

Temp agreed that Ameche's physical fitness made him a good defensive player.

"Alan was a very good linebacker. . . . He played behind me so he didn't have much work to do," Temp joked. "I made his life easy.

"He was in such great shape. You never saw him huffing and puffing and wanting to leave the game. Obviously, playing linebacker hurt Alan's production because he was on the field almost the entire game. And in the fourth quarter you tend to take the path of least resistance.

"But I never heard him complain. In fact, I'm sure he liked playing defense. It finally gave him the chance to hit somebody back."

In Ameche's four years at Wisconsin, the Badgers would go 4–0 against Marquette with a combined score of 129–50. But in the second game of their 1953 season, the Badgers were fortunate to escape with a 13–11 victory, and Ameche was the man to thank for saving the day.

In a game played in the mud and the rain of Camp Randall Stadium, Ameche rushed for 112 yards in 21 carries. He tied the game at 7–7 with a

3-yard run in the second quarter and ran 21 yards for the winning touch-down in the third quarter.

The Badgers had risen to number sixteen in the AP poll following their victory over Penn State in the opener, but their lackluster showing against Marquette knocked them out of the still fluid early-season poll. The un-ranked Badgers would travel to Los Angeles for a rematch with UCLA, which had handed them a 20–7 loss while shutting down Ameche in 1952.

The Bruins followed much the same game plan, shutting out the Badgers, 13–0, while holding Ameche to a net of 50 yards in a Saturday night game. Jim Miller, a sophomore from Eau Claire, had by now taken over the quarter-back position from the journeyman senior Vergetis. Miller was a good run-ner and good athlete but not a particularly adept passer, and it was becoming apparent that opponents were bunching up the middle of their defenses to stop Ameche.

Wisconsin went on the road in the fourth week of the season to open its Big Ten season at Purdue, the team it had shared the Big Ten title with in 1952, and it was clear the Boilermakers had seen the film of the UCLA game. Although Ameche was held to 58 yards in 16 carries and no touchdowns, he wasn't really needed in the contest.

The star on this day was Miller, who although completing just two of six passes for 38 yards and one interception, ran for 88 yards in five carries. The young quarterback scored two touchdowns, including a 50-yard scramble.

Clary Bratt also had a strong game, with four carries for 113 yards, one of which was a 76-yard-run that set up Miller's first touchdown. Gary Messner played a strong game defensively, having an early fumble recovery and inter-ception that helped Wisconsin lead 21–0 in the third quarter.

The Badgers were still unranked, but with a nice victory at Purdue under its belt and the quarterback situation seemingly settled after Miller's strong outing, it appeared that things were on the upturn. Ohio State was next, and while the Buckeyes were a good, solid team, they were a year away from greatness. In 1954 they would give Woody Hayes his first national cham-pionship, but in 1953 the Buckeyes were still unranked when they visited Madison and didn't even figure in the Big Ten title picture.

So what happened? The Buckeyes upset the Badgers, 20–19, putting a huge hole in Wisconsin's hopes to repeat as Big Ten champions. In those days, when Big Ten teams played just six conference games per season, there was a very small margin for error.

Fortunately for the Badgers, powerful Michigan State, competing in its first season as a Big Ten member, would suffer its first loss of the season to

Purdue, 6–0, on the same day, October 24, 1953. But Illinois, ranked number three in the nation, remained undefeated and loomed as the favorite to win the Big Ten.

Ameche played a strong game, rushing for 73 yards in 16 carries, before almost 53,000 at Camp Randall, but it wasn't enough. The Buckeyes' Howard "Hopalong" Cassady scored the game's first touchdown, dragging Wisconsin defenders for 7 yards.

The Badgers managed a 12–7 halftime lead, though, after Miller scored on a 12-yard run and a 5-yard pass to Norb Esser. The Badgers were unsuccessful on both extra-point attempts, which would later haunt them.

Wisconsin went up 19–7 in the third quarter as Miller scored on a 10-yard quarterback option and this time made the extra point. After an Ohio State touchdown made the score 19–14, Ohio State quarterback Dave Leggett threw a 60-yard pass to Cassady for the winning score with 2:31 left in the game.

With games against Iowa and Northwestern, two of the conference's weaker teams, to follow, Wisconsin had three weeks to prepare for the Illini. The Badgers got back on track the following week against the Hawkeyes with a tougher-than-expected 10–6 victory in Madison, in which Ameche rushed for 76 yards in 22 carries but no touchdowns.

The Badgers dominated the game, outgaining the visitors 374–170, but trailed 6–3 in the fourth quarter. The Hawkeyes' only score of the game was a 36-yard touchdown reception by Dusty Rice from quarterback Jerry Reichow in the second period.

With eight minutes left in the game, Miller (10 for 23, 211 yards, and 2 interceptions), threw an over-the-middle pass intended for Harland Carl that appeared to be intercepted by Iowa's Pinky Broeder. Broeder batted the ball in the air twice, but then slipped as Carl picked the ball out of the air and ran 38 yards for the winning touchdown.

There wasn't nearly as much drama the following Saturday, when Wisconsin trounced the winless-in-conference Northwestern Wildcats, 34–13. Ameche had a strong game, rushing inside for 84 yards in 17 carries, including one touchdown.

The Badgers had pretty much avenged their heart-breaking loss to Illinois in 1951 with their 20–6 victory in 1952. But they could deny Illinois a Rose Bowl trip again with a victory over the still-unbeaten Illini in 1953.

A sidelight to the contest would be the showdown between Ameche and J. C. Caroline, the two best backs in the Big Ten that season, if not the nation. It was a contrast in styles between the speedy Caroline, who would later go on to stardom as a cornerback for the Chicago Bears, and Ameche's bruising inside running.

The attractive matchup drew national media attention, including the legendary sports writer Red Smith, who at the time wrote for the *New York Herald-Tribune*. His syndicated column also appeared in the *Milwaukee Sentinel* from time to time.

In his column after the game, Smith contended that Williamson and Penn State's Rip Engle had been tipped off about Caroline by the South Carolina head coach, Rex Enright, when Caroline was a high school player in South Carolina. Caroline, who is black, couldn't attend South Carolina, which still was segregated at that time. So Enright told Williamson and Engle, who were his coaching opponents at an annual Blue-Gray game in Montgomery, Alabama, about the talented prospect. But neither Engle nor Williamson followed up on Enright's advice.

The immortal Smith wrote:

It requires no great gifts to imagine Williamson's feelings when Caroline caught Wisconsin's opening kickoff and rushed 32 yards up the middle to send Illinois plunging toward a touchdown and a lead of 7 to 0.

It turned out, however, that it had been an unnecessary precaution to take away Williamson's belt and suspenders and remove all sharp objects from his reach before the game. The Wisconsin coach will not seriously contemplate suicide until a year from next June when his fullback Alan the Horse Ameche is turned out to pasture.

Caroline is a bright and gifted boy but Ameche is a man, and this was a game to split them out. Man's inhumanity to man was never more shockingly demonstrated. Wisconsin's red horde heaped red ruin on the unbeaten leaders of the Big Ten. The joy ride toward the conference championship and the Rose Bowl halted at the sign of the Flying Red Horse.

Translated, Wisconsin thumped the number-three-ranked Illini that day, 34–7. Caroline had a personal victory that afternoon in Madison, rushing for 83 yards in 25 carries to break Ameche's conference season rushing record of 774, set in 1951. But it's doubtful Caroline did any celebrating that day.

Smith's wonderful column continued:

Before the game, a man named Bob Zuppke, Illinois coach emeritus who schooled (Red) Grange in violence, had confided the opinion that Caroline was a better halfback than Old 77 himself. If this was the new Grange last Saturday, then Ameche was a couple of guys named Nagurski and Nevers.

The Blur, as they call Caroline, is wonderfully fast. He has the uncommon ability to run about as well to his left as to his right. Controlling him is like beating out a brush fire, and Wisconsin's ends did a magnificent job. On defense he is a willing tackler with plenty of bounce. When he tried to tackle, he bounced.

According to the Wisconsin roster, Ameche weighs 205 pounds but his weight was quoted elsewhere at 235 and he looks all of that. He is an erect runner, the sort whom a low tackle ought to cut down, but he sprays tacklers. Using the winged-T and the conventional T-formation, Wisconsin employs Ameche the way Tony Zale used his left hand. He punishes the mid-section until the defense doubles up in pain, then he feints at that flinching middle while a swifty like Harland Carl or Jerry Witt sweeps wide with a pitch-out.

That's how Wisconsin got in front, Carl going 40 yards around his left side for the winners' second touchdown. Wisconsin stayed in front by stopping Caroline on a vital play. Perhaps it was the game's key play, the decisive one, for there'd been no defensive operations worth mentioning up to that one. This is a characteristic common to many games in this first season since the return to one-platoon football. Most coaches start their 11 best offensive players and depend on incantation and prayer for defense.

Illinois had marched to a score from the opening kickoff and Wisconsin had marched right back for a tie. After Carl put Wisconsin ahead, Illinois received and went barreling down to the Wisconsin 12 yard line, where it was fourth and four to go.

Ordinarily Caroline's speed will take him that far before the defense can intercept him. This time, though, he flashed around the sideline, tried to turn and encountered Ron Locklin, the Wisconsin end. J.C. was like a fat lady in the shopping rush hurrying around a corner with her arms full of Christmas packages. They picked up his initials all over the field.

From that moment Wisconsin had control, kept applying pressure until Illinois came unstuck in the fourth quarter. Three touchdowns in that last period made the score a shocking 34 to 7.

The Illinois kids were in a panic. Their fine back, Mickey Bates dropped a screened pass on fourth down. They fumbled. They threw passes into Wisconsin paws. They itched with shuddering nervousness and it was easy to understand why.

By that time they thought they had Ameches crawling all over them.

Smith's nonpareil prose notwithstanding, it was one of the greatest victories ever for Wisconsin football. Not only did the Badgers crush the number-three team in the nation, they thrust themselves back into the Big Ten title picture in a season for them that had contained many more questions than answers. The only thing standing between the Badgers and at least a share of the Big Ten crown was a victory over Minnesota in the season finale.

Led by Ameche's 145 yards in 17 carries, the Badgers had piled up an almost unbelievable 383 rushing yards against Illinois. Wisconsin had attempted only three passes in the game, but they weren't necessary with the running game clicking as it did. Carl had one of his finest games, rushing seven times for 103 yards, including that 40-yard touchdown run that put Wisconsin ahead for good, 14–7.

Miller was proving to be a good fit at quarterback as well. He had scored twice on short sneaks and contributed on defense with an interception. Witt provided the highlight of Wisconsin's three-touchdown fourth quarter with a 41-yard touchdown burst.

The Badgers knew going into the final week that a return trip to the Rose Bowl was out of the realm of possibility, because even if they tied for the championship with Michigan State or Illinois, the Big Ten would certainly send either of those to Pasadena over Wisconsin. It had been two years since Illinois represented the conference at the Rose Bowl, and Michigan State, in its first season in the conference, had never been to Pasadena.

But the Badgers, who had skyrocketed from out of the poll to number eight in the nation with the upset of Illinois the previous week, were in no way prepared for their fate in the final week of the 1953 season. Despite astronomical odds to the contrary, Wisconsin and Minnesota would play to a 21–21 tie for the second straight season.

Because Illinois bounced back with a 39–14 drubbing of Northwestern, and Michigan State escaped, 21–15, over Michigan, they shared the Big Ten title at 5–1, with the Spartans being awarded the Rose Bowl berth. The tie would cost Wisconsin, which finished at 4–1–1 (6–2–1 overall), a second straight shared title.

Playing on a frosty field in Minneapolis on November 21, Minnesota scored on its first possession, covering 77 yards and capped by Paul Giel's touchdown run. Jim Miller had his best passing game of the season, throwing touchdown passes to Norb Esser (54 yards) and Jerry Witt to stake the Badgers to a 14–7 halftime lead.

Minnesota scored a pair of 1-yard touchdowns in the late third quarter and early fourth quarter to regain the lead at 21–14. Miller, who was 7 of 11 passing for 174 yards, engineered an 82-yard tying drive, capped by Ameche's 3-yard touchdown run with 6:15 left in the game. Billy Miller kicked his third consecutive extra point to tie the game. Ameche was one of four Badgers to play the entire 60 minutes.

The Badgers were lucky to escape with the tie because Minnesota had one last drive left. With 75 seconds remaining in the contest, Ameche clobbered Minnesota fullback Melvin Holme, who fumbled at the Wisconsin 2-yard line. It was recovered by Wisconsin's second-string center Bill McNamara, effectively ending the game.

It also marked the final game for Minnesota's Paul Giel, who in the course of the game set a Big Ten record for total offense.

From a statistical standpoint, it was a so-so year for Ameche. He had 165 carries, 40 fewer than he had in 1952, for a net of 801 yards. But his 4.8 yards per carry was higher than the previous season, although not as high as his 5.2 average as a freshman. He had just five touchdowns on the season.

The honors, however, began to pile up in earnest after the 1953 season. Ameche was named first-team all-American by seven organizations including the Football Writers Association, *Look* magazine, and Paramount News. He also won the Walter Camp Memorial Trophy and Italian player of the year, and was runner-up to Giel in the *Chicago Tribune*'s Big Ten player of the year voting.

Writing for the *Milwaukee Sentinel* after the upset of Illinois, Frank Graham said of Ameche's 1953 season: "Ameche is the kind of kid for whom football was invented. He enjoys hitting and being hit, and it required the abolition of the two-platoon system to bring out the best there was in him.

"No one ever taught him to tackle until this year, but there wasn't much Bob O'Dell, the backfield coach, had to teach him. He's a nice kid, gentle and considerate of his classmates and all others on the campus when he's off duty, but once he puts on that football suit he is sparked by a lust for violence and a ball carrier who falls into his hands is marked for destruction. Imagine having a boy like that on your squad and not using him on defense for two years! On the other hand, now that the situation has been corrected, imagine having a boy like that on your squad for another year, this 20-year-old destroyer being a junior."

14

The Home Stretch

THE COVER PHOTO OF THE OCTOBER 24, 1954, *Milwaukee Sentinel* Sunday magazine was one that begged to be scrapbooked. The Frank Stanfield photo featured big, bad all-American bruiser Alan Ameche outside his modest Madison abode at 131 Craig Avenue with his sixteen-month-old fellow bruiser Brian in tow. Both are wearing big white "W" monograms on their cardinal-red jackets.

Inside the home was Alan's wife and Brian's mommy, Yvonne, with the family's newest addition, six-week-old Alan Jr., who had joined the family in the off-season. We discover from the article that Alan's parents, Augusto and Elizabeth, who had moved to Madison a year earlier, were now gone, leaving shortly after Alan Jr. was born for an extended (two-year) visit to their native Italy.

"I'm afraid that I won't be able to match his mother's cooking," Yvonne told *Sentinel* reporter Ingrassia with a chuckle.

Yvonne might have been chuckling for two reasons. First, she didn't even attempt to compete with her mother-in-law when it came to cooking Italian. Second, although she didn't say so in the article, she was very happy to see her hard-to-get-along-with mother-in-law leave for the other side of the world.

Yvonne, whose father, Mike Molinaro, was half Italian and whose mother was of German extraction, revealed that she had never cooked spaghetti. Alan would have to quench his appetite for Italian food at Lorenzo's, his favorite campus restaurant in Madison.

The tenor of the quite-revealing article is that being a superstar college football player, especially a married player with two babies at home, is anything but glamorous for both the player and his wife. We learn the following about the Ameches:

Ameche was a great father, but not particularly keen on changing diapers.

"Oh no, Lino's definitely boss around here," said Yvonne when asked if he does his share of diaper changing. "Lino always has a sore shoulder when the baby has to be rocked."

A slew of Stanfield's photos reveal that Yvonne was just kidding about her husband's parenting skills. Ameche is shown rocking and feeding Alan Jr. while another photo shows him pitching a football around with husky blonde Brian.

There was no glamour in living in a two-bedroom, one-bath unit in the Blackhawk housing project on Madison's west side.

"Not what it's cracked up to be," Yvonne said. "Naturally, I'm proud. And I got real excited the first few times I saw him in a game or picked up a national magazine and saw his picture. But that doesn't thrill me anymore.

"We have so little real home life. The phone or door bell is always ringing. Why, just the other day a photographer stopped by at 7 a.m. to get pictures for a national magazine.

"Not that I mind it, but it's another indication that our life isn't our own. We don't have any privacy, not even when we are out to dinner. Someone is always coming over to our table."

College football stars were anything but coddled.

We learn from Ingrassia's article that although he was a senior (majoring in physical education), Ameche had 7:45 a.m. classes on Monday, Wednesday, and Friday and was up by 7:30 a.m. the other two weekdays.

Yvonne generally prepared him one meal per day—breakfast. A typical breakfast for the big-eating Ameche would include ham and eggs, toast, apple pie, and milk. If he was running late, just fruit juice.

"I'm usually feeding the baby, so I make breakfast for Lino," Yvonne said.

During the season, Ameche ate dinner with the coaches and other players at the training table and was only able to make it home for lunch on Wednesdays and Fridays.

Stress was a daily occurrence at the Ameche home.

Yvonne told a story revealing the unbelievable pressure exerted on not only her but also her young husband's shoulders.

"Lino is so nervous, he's awful around the house. He's hard to live with during the football season.

"Before the Rice game [October 9, 1954] I had just finished feeding the baby and was going to bed when Lino started shouting numbers of plays and thrashing around in bed. He didn't remember a thing the next morning."

Ameche had at least one less to thing to worry about in his senior year—his nose. In his junior season he had been fitted with custom-made, extra-broad shoulder pads, and for his senior year he was fitted for a face mask. In the next few seasons, face masks would become mandatory equipment, but in 1954 Ameche was one of the first players to be seen wearing one of the awkward-looking safety devices.

"Alan was the first guy on the team to wear a face mask," said teammate Jim Temp. "He had that nose. Helmets would come down on his nose. He always went around with scabs and blood on the bridge of his nose.

"It was made of plastic. I remember he had trouble breathing with the original design so they modified it until they got it right."

On the classroom front, Ameche apparently had things figured out as well. According to a profile in *Parade* magazine that appeared just before his senior season, Ameche had achieved just under a B average in the College of Education, where he was studying physical education.

"Of the seven Kenosha boys who came to college with him his high school grades were lowest," the article, written by Henry J. McCormick claimed. "He is proud that his college grades are the highest."

Ultimately, Ameche was the only one of the group who would finish at Wisconsin in four years. Nicolazzi would come back and finish after a stint in the Army, and Shwaiko, after missing the 1953 season for academic reasons, would return in 1954 and 1955 to play key roles with the team.

As for Ameche, as much as he was loved and respected by his teammates, he was never chosen to lead the Badgers as captain. Make no mistake, there was no jealousy on the Badgers between Ameche and the rest of the squad, but he was just not the sort to lead the team in cheers.

"That was the thing about Alan," Jim Temp recalled. "He wasn't necessarily a leader in the sense of a rah-rah kind of person. But he played football like you can't believe."

Although Ameche was never elected captain by his Wisconsin peers, that doesn't mean he wasn't the most respected member of the team. In interviews with his teammates from Kenosha through the Baltimore Colts, Ameche was universally respected and liked by his teammates.

"The thing you could always be sure of with Alan was that he was never going to quit," said Roger Dornburg. "He was a big, tough bird who always gave it his all. He had a ton of talent but he had toughness and heart, too.

"He was the star of the team but no matter what your status was on the team, Alan treated everybody the same, with respect. He was always friendly to everybody and everybody on the team liked him."

In Booton Herndon's *Sports Illustrated* article, Gary Messner, the captain of the 1954 team, summed up how the Badgers felt about Ameche.

"Al is the most popular man on the team. He makes our jobs a lot easier. You can block a man a lot better when he's looking at somebody else.

"He was the greatest football player I've ever seen, including the current crop," Messner would say after Ameche's death.

"Nobody had to do a great deal of blocking for him, quite frankly. There aren't a lot of guys who could do it all but he could."

The biggest question mark heading into the 1954 season was who would hand off the football to Ameche. Miller acquitted himself quite well, especially as a runner, in taking over the job in 1953. But Haluska's leg was now 100 percent healed, and he was deemed a better passer than Miller.

Clearly, Williamson had a tough decision to make, so he did the only logical thing he could do. He deferred a decision and decided that the quarterback situation would be handled by committee in 1954.

For the most part, his nondecision worked out well. Despite being part-time, Miller's passing stats improved over the course of 1953—he was 46 of 88 for 608 yards and five touchdowns in 1954. Haluska also saw plenty of action, mostly in relief, completing 36 of 75 for 505 yards and two touchdowns.

Even Williamson, who had been the voice of doom and gloom before the 1953 season, fairly gushed when assessing his team's prospects for 1954. The only thing curbing his enthusiasm was the loss of halfback speedsters Harland Carl and Jerry Witt.

"Our backfield situation is good," stated Williamson. "We have fine hopes at quarterback and a real fullback. Our halfbacks, while not as experienced except for the two starters (Bob Gingrass and Clarence Bratt) are fairly strong. But we don't have the breakaway speed we had there last year."

As for Ameche's weight, a surprisingly popular topic of conversation during his four years in Madison, Williamson lent Ameche's preseason weigh-in a circus atmosphere, with a certified public accountant on hand to accurately record the number. Ameche weighed in at 210, which was within a few pounds of his playing weight all four seasons.

Apparently the six weeks Ameche had spent at Fort Eustis in Texas for ROTC training did him a world of good. According to the Wisconsin sports information department, Ameche had ballooned up to 230 pounds at the start of spring drills.

"He's quite a football player," said Williamson, going out on a limb at the weigh-in.

"Greater things are expected of him this fall, but I want to relieve him much more with Charlie Thomas, who has shown great improvement on both offense and defense."

It should be noted that Williamson said almost exactly the same thing about Thomas, Ameche's backup from Evanston, Illinois, the previous preseason but then proceeded to play Ameche an average of 55 minutes per game in 1953.

With Miller at quarterback, the Badgers opened the season ranked number ten and didn't disappoint anyone in their season opener against perennial in-state rival Marquette on September 25. Ameche rushed for 107 yards in 18 carries as the Badgers cruised to a 52–14 victory. Ameche scored a touchdown on a 1-yard plunge and also had a 47-yard dash.

Bratt staked Wisconsin to a 13–0 early lead in the contest with the game's first two touchdowns, but Marquette took a short-lived 14–13 lead early in the second period.

With the Big Ten back to ten teams again with the addition of Michigan State in 1953, it was decided that each team would now play seven conference games. That meant dropping a nonconference game so that each team would still play a regular season schedule of nine games.

For the first time, Wisconsin would play Michigan State in conference play in 1954. The Badgers, who had moved up to number five after manhandling Marquette, would shut out the Spartans, 6–0, in a game that rekindled memories of the Hard Rocks.

It was a great day for Kenosha in East Lansing, Michigan, in the matchup between the Big Ten's last two representatives to the Rose Bowl. Ameche would have what would prove to be his most productive game of the season, 127 yards in 17 carries, scoring the game's only points on a 28-yard run in the second quarter. Ameche appeared to be stopped when hit by two Michigan State defenders at the 5-yard line, but his momentum carried him into the end zone. Miller's 38-yard scramble on the previous play had set up the winning touchdown.

Paul Shwaiko was the star on defense. He intercepted an Earl Morrall pass deep in Wisconsin territory with five seconds left in the game to blunt Michigan State's last hope.

The victory over Michigan State catapulted the Badgers to the number-three ranking and into the national spotlight. Their October 9 game with Rice and halfback Dick Moegle was to be televised nationally, an extreme rarity in 1954.

The game was a rematch of the 1952 contest in Houston and was billed as "Workhorse versus the Racehorse." The Owls were ranked number eleven coming into Madison, and Moegle was fresh from Rice's 41–20 win over Cornell, in which he had carried just six times; however, he had gained 168 yards (28 yards per carry), scored four touchdowns, and caught two passes for 28 yards.

Moegle would have a fantastic college and pro football careers but would always be remembered for one play in the 1954 Cotton Bowl in Dallas. He appeared to be on his way to a 95-yard touchdown when Alabama's Tommy Lewis came off the sideline to tackle Moegle in front of the Crimson Tide bench. After a conference by the game's officials, Moegle was awarded a touchdown in what would be one of the most replayed plays in college football history.

The first-ever meeting between the intersectional rivals in Houston had featured off-field drama when Williamson denied Ameche a starting role because "he hadn't earned it." The 1954 game would keep the drama on the field, where it belonged.

Trailing 7–6 in the fourth quarter, the Badgers were thwarted twice by a surprisingly stout Rice defense. The first time, Wisconsin's drive halted at the Rice one and at the Owls' five the second time. Both times, Rice took over on downs.

But the third time was the charm, as Ameche crashed into the end zone with the winning touchdown with 55 seconds left in the game. In the battle of unbeatens, Wisconsin prevailed, 13–7.

The winning drive, which lasted 12 plays, started at the Rice 40 with 5:49 left in the contest. On a third and five from the 35, Miller broke loose for a 10-yard run to the Rice 25.

An 8-yard pass to Jim Temp and a 3-yard run by John Bridgeman gave Wisconsin a first down at the Rice 14. After runs of 4 yards by Ameche, 2 by Bridgeman, and 3 by Ameche again, the Badgers faced a fourth and one at the Rice five with the game on the line. On what would be the key play of the game, sophomore Pat Levenhagen crashed off the right guard for three yards and a fresh set of downs.

Levenhagen got to the one on the next play, and from there Ameche plowed over the right tackle for the winning touchdown. Buzz Wilson kicked the extra point.

Ameche, who rushed for 90 yards in 21 carries, also scored the Badgers first touchdown from 2 yards out in the first quarter. It was Wisconsin's first possession of the game, but Wilson's extra point missed.

Rice took the lead at 7–6 midway through the first period on a 20-yard pass from quarterback John Nisbet to Lamoine Holland, who was alone in the end zone. Phil Harris's conversion kick gave the Owls a lead that stood up until the game's closing seconds.

Wisconsin dominated statistically, gaining 22 first downs to Rice's 14 and outrushing the Owls, 236 to 144 yards.

The victory vaulted Wisconsin to number two behind number-one Oklahoma, but the schedule was hardly getting easier. In the next two weeks, Wisconsin would host number-five-ranked Purdue and then travel to Columbus to play number-four-ranked Ohio State.

In the Purdue game, which featured the passing of Len Dawson versus the rushing of Ameche, the Badgers prevailed, 20–6, to move to 4–0. Purdue, which the week before had been tied by number-six Duke, suffered its first loss of the season as Ameche rushed for 73 yards in 18 carries. Ameche scored Wisconsin's second touchdown on a three-yard run.

As crucial as the Purdue victory was, a win over Ohio State on October 23, in a battle of unbeatens, would have been even more important. The game was in Columbus, a place where Wisconsin hadn't won since 1918.

The Buckeyes were Williamson's personal nemesis as well. In his five years at Wisconsin, he had compiled a fantastic 21-7-4 record, the best in the league. His personal record against the Buckeyes to that point, however, was 0-4-1. A 6-6 tie in 1951 had cost the Badgers a Big Ten title, and a 20–19 loss in 1953 cost them another title.

Even in 1952, the year of the Badgers' first-ever Rose Bowl appearance and conference co-title (with Purdue), Ohio State had marred the Badgers' season by handing them a 23–14 loss. Just once Williamson would like to beat the Buckeyes—unfortunately, it was not to be. Before being promoted to the Wisconsin athletic director's job after the 1955 season, Williamson would retire from coaching with a 0-6-1 record against the Buckeyes.

There would be no shame in losing to Ohio State in 1954. The Buckeyes would be the team of destiny, going undefeated (10-0) and winning the national championship by beating Southern Cal in the Rose Bowl. The Badgers were the fifth notch in their belt, 31–14.

Ohio State's strategy of shutting down Ameche worked perfectly. He had perhaps his poorest game of the season, rushing for just 42 yards in 16 carries, and for the first time in five games, he was kept out of the opponent's end zone. Ironically, the Badgers came into the contest with the number-one defense in the Big Ten, while Ohio State had the number-one offense in the nation.

Ohio State led 7–3 at the end of the first quarter, and as was the case the previous year, Cassady was again the culprit. He intercepted a pass by Jim Miller, Miller's first interception of the season, and returned it 88 yards for a touchdown. Cassady's play changed the momentum of the game.

Williamson continued his system of rotating quarterbacks, starting Miller but going to Haluska if the situation called for a passer. Haluska relieved Miller in the second half and was effective, prompting Ohio State coach Woody Hayes to call Haluska "the best passer we've seen all fall."

The Badgers, apparently wearing down in the fourth quarter, allowed three touchdowns as the Buckeyes pulled away in the end. Ameche would never get untracked in the contest, but that was par for the course in his four games against the Buckeyes.

Ameche would finish with 75 carries in his career against Ohio State but not one touchdown. The only other Big Ten team to "shut out" Ameche was Michigan, a team that wasn't on Wisconsin's schedule for Ameche's four years in Madison.

Ameche was said to have had a great admiration for Hayes and apparently often wondered what it would have been like to play for the controversial coaching legend. Apparently, the admiration was reciprocal on the part of Ohio State. Before the game, Ohio State assistant coach Esco Sarkkinen, who had watched Ameche on film at least three games per year for four years, had this to say about the Wisconsin fullback: "Ameche is the greatest fullback on the North American continent today. He is powerful, he's shifty, and he's fast and he's all of them all of the time. He's big, too, but he doesn't need to be. Not with that heart."

The loss to Ohio State dropped Wisconsin to 4–1 on the season and to the number-eight national ranking. Unfortunately, the Badgers were on the road again the following week at unranked Iowa, a place where it was never easy to win. But the Badgers had won five straight times versus Iowa, and 9 of their last 11 meetings.

Unfortunately for the Badgers, this time the Hawkeyes broke the losing streak, 13–7, and effectively ended Wisconsin's hopes for a Big Ten title in Ameche's senior season. No one could pin this loss on Ameche, who had one of his best games in a Wisconsin uniform. He played all 60 minutes, carrying the ball a season-high 26 times for 117 yards.

The Hawkeyes went up early, 13–0, but Ameche led a second-half comeback. In the third period he appeared to score on a 22-yard run, but the referees ruled that his knee touched down insde the Iowa 1-yard line. Ameche scored on the next play to bring the Badgers to within 6. Wisconsin penetrated deep into Iowa territory in the fourth quarter, but the drive was halted by a fumble. Iowa controlled the clock for the game's final five minutes to preserve the victory.

Even in the final weeks of his collegiate career, Ameche was not into personal glory, but in reality that was all that was left for the Badgers in the final three weeks of their 1954 season. With struggling Northwestern next on the schedule, the long-time *Chicago Daily News* sports writer John Carmichael encapsulated Ameche's career at Wisconsin. Carmichael pointed out that through 34 college games (including the Rose Bowl) Ameche had gained 3,260 yards in 671 rushing attempts, "a record that nobody may ever approach." Carmichael further stated that Ameche never missed a game because of injury, lost just 14 fumbles in those 34 games, while his teammates had lost 42 over the same span, had been thrown for an aggregate of just 93 yards in losses, and "absorbed the requirements for single-platoon play so effectively that he has become one of the finest linebackers in Big Ten circles."

The Badgers put a halt to their slide, dominating the mistake-prone Wildcats, 34–13, in Madison. Ameche suffered an ankle injury in the contest but not before becoming the NCAA's all-time leading rusher. Before leaving the game, Ameche had rushed for 59 yards in 17 carries giving him a career total of 3,186 yards, breaking the record of San Francisco University's Ollie Matson (1948–1951) of 3,166 yards. Ameche had two long gains that were nullified by penalties, but he did score one of the Badgers' five touchdowns.

"The big moose is one of the greatest—certainly a handy man to have in the backfield," Wildcats coach Bob Voigts told the Associated Press after the game. "You can't concentrate on just stopping Ameche either or you'll be knocked apart by the other backs."

Northwestern lived up to its reputation as a team that could move the football, but they were also self-destructive. The Wildcats turned the ball over five times—three lost fumbles and two interceptions—and the Badgers took full advantage. Sophomore Billy Lowe was Wisconsin's leading ballcarrier, with 68 yards in seven carries, including Wisconsin's first touchdown on a run of 23 yards that saw him break two tackles.

In addition to taking over as college football's all-time leading rusher, Ameche also took over the Big Ten rushing lead with his relatively modest performance against Northwestern. It is not known if anyone in Madison was concerned that the ankle injury might hamper Ameche's chances at winning the Heisman Trophy or if anybody cared, for that matter. The hype that surrounds the award today is ten times what it was in 1954. There was certainly some interest in the award, but not weekly analysis pieces on who the front-runners were. Based on his four-year body of work, Ameche was certainly a favorite to win, but the injury in his stretch run made him anything but a shoo-in.

Ameche didn't practice with the squad in the week leading up to the November 13 Illinois game in Champaign. It was also reported that Ameche had a touch of the flu and that Williamson told Ameche's understudies, Charles Thomas and Glenn Bestor, to be ready to play. Illinois star J. C. Caroline was also deemed questionable for the game because of a nagging shoulder injury, and the Badgers were rated as a two-touchdown favorite against the Illini, who were still winless in the Big Ten.

The mystery ended when Ameche lined up in the Wisconsin backfield to start the game before a sellout Memorial Stadium crowd of 71,119. But, alas, he was only there as a decoy. He lasted seven plays, never touching the ball, before being replaced for the day by Thomas.

The Badgers won, 27–14, scoring three touchdowns in the fourth quarter. It was the first time since 1919–21 that Wisconsin had scored three straight victories over the Fighting Illini. But it was no way for a Heisman Trophy candidate to put on a stretch drive. Ameche had one last chance to impress the Heisman voters in his final college game against Minnesota, but the Golden Gophers were a vexing bunch, to say the least.

Minnesota came into Madison that year with a 4–1 record and a chance to tie Ohio State in the Big Ten loss column, although the Buckeyes had clinched the title outright, by virtue of winning their first six conference games. The Buckeyes made the point moot by crushing rival Michigan, 21–7, in the final week.

The Badgers, who would finish the season ranked number nine in the AP poll, left no doubt on this afternoon, crushing the visitors from Minnesota, 27–0. Like Northwestern two weeks earlier, the Golden Gophers would be a victim of their own incompetence, throwing seven interceptions, a Big Ten record.

Badger senior halfback Clarence Bratt grabbed four of the errant throws, also a Big Ten record. Wisconsin took full advantage of the fact that Minnesota was down to its third-string quarterback, stacking eight defenders on the line of scrimmage and daring reserve Don Swanson to throw the football. Gophers starter Gino Cappelletti, who would go on to play professionally for the old Boston Patriots, had been sidelined for the remainder of the season with a dislocated elbow the previous week against Iowa.

As for Ameche, it was a bittersweet ending to his brilliant collegiate career. Despite hobbling noticeably on his still bothersome and heavily bandaged right ankle, Ameche gamely carried 13 times for 26 yards and two touchdowns.

Perhaps sensing that Ameche needed touchdowns to boost his Heisman candidacy, Williamson obliged by giving him scoring opportunities aplenty in the first half. Leading 7–0, Ameche failed to score from a yard out on the last play of the first quarter. But on his second chance, on the first play of the second quarter, Ameche scored from the same distance.

After a blocked punt by Gary Messner was recovered by Norm Amundsen at the Gophers' four-yard line, Ameche was given another chance. This time he scored on the first try, through the right tackle, at 12:58 of the second period. It was the twenty-fifth and final touchdown of his career at Wisconsin.

Ameche returned to the game in second half but left the field for the final time when he came up hobbling after a pileup with 6:52 remaining in the third period. He left the field to a standing ovation from the sellout crowd of 53,131, one that included a large contingent of placard-carrying fans from Kenosha.

A famous photo by a United Press photographer, Leonard Fulce, shows Ameche, head bowed and covered by a cloak, sitting on the Badgers bench as the final minutes of his spectacular career ticked away. When the final gun sounded, Ameche was honored by his teammates, who carried him on their shoulders off the Camp Randall playing field.

Although he had gained only a relatively modest 26 yards in his finale, Ameche finished his college career with 3,212 in 673 carries. Both were NCAA records. His 133 yards in 28 tries at the 1953 Rose Bowl weren't included in the final total.

Despite the ankle injury and despite having the least productive season of his college career, Ameche won every postseason honor imaginable. He won the Heisman Trophy, again won the Walter Camp, which was now awarded by *Collier's* magazine to the player of the year, was voted Wisconsin's MVP by his teammates for the second consecutive year, won the *Chicago Tribune*'s Big Ten MVP award, and won the United Press' Back of the Year award. He was also named to every first-team all-American team and to the All–Big Ten team.

Ameche's NCAA records have been broken many times over, but the Football Bowl Series (FBS) rushing yardage record remains in the hands of another Badger—the great Ron Dayne, who from 1996 through 1999, rushed for 6,397 yards. In 1999 he also became the second University of Wisconsin running back to win the Heisman.

There was so much excitement generated over Dayne's record-breaking career that his name and number, 33, were the first to be placed on Camp Randall's ring of honor at Wisconsin's final home game on November 13, 1999.

Ameche's name and number, 35, were added the following season on September 9, 2000, during halftime of the Badgers game with Oregon. But the fact that Dayne's name and number were immortalized on the facade before Ameche's doesn't sit well with some Wisconsin old-timers and friends of Ameche.

"Nobody liked it when they put Dayne's name up in the ring of honor before Alan's," said Mario Bonofiglio, Ameche's close friend and teammate in high school and college. "You put Dayne up there before Ameche . . . that's just nuts. Alan won it in 1954 and they wait until after Dayne wins the Heisman to put him in the ring of honor?

"A lot of people in Madison went nuts when they saw that. People called me from Madison. They couldn't believe [Ameche] wasn't up there first."

But according to Ameche's oldest son, Brian, the family holds no ill will toward the University of Wisconsin. The elder Ameche's last official visit there was in 1984 to present the athletic director, Elroy Hirsch, with a replica of his Heisman. Until his death in 1988, Ameche frequently helped the Badgers' recruiting efforts whenever asked.

"It didn't bother me that Ron Dayne went in first," Brian said. "I don't believe it was an intentional slight there, just a mistake.

"I went back to Madison to speak at halftime once and when I realized that everybody was listening to me and the place was silent, I choked on my words. I was like, uh, uh, uh . . . and I think to this day, that the people, to cover my embarrassment . . . they applauded for me.

"I think that's the earnestness that the Midwest is known for. I finished my speech and they applauded again. When I was walking back through the stands to where I was sitting, people were reaching out and touching me. 'It was a very lovely speech. Thanks for coming. We're so happy you are here.'

"It was just a great experience."

15

Holding the Heisman

ALAN AMECHE DIDN'T KNOW IT AT THE TIME, but he had been a finalist for 1953 Heisman Trophy. He might have never known except for the fact that he won it in 1954.

To say that the Heisman and all its machinations have moved in mysterious ways would be an understatement. The honor, since 1935 reserved for America's best college football player, has been awarded to some of the sport's truest football heroes, like Iowa's Nile Kinnick in 1939, and some of its most notorious, like Southern Cal's O.J. Simpson in 1968. The award has gone mostly to the deserving, but it did, on a few occasions, go to the undeserving.

In 1954 there may have been a few players with gaudier portfolios than Ameche, but there were none more deserving. In his four years at Wisconsin, with the help of a coach and teammates who believed in rock-ribbed defense, Ameche turned things around. He was the public face of a program that before his and Ivy Williamson's arrival had little to publicize.

Ameche's statistics in 1954 were . . . not so great. That will happen to you when a misguided rule legislates that you must be on the field taking lumps for 55 minutes per game and you sit out nearly two games because of injury. Ameche's best years statistically at the collegiate level were behind him by the time he was through his sophomore season.

To summarize his career at Wisconsin, Ameche played in all of Wisconsin's 37 games from 1951 through 1954, including the 1953 Rose Bowl game. There were two games, however, Marquette in 1951 (one carry) and Illinois in 1954 (no carries), in which he had just one carry combined.

In 1951 and 1952, with 824 and 946 yards, respectively (not including the 133 yards he netted at the Rose Bowl), Ameche piled up 1,770 yards in his first two seasons. He rushed for 801 yards and 641 yards in his junior and senior seasons, giving him a total of 1,442 yards in the second half of his career—a difference of 328 yards.

A strong case could have been built for Ohio State's Howard Cassady to win the Heisman in 1954. He had rushed for 609 yards and added 137 receiving yards, and he was a great defensive back. It may be a legend, but it has been written that Cassady never allowed the man he was covering to catch a pass in his time at Ohio State.

The biggest argument for Cassady was the team he played on. Cassady was the undisputed star of Ohio State, which was undefeated and number one in the nation in 1954. Ohio State convincingly beat Wisconsin in 1954, and Cassady outplayed Ameche in the contest.

Ameche, Cassady, and Notre Dame quarterback Ralph Guglielmi were all unanimous choices to the Associated Press All-American Team. Guglielmi had a nice season in 1954, completing 68 of 127 attempts (53.5 percent) for 1,162 yards. For Ameche and Guglielmi, it was 1954 or broke because both were seniors. As a junior, Cassady had one more chance in 1955, and he did ultimately win the Heisman that year.

A total of 1,318 sports writers and sportscasters voted in 1954. Ameche garnered 1,068 votes to the 838 of the runner-up, Oklahoma center Kurt Burris. Cassady finished third with 810, and Guglielmi was fourth with 691.

The Heisman has evolved over the years, and in 1954 only the winner made the trip to New York for the presentation. Now, all the finalists come to New York, and the winner isn't known until it is announced in a hopefully dramatic, made-for-television event.

It was when Ameche learned that he had won the Heisman that he also learned that he had finished sixth in the 1953 voting. Notre Dame's John Lattner would capture the award that year, followed in order by Minnesota's Paul Giel, Paul Cameron of UCLA, Bernie Faloney of Maryland, and Bob Garrett of Stanford.

"It's funny, isn't it?" Yvonne Ameche would say later. "You would think for an award as big as the Heisman somebody would have told him."

Notre Dame's publicist, Charlie Calahan, apparently felt that Guglielmi should have won the 1954 award and the only thing holding him back was that the voters didn't want players from the same school to win the award in consecutive years.

"If Johnny Lattner had not won the Heisman Trophy last year, I'm sure Ralph Guglielmi would have won it this year," Calahan was quoted as saying. "They don't like to give it to the same school two years running."

But, as the *Wisconsin State Journal* columnist Henry J. McCormick pointed out, Yale's Larry Kelley and Clint Frank won the award in 1936 and 1937, and Army's Felix "Doc" Blanchard and Glenn Davis won it in 1945 and 1946.

Most observers of college football of that era agree that the Heisman was more of a lifetime achievement award for one's body of work rather than just a one-season honor. Rudy Riska is the director emeritus of the Heisman Trophy and the unofficial Heisman historian. He agrees with that view.

"A lot of times in those days it was based more on the career—two or three years together," Riska said. "The voters looked at the fellow's career, what he meant to his team over the years. I think that was the standard at that time with voters.

"Look at a guy like Angelo Bertelli," said Riska of the 1943 winner from Notre Dame. "He had a great junior year, then in the middle of his senior year he had to go into the Marines.

"He only played six games, yet he won the Heisman. He'd come back for the awards ceremony every year, and I think he kind of felt he didn't deserve the award because he hadn't played in that many games his senior year. But he won it based on his career."

Ameche's teammates agree that the award was more of a cumulative thing than it was for what he did in 1954. They also feel that his production would have been much higher if he hadn't been forced by the one-platoon rule to play upward of 55 minutes per game his last two years.

"If you ask me, it was definitely a cumulative thing," said Jerry Wuhrman. "I think the voters were going by total yards for a career and that's why he got more recognition as a senior even though maybe his statistics weren't as strong as when he was a freshman and sophomore. And the team didn't perform as well when he was a senior either."

Added Jim Temp: "I'll say this . . . Alan definitely deserved the Heisman for what he did in his career. I was just proud that I had the opportunity to play with him and alongside him."

Even though the Heisman was a national award and the first honoree, in 1935, was Jay Berwanger from the University of Chicago, most of the voters were sportswriters and from the eastern part of the country.

"Sportscasters weren't even given a vote," said Riska. "Nobody complained about it, but there was definitely more representation in the East than there was with the rest of the country. We found that there were newspapers with 9 or 10 guys from one staff voting.

"At one point there were almost 2,000 voters and all of them were with newspapers. We wanted to make sure it was guys who actually covered teams and saw the games."

The eastern bias certainly explains how Yale players Larry Kelley and Clint Frank won back to back in 1936 and 1937. In one of sports' greatest blunders, TCU's legendary Sammy Baugh finished fourth to Kelley.

The eastern bias had been brought into balance by the time Ameche came along in the 1950s. Television still wasn't much of a factor, because at that time only one national game was shown every Saturday, and most of the voters missed it because, if they were doing their jobs, they were covering a game somewhere else.

One factor for some voters might have been a catchy nickname. Starting with Alan "the Horse" Ameche, followed by Howard "Hopalong" Cassady and Paul "Golden Boy" Hornung, there were three memorable nicknames in three consecutive years from 1954 through 1956.

It may seem odd now, because today the Heisman award milks the event for every ounce of drama, but when Ameche won it, he actually knew he had won it more than a week in advance. It was already known that he was the winner when he went to New York for the National Football Writers Association All-American dinner for *Look* magazine on Saturday, December 4.

Ameche and the Outland Trophy winner, Bud Brooks of Arkansas, were the only two players asked to speak at the lavish dinner at Gene Leone's restaurant. After an appearance on the *Jackie Gleason Show* on Saturday night, Ameche caught a flight back to Madison on Sunday afternoon.

By the time he returned days later to claim the Heisman on the following Thursday, he had already had his national press conference via "squawk box," the precursor to today's conference call, effectively upstaging himself and the award ceremony.

Ameche arrived in New York on Tuesday to have his official portrait taken, and Yvonne was flown out the next day, escorted by the Wisconsin backfield coach, Bob O'Dell.

"When we got off the plane, we were met in New York by a big limousine," Yvonne recalled. "My eyes were this big.

"We were taken to the 21 Club for dinner and Alan was already there. It was a very famous club, like the Stork Club. Having dinner at the next table from us was Aristotle Onassis and Maria Callas.

"I was one of the first women ever to stay at the Downtown Athletic Club [site of the Heisman presentation] because none of the previous winners had been married. We took the limo everywhere when we were in New York.

"It was just very exciting, but there wasn't all the hype there is now. There aren't all the flashbulbs and things you see with the ceremony now."

Wisconsin was represented by Ivy Williamson and the state's lieutenant governor–elect, Warren Knowles.

Williamson told the Associated Press that he always told Ameche, "You can be a great football player . . . you can be a great guy. But you have to prove it yourself.

"He has proved it."

Knowles said the state of Wisconsin was proud of Ameche and grateful to the sportswriters for selecting him.

Ameche's speech itself was pretty much boilerplate. According to the Associated Press story of the event, Ameche said he was "proud and humble." He was proud because it was the "finest award he ever has, and probably ever will, receive." He said he was humble because "I know many other deserving players could have received this honor."

Ameche thanked a number of people who had aided him in his career, including Kenosha High School coach Chuck Jaskwhich and Williamson. "But," he added, "I want to thank the most understanding and helpful one of all, my wife." AP added, "Pretty Yvonne, mother of Al's two sons, was at his side to share his glory."

Ameche told the audience that he hoped to play professional football but cautioned that the U.S. Army might be in his future. He was in Wisconsin's ROTC program and would have been eligible for a commission upon graduation (but he flunked his entrance physical exam).

Seated at the speaker's table that night with Ameche and Yvonne were Jay Berwanger, the first Heisman winner in 1935; Doc Blanchard, the 1945 Heisman winner; Chuck Jaskwhich; and O'Dell.

Apparently, Ameche handed the trophy over to Madison restaurant owner Bob Leske, and it remained on display in his Madison steakhouse for four years before Ameche retrieved it. The Ameches never displayed the trophy in their home until the family purchased a larger home in the late 1960s, when Alan's playing days were long over.

"I don't remember where [the Heisman] was all those years, but I'm sure we had it somewhere," Yvonne said. "We had six kids to worry about, too, remember?

"Alan was a very modest man. He never wore his [NFL] championship ring or his letterman's jacket from Wisconsin. In fact he gave it [the jacket] to a priest later on.

"We eventually put [the Heisman] on display in the house sometime in the late 1960s," Yvonne said. "I remember I won an award for needlepoint and we hung that from the arm of the Heisman."

Some who knew Ameche said that the reason the trophy was kept out of sight for years was because of his sons. He didn't want them to have a daily reminder of the expectations cast upon them by their father's award.

"It might have been because of the kids. Who knows what his thinking was then," Yvonne said. "I'm sure that might have had something to do with it."

In 1954 the Heisman committee awarded just one trophy—to the player. What he chose to do with the trophy was his business. Leon Hart, the 1949 Heisman winner from Notre Dame, donated his trophy to his alma mater, and Ameche would eventually do the same for Wisconsin.

"Back then all the player got was a trophy," Yvonne said. "Leon Hart had given his to Notre Dame and Alan wanted to donate his to Wisconsin, so they went before the Heisman committee and asked that two trophies be given each year—one to the player and one to the school."

Riska said the lobbying by Ameche and Hart carried plenty of the weight with the committee.

"A lot of the guys wanted to give their trophies to their schools, but they didn't want to give them up either," Riska said. "I can't remember when it was, but the committee decided to give out two—one to the player and one to school—and they made it retroactive to the beginning.

"Plus, a Heisman ring was created, too. You can't carry the trophy around, that's for sure, but they thought the players should have something to show off. Like I said, there has been a lot of tweaking to the Heisman award over the years, a lot of positive changes made."

The *Milwaukee Sentinel* sports editor, Lloyd Larson, had some nice words to share with his readers about Ameche's postseason honors.

The thing that makes all this recognition business double wonderful is the manner in which Alan Ameche the man has received all the acclaim coming to Alan Ameche the football player.

He is taking it in stride just as he took every bit of publicity during his remarkable four year varsity career. The Horse has his feet firmly planted on the ground just as exactly as they were planted when he came out of Kenosha High School to make his first bid for fame as a Badger freshman in the fall of 1951.

That's the real test for an outstanding athlete: Does the hat size increase with increasing fame or does he stay level, modest and humble? Everybody who has come in contact with Ameche will tell you that he falls into the latter class.

In my mind, that's more important than all his thrilling runs, his blocks and tackles, his breath-taking exhibitions of lowering the boom, as they say in football when a man drives into an opponent with all the power he can muster in fighting for those precious extra yards.

So here's to Alan Ameche, the type of All-American the world needs!

So beyond the statistics and the hype, just what was it that made Alan Ameche the best football player in the land in 1954? Here are a few opinions of his teammates, the players whose unenviable task it was to try to tackle Ameche every day in practice.

Jerry Wuhrman: "Well, for one thing there was no finesse in Alan's style. He was more standup than most running backs, but it was just hard straight ahead football.

"The thing that made him so hard to tackle was that he had these enormously huge, strong thighs and a very strong upper body. He was able to overpower a lot of tacklers because he was a very big man for a running back of that time, and certainly defensive players then weren't as big as they are now."

Roger Dornburg: "His running style was different. He had kind of a wobble to him or something. He ran side to side, like he didn't know where he was going, but all the time he was running like a tank. He was so hard to tackle and when he hit you, he let you know it.

"He didn't even have to lower his shoulder. He was so muscular and tough, he'd just kind of run over you by running into you if that makes sense. When he'd hit you, it was like hitting a piece of iron or something.

"You had to just hit him and grab a hold of something. Alan was as good as anybody I ever played against."

Mark Hoegh: "His running style with his knees so high, if you got to him before he got to the line of scrimmage, you had a pretty good chance to bring him down. But once he got to the line of scrimmage and past, it was tough to bring him down.

"He ran high, but he was so powerful, over 200 pounds of muscle. His knees were always so high that you'd have to get both legs or you were going to catch one in the head or the face with the other."

Jim Temp: "Alan wasn't the greatest speedster. It was his strength. He had enormous strength in the legs and above the waist, too.

"But the thighs were like weapons. You hit a guy like that and you'd better have a clean shot at him or he will run right over you every time."

When Ameche left Wisconsin, he had literally rewritten the Wisconsin and the NCAA record books.

- Ameche broke the Wisconsin single-season rushing record in both his freshman (824 yards) and sophomore (946 yards) years. The record had been held previously by Elroy "Crazylegs" Hirsch from 1942 (767 yards).
- Ameche broke the Wisconsin career rushing record with 3,212 yards (not including the 133 yards he gained in the Rose Bowl). The record of 1,748 had been held by Ben Bendrick from 1945 through 1948. Ameche had actually eclipsed that record after his first two seasons.
- Ameche broke the Wisconsin career scoring record with 150 points on 25 touchdowns. Pat Harder had held the record, scoring 121 points in 1941 and 1942. Ameche's 54 points in 1954 were exceeded only by Harder's 72 points in 1941.
- Ameche's 3,212 yards also broke the NCAA record for career rushing yards. The record of 3,166 had been held by San Francisco University's Ollie Matson from 1948 through 1951. Ameche's 673 carries at Wisconsin were also an NCAA record.
- Ameche ran for 100 or more yards 16 times in his collegiate career. He also ran for 200 against Minnesota in 1951.

Ameche left Madison and the state of Wisconsin in 1954, never to live there again. But the honors from his playing days at the University of Wisconsin kept rolling in for years to come.

- In 1969 Ameche was named Wisconsin's all-time greatest player by a vote of Badger fans. He was also named to Wisconsin's all-time team at that time and had already been named to the Wisconsin State Hall of Fame and the National W Club Hall of Fame and had received the Wisconsin Alumni Association Distinguished Alumni Award.
- In 1975 Ameche was inducted into the College Football Hall of Fame, which is now located in South Bend, Indiana.
- In 1980 he received the NCAA Silver Anniversary Award, which recognizes former players for distinguishing themselves off the playing field.
- In 1984 Ameche presented his Heisman Trophy to Athletic Director Elroy Hirsch at the halftime of the Northwestern game.
- In 1991 Ameche was one of thirty-five charter members inducted into the UW Athletic Hall of Fame.
- In 1992 Ameche was inducted into the College Sports Information Directors Academic Hall of Fame.

- In 1997 Ameche was named to the first GTE Academic All-America All-Time football team. Joining Ameche on the first team were such greats as Lance Alworth, Raymond Berry, Dave Casper, Fran Tarkenton, Pete Dawkins, Merlin Olsen, Lee Roy Selmon, Randy Gradishar, and Sam Huff.
- In 2000 Ameche's number, 35, was retired from the University of Wisconsin, and his name was added to Camp Randall's facade.
- In 2004 Ameche was inducted into the Rose Bowl Hall of Fame.

16

Moving On, Again

NOBODY IN THE MEDIA EVER ASKED Alan Ameche if it bothered him that he was given every honor a football player could ever ask for except one—captaincy of the University of Wisconsin team. But, as it turned out, he would get it before graduation.

There was still some college football left to be played for Ameche, starting with the North-South All-Star game in Miami's Orange Bowl on December 25, 1954. Ameche and Notre Dame tackle Frank Varriachione would cocaptain the North team, coached by Ivy Williamson, and Miami quarterback Carl Carrigus and Oklahoma center Kurt Burris would share the captaincy of the South, coached by Miami's Andy Gustafson.

The South strategy, according to pregame reports, was simple: Stop Ameche. According to an Associated Press report, Burris, the runner-up to Ameche in the Heisman voting, "made no secret of the fact that he's anxious to take a crack at stopping 'The Horse.'"

The South team, in the person of Maryland coach Jim Tatum, Gustafson's assistant for the week, even tried a little psychological warfare on Ameche in the days leading up to the Christmas night encounter.

"We know Ameche is hard to stop," said Tatum. "But we're counting on him to stop himself. I figure we'll get the ball three times on fumbles."

Obviously Tatum was exaggerating because there was nothing in Ameche's past that would indicate he was a fumbler. According to Art Lentz, the longtime head of Wisconsin's Sports News Service, in Ameche's four years at Wisconsin he accounted for 39 percent of Wisconsin's rushes, 46.3 percent of its yardage (over 6 yards per carry), and just 25 percent of Wisconsin's fumbles.

Apparently Tatum, who claimed he was being serious, wasn't peppered with follow-up questions by the press because there was no further explanation of why he thought Ameche was prone to fumble. Tatum pointed to Burris and Miami's Ernie Tobey, two of the South team's best linebackers, as a possible explanation.

When asked to respond to Tatum's "out there" statement, Williamson was rather bemused, chuckling when told what Tatum had said.

"No, I can't go along with him on that," Williamson said. "Why, I don't recall Ameche fumbling three times all season."

Williamson did, however, agree with the oddsmakers who installed the South as a 7-point favorite in the contest. As it turned out, Williamson was wrong because the North beat the spread, but lost the game, 20–17.

Ameche played a strong game in defeat, rushing for 88 yards in 14 carries and no fumbles. True to its word, the South's defense ganged up on Ameche. The star of the game was Maryland fullback Dick Bielski, who rushed for 105 yards and a touchdown for the South.

There was one final game to be played, the Senior Bowl Classic in Mobile, Alabama, a month later in January 1955. Again, the game was billed as showdown of fullbacks—Ameche versus Bielski. The game served the double purpose of the players' last college game and their first professional game. Members of the winning team received $500 apiece while the losing players earned $400. The coaches were professional head coaches—the Cleveland Browns' head man, Paul Brown, for the North squad and the New York Giants' Steve Owen leading the South team.

"I am confident Bielski is the equal of any fullback who will play in the Senior Bowl game," said Owen, when asked to compare Bielski and Ameche.

Brown responded: "[Ameche] is much faster than I thought and much faster than most people believe."

The North entered the game with a three-game winning streak, but again, the South appeared to have the stronger lineup, with four all-Americans—Frank McDonald, Miami, end; Rex Boggan, Mississippi, tackle; Bud Brooks, Arkansas, guard; and Burris. Ameche was the North's only all-American.

With Ameche leading the way, the North had a 6–0 halftime lead. But the South broke the North's winning streak, 12–6, as Southern Methodist's Frank Eidom and Bielski teamed up to gain 260 yards on the ground. Auburn quarterback Bobby Freeman won the MVP award, leading the South on two long touchdown drives in the second half. A record crowd of 30,030 attended the game.

The transition period from Madison to professional football was obviously a very busy time for the Ameche family. In addition to the two all-star games, Ameche was working out regularly to stay in shape for the certainty that he would play professional football. Plus he was continuing his schoolwork, try- ing to maintain his B average in physical education. Ameche wouldn't grad- uate on time in 1954 but would return to Madison after his rookie season in Baltimore to earn his diploma.

On the home front, Yvonne was kept more than busy chasing after Brian and Alan Jr. Soon she would be pregnant with Cathy, the couple's third child.

And back home in Kenosha, the people were very proud of their favorite son. Kenosha is a city that likes banquets and testimonials, but the one the city threw on January 12, 1955, at the Eagles Club, the site where Ameche was to have cut his teeth as a Golden Gloves boxer, was colossal. Tickets went on sale two weeks ahead of time, and all 1,000 tickets were sold out two days after they were put up for sale. To say it was the social event of all-time in Kenosha would not be an exaggeration.

The entire Wisconsin football staff—Ivy Williamson, Milt Bruhn, Bob O'Dell, George Lanphear, Paul Shaw, Fred Marsh, the UW athletic director Guy Sundt, and the UW sports publicity director Art Lentz—was there. Chuck Jaskwhich and Barton Groves, who had coached Ameche at Washington Junior High, were in attendance, along with the immortal Don Hutson of the Green Bay Packers, Chicago Cardinals ends Don Stonesifer and Tom Bienne- man, Cardinals coach Joe Stydahar, Milwaukee Braves shortstop Johnny Logan, Marquette football captain Tom Braatz, and Chicago White Sox pitch- ing coach Ray Berres.

The media was well represented by Jerry Pfarr, the new sports editor of the *Kenosha Evening News*, the Associated Press's Chris Edmonds, United Press' Ed Sainsbury, Lew Cornelius of the Madison *Capital Times*, Roundy Cough- lin of the *Wisconsin State Journal*, Tony Ingrassia of the *Milwaukee Sentinel*, and a crew of photographers and reporters from *Life* magazine. The *Milwau- kee Sentinel* sports editor, Lloyd Larson, was the toastmaster for the evening, and the *Milwaukee Journal* sports editor, Oliver Kuechle, wrote a poem for the occasion.

Alan Ameche Day in Kenosha began at around 5 p.m. with an assembly outside Kenosha City Hall. There Ameche was awarded the key to the city from R. Merrill Rhey, Kenosha's city council president. Rhey also presented Ameche with a scroll naming him an honorary citizen of Kenosha "wherever he shall reside."

Ameche boarded a fire truck with Yvonne and oldest son Brian for a short ride through Kenosha's downtown to the lakefront Eagles Club. Before departing, Ameche tipped his fireman's cap to the crowd and said, "This is my first ride on a fire truck."

Ameche would soon experience another first ride, which would make the fire truck seem very mundane. Jim Barnhill of the *Kenosha Evening News*, the general chairman of the event, introduced Ameche, who made his grand entrance to the event wearing a broad-brimmed cowboy hat and sitting atop a 1,500-pound Palomino horse.

Yvonne, who admitted she was afraid of horses, was rightly afraid of what the real horse might do to the man called Horse. In his account for AP, Edmonds recorded Yvonne's comment that "[Ameche's] never been on a horse in his life. Never in his life."

Ameche's grand entrance made for a great photo opportunity, but it also created some unintended consequences for the Eagles Club. The Palomino objected vehemently to the ride in the tiny (6-feet by 5-feet) elevator to the third floor of the Eagles Club ballroom and took out his displeasure on the walls of the elevator. It might have seemed funny at the time, but it was no joke when the Eagles Club sent the Ameches the bill for the damages caused by the horse.

"Yes, they sent us the bill," Yvonne said. "That was really something."

Ameche would later tell the story to his best friend with the Baltimore Colts, Gino Marchetti, who remembered the incident.

"Alan said it cost him about $300 or $400," Marchetti said. "That was a lot of money for that time. . . . That's a game salary back then."

"But Alan wasn't mad. He was laughing when he was telling the story, he thought it was funny. But that was his sense of humor."

Fortunately for the Ameches, their bank account was in much better shape following the testimonial. One of the other highlights of the evening was the lavish gifts showered on the young couple. Among them were a complete men's wardrobe, a watch, toys for the babies, and a brand new Hudson Hornet, the first ever to be produced at Kenosha's American Motors plant. But nothing topped the ribbon with $3,212—one dollar for every yard gained by Ameche at Wisconsin. Dan Viola, the man in charge of collecting the donations, estimated that the total value of the gifts was almost double the $3,212 number. The dollars were strung together in two lines stretching the breadth of the banquet hall, and Alan and Yvonne each reeled in one of the strings for deposit in a huge bushel basket. It was another great photo opportunity.

"At that time we were so poor, so it meant a lot to us," Yvonne said.

However, she wasn't as enamored of the Hudson, which bore the license plate B (for Badgers) 35 (Ameche's number at Wisconsin).

"It was a terrible car," she would say later. "I had to learn how to open the hood and flip the thing to get it started."

Apparently, the American public agreed with her about the Hudson, which was manufactured from 1909 to 1954 in Detroit. Hudson merged with Nash-Kelvinator in 1954, forming American Motors, but the Hudson was discontinued after the 1957 model year.

Edmonds's story on the proceedings claimed that Yvonne was more nervous than Alan, although he was the one who would eventually have to make the speech that everyone came to hear.

"She looked tired and she admitted she was.

"'And all those faces out there,'" she whispered. "'I'm frightened to death. I can't eat a thing.'

"She ate her chicken and finally relaxed. She leaned over and squeezed [Ameche's] hand and they exchanged glances, the kind that mean 'You'll be all right.'"

Apparently Yvonne eventually got over her fear because in later life she became quite a public speaker. But on that night, she was spooked by the whole horse thing.

"Is that horse really ours?" she said to Edmonds. "What will we do with it? I'm afraid of horses."

Apparently Yvonne didn't realize that the horse was just a little symbolism for her husband's nickname, and Edmonds good naturedly played along with her. Jerry Pfarr's column in the Kenosha Evening News ten days after the event told the whole story.

"My goodness," she said. "How will we get it to Madison?"

"You can put it in the back seat of Alan's new car," joked Edmonds.

"What will we do with it when we get it home?" wondered Yvonne.

"Well, you can always keep it in the living room, behind the sofa," suggested Edmonds.

"Finally, Yvonne decided they would give it to Badger assistant coach George Lanphear, the man who first nicknamed Alan 'The Horse.'"

The evening's program began with a seven-minute film featuring the Ameches at home and highlights of Alan's career at Wisconsin. Next up were short talks by Jaskwhich and Williamson.

"Lino—to me he'll always be Lino—has remained humble despite having every reason in the world to acquire a big head," said Jaskwhich. "He is a credit to this wonderful town and an inspiration to this city's young athletes." Jaskwhich received one of the largest ovations of the night.

"Al's record speaks better than I can," said Williamson. "To say that he is a truly a great football player, I think, is an understatement.

"He has done a remarkable job on the football field, in the classroom and as a husband. And you people in Kenosha have a lot to do with his success. I know you are going to be behind him in the future."

That left just Ameche to be heard from and those in attendance that night say they will never forget the young man's emotional speech. He started by thanking "the people I grew up with, the people I learned to love.

"This is an evening I'll never forget. I've been very fortunate up until now and this is the climax of everything, from the people in my own hometown, the people that I love. I'm very proud that I came from this town.

"I only hope that someday I will be able to thank each one of you personally. I owe you all a debt of gratitude, but above all I should thank my wife Yvonne, who has helped me so much."

Toastmaster Lloyd Larson concluded the proceedings by naming it "without question, the finest testimonial banquet I've ever attended."

One of several stories that appeared in the *Kenosha Evening News* the day after the testimonial asked several of the participants to give their thoughts about Ameche. The unbylined story provided several interesting comments.

Art Lentz, University of Wisconsin publicity director: "No one at Wisconsin has ever compiled such a record or is more deserving of All-American honors than Alan Ameche. Never once has he uttered one word that would reflect badly upon his home state or his hometown. And his wife, Yvonne, is an all-American on the distaff side."

Bob O'Dell, Wisconsin backfield coach: "I don't know what everybody is so doggone happy about. Now, I'll have to go to work. He's made a great backfield coach out of me."

Guy Sundt, Wisconsin athletic director: "I have never seen an individual do such a job as Al has . . . not only as a football player, but as a leader and an inspiration to his fellow students."

Ivy Williamson, Wisconsin football coach: "After the Minnesota game in Al's freshman season, I told him he could have a great career but that he would have to face many problems and that his time wouldn't be his own. He replied 'You know Coach, that doesn't bother me very much.'"

Jim Barnhill, general chairman: "I am only unhappy that space didn't permit more than 1,000 to attend the banquet. I want to thank all of you who helped carry the ball. We are all very proud of Al."

To expand on Barnhill's point, the event could have been much larger if there had been more room at the Eagles Club, but still it was probably the largest such gathering ever in the history of Kenosha.

According to still another unbylined *Kenosha Evening News* article, a crew of 16 women spent two full days preparing the chicken dinner for the 1,000 guests that night. A total of 500 chickens and nearly 500 pounds of potatoes were prepared that night.

A serving crew of 36 waitresses made sure the dinners were distributed efficiently. Decorations for the hall, which included a 12-foot football hung from the ceiling, and pennants from each Big Ten school, direct from Camp Randall Stadium, were provided through the cooperation of the University of Wisconsin and the Madison Chamber of Commerce.

Reporters at the testimonial took advantage of their access to Ameche to ask him about the validity of reports that he was considering an offer to forego professional football and be a professional wrestler. A Des Moines, Iowa, wrestling promoter named Pinkie George was circulating stories that he would pay Ameche $100,000 to wrestle for him.

George claimed he had contacted Ameche through intermediaries. He even went so far as to say, "I don't have fundamental objections if Ameche also wants to play pro football. But in that event, I could offer him only 50,000 for about six months of wrestling a year."

At one point, George went so far as to say that he planned to meet with Ameche in Milwaukee and offer him a $25,000 down payment to "seal the bargain."

"He's a big, rugged boy and he can do anything well," the self-promoting George said. "He has done some wrestling and I know he would make a good professional wrestler. He would even be good at marbles if that's what he wanted to do."

Yvonne seemed to see through George's phony publicity stunt before the gullible press caught on to the scam.

"I can't picture him a wrestler," she said of her husband. "I really don't think he will go for it.

"He's never mentioned the game and I don't think he's the type."

The story first started making the rounds soon after Ameche accepted the

Heisman Trophy in December. According to an Associated Press story at the time, Ameche was contacted at home about the reports of a $100,000 offer, and he claimed it was the first he had heard of it.

"With that kind of money being thrown around, naturally I'd like to look into it," Ameche said in December. "In fact, I don't have any objections to most things that I can make $100,000 at."

But a month later at the testimonial, Ameche seemed to permanently quash George's stunt.

"The offer doesn't amount to that much," said Ameche when reporters tossed out the $100,000 figure that night. "As I understand it, the fellow from Des Moines merely said I could probably make $100,000 a year in professional wrestling."

Apparently professional wrestling did hold a place in Ameche's heart, however. He refereed several professional matches in Milwaukee and Chicago before beginning his professional football career. An Associated Press story appearing in the *Milwaukee Journal* bore the headline "Alan Ameche steals show as referee in mat dispute."

According to Yvonne, Ameche was very serious about his involvement with pro wrestling.

"We needed the money because we had two young children and another one on the way when he did the wrestling matches [officiating]," she said.

"I can tell you this much. When he signed his contract with the Colts, he had put into his contract that he could do professional wrestling in the off-season if wanted to. It never happened, but it was there.

"So if it was in his contract with the Colts, he must have been serious about it."

The other big rumor floating around Ameche after winning the Heisman was that several teams from the Canadian Football League were hoping to snatch him to play in their league. Apparently the Montreal Allouettes and the Winnipeg Bombers were the most aggressive of the Canada teams in pursuing Ameche, according to a story by Tony Ingrassia of the *Milwaukee Sentinel*.

"Ameche is a great football player and a cinch to make good in the pro ranks," said Dr. C. (Peahead) Walker, Montreal head coach. "He's a fine boy, besides and we're going to make a strong effort to land him.

"I've talked a bit with Al, but I don't feel I should bother him while all these festivities [All-American events] are going on. You can say, however, that he has a definite offer. I intend to watch him play in the North-South Shrine game and will go into more details with him later at Madison."

Walker seemed to recoil a bit when Ingrassia asked him for details.

"How much did I offer him? I can't reveal any figures of course. You know you've got to do a lot of dickering with boys before you sign them. But I can tell you I'll make a very attractive proposition. The Canadian fans like name players and we want Ameche badly in Montreal."

Ameche knew of the Canadian speculation but apparently didn't pay much attention to it. He said that any deal with a Canadian team was out, "until I find out what's going to happen here in the states," Ameche said in a United Press story. He also said he would prefer playing in the United States, "unless the financial difference is too great."

But in the end, like the professional wrestling talk, the Canadian football talk was just that . . . talk. Yvonne Ameche doesn't even remember any discussion of Ameche going to Canada to play football.

"I don't know anything about that," she said.

What she does remember is that both she and her husband wanted to stay in the Midwest when it came to playing professional football.

"Originally we wanted to stay close to home," Yvonne said. "Alan would have loved to play for the Packers or the Chicago Bears."

On the plus side, Ameche didn't stay on the draft board for long. He was the third pick of the NFL draft on January 27, 1955, going to the Baltimore Colts. The Colts, just two years into their existence in the NFL, also had the first pick of the draft, a so-called bonus pick, in which they chose quarterback George Shaw of Oregon. The Chicago Cardinals chose Oklahoma end Max Boydsten with the second pick.

Prior to the draft, Ameche had only said, "I have no real preference, but it would be nice to stay in the Midwest." There was no ESPN or live coverage in 1955, so the Ameches got the news by telephone at their Madison home.

"We were both crushed," said Yvonne, recalling the news that Ameche had been drafted by the Colts. "I didn't want to have to leave the Midwest. My mother was very ill at that point. I didn't want to go that far away and neither did he."

If he was disappointed by being drafted by the Colts, who were 3–9 in 1954, he covered it with a big smile at his contract signing. Days after the draft, Ameche signed a two-year deal with the Colts and then posed with the contract in hand with his advisor, John J. Walsh, who was also an attorney and the University of Wisconsin's boxing coach, and Colts president and general manager Don Kellett. The signing took place in Walsh's Madison office.

"I am glad that I have signed," said Ameche in the United Press article that accompanied the photograph. "And I am happy to learn they have no intentions of trading me."

As expected, the Colts immediately announced that Ameche would concentrate on playing fullback with the Colts and leave his defensive career behind. While the terms of the deal were not released, the story related that "a conservative estimate is that it provides for a minimum salary of $12,500 per year." That figure was contradicted later in Ameche's career, when he revealed that he had earned $15,000 in his rookie season.

Kellett did reveal that the Colts were reluctant to offer more than a one-year deal and that Ameche had asked for a three-year contract. The two-year deal, according to Kellett, represented a compromise.

The only contract detail that was revealed was that restrictive clauses regarding off-season activities had been stricken from the contract, thus allowing Ameche to participate in professional wrestling if he so desired.

"We are pleased to have Ameche with us," said Kellett. "And we think he'll give us the offensive punch we need. We think we had a pretty good defensive team last year.

"It's probable that Alan will be on the College All-Star squad so he will be joining us after we have begun practice. Our new rule which allows a team to retain 35 instead of 33 players for the first two [exhibition] games if those players were on the All-Star squad will be a help."

The Colts training camp in those days was the campus of Western Maryland College at Westminster.

Joining Ameche on draft day were six of his Wisconsin teammates. End Jim Temp went to the Green Bay Packers in the second round; guard Norm Amundsen went to the Packers in the sixth round; end Ron Locklin went to the New York Giants in the sixth round; back Clarence Bratt went to the Chicago Bears in the twelfth round; tackle Jerry Cvengros went to the Los Angeles Rams in the twenty-first round; and back Bob Gingrass went to the Philadelphia Eagles in the twenty-seventh round.

There were 30 rounds of the 1955 NFL draft, but the league at that time consisted of just 13 teams. The steal of the draft that year came in the ninth round, when the Pittsburgh Steelers chose unheralded Louisville quarterback Johnny Unitas.

Alan Ameche, big man on the University of Wisconsin campus. (Ameche family photo)

Ameche peruses *Collier's* magazine with Wisconsin teammate Gary Messner after the publication named Ameche college player of the year. (Ameche family photo)

Yvonne and Alan admire
the Heisman Trophy.
(Ameche family photo)

"The Horse" made a grand entrance at his Kenosha testimonial dinner.
(Milwaukee Sentinel)

The Ameches reel in the dollars at Alan's coming out party. (United Press)

Kenosha showed its generosity to its favorite son by rewarding him with the first Hudson (complete with vanity plates) to be manufactured in Wisconsin. (Ameche family photo)

Ameche gets the word that he's been drafted in the first round by the Baltimore Colts. (Milwaukee Sentinel)

Ameche barrels into the end zone with the winning touchdown in the Greatest Game Ever Played. (Ameche family photo)

The Ameche family in 1964 (*from left*): Brian, Cathy, Yvonne, Beth, Alan Jr., Alan Sr.,
Paul, and in front Michael and Duke the dog. (Philadelphia Sunday Bulletin)

The Ameche sons, Lynn and Alan, celebrate their mother's Mother of the Year award in Kenosha. (Ameche family photo)

Ameche shares a lighter moment with (*from left*) Buddy Young, Gino Marchetti, and Weeb Ewbank in New York. (New York Athletic Club photo)

In a reunion meeting in New York's Central Park twenty years after the Greatest Game Ever Played, Colts quarterback Johnny Unitas was said to have told his teammates, "We beat the —— out of them twenty years ago, and now we're going to do it again." The Colts, assembled here, did just that. The Colts were (*front row left to right*) Lenny Moore, Ameche, Unitas, and Raymond Berry; (*back row left to right*) Steve Myhra, Art Donovan, Gino Marchetti, and Jim Parker. (Ameche family photo)

Alan Ameche, successful businessman and patron of Philadelphia arts.
(Ameche family photo)

17

Weeb's Tangled Web

O RDINARILY, GINO MARCHETTI PROBABLY NEVER would have remembered the first time he laid eyes on Alan Ameche. But fifty-six years after the fact, he still remembers the moment with crystal clarity because of the conversation that accompanied the sighting.

"It was really strange," said Marchetti, the Baltimore Colts Hall of Famer and arguably the greatest defensive end ever to play in the NFL. Marchetti was a World War II veteran who was a machine gunner at the Battle of the Bulge and would later in life be Ameche's business partner.

"I remember it was before camp opened, and I was walking with [Colts coach] Weeb Ewbank. We were coming from a meeting and heading to chow, and Alan was walking ahead of us.

"I remember it because Weeb made a really strange comment that stuck with me over the years. He sees Alan in front of us and he says, 'There is our big draft choice. He was babied in college. He was spoiled at Wisconsin. They didn't baby you in college, did they Gino?' Weeb asked me. I told him, 'No, I wasn't babied.'"

It might have only been a first impression, but apparently for the inflexible Ewbank, it was his lasting impression of Ameche. Despite what Ameche would accomplish on the field for the Colts, and his feats were borderline Hall of Fame caliber, Ewbank would ride him mercilessly and, eventually, right out of the league. It's safe to say that the feelings between the two men were mutual, and that animosity ruined what should have been six of Ameche's happiest years on Earth.

"It was so strange because here Weeb hadn't even had a chance to know the guy and he'd already made up his mind about him," Marchetti said. "The really strange thing is that Weeb never changed his mind about Alan. He never, never liked Alan for some reason, and I never could figure it out.

"Alan worked hard, he played hard, he was a good blocker. He did everything that was asked of him, but Weeb would never give the guy a break.

"The only thing I can think of is one thing. Alan had a habit of always being barely late for everything . . . meetings, practice, pregame meals. Things like that really bothered Weeb. Alan would come out to practice sometimes with his shoes untied and he'd have to bend over to tie them up on the field. All of those things bothered Weeb and put a strain on their relationship."

The Ameche-Ewbank feud was common knowledge among Colts insiders, and it really was an anomaly. To a man, the Colts will tell you that there was a genuine camaraderie on the squad. Like every team, the players came from all walks of life, but this was a group that genuinely practiced and believed in the team concept.

"I know that Weeb had an attitude toward Alan, and to this day I don't understand it," said another Ameche friend and Hall of Fame wide receiver, Raymond Berry. "I have my theories about it, but I honestly don't know for sure.

"There is no question that Weeb's attitude toward Alan was not good and not healthy for the team, and in the long run it proved costly to the Baltimore Colts and Weeb Ewbank.

"Alan came in here as Heisman Trophy winner and he had a personality that was very extroverted, and he had a tremendous sense of humor and laughed a lot. I think maybe Weeb took that as not caring or being too lackadaisical, but that just wasn't the case.

"Alan's personality gave the appearance of being very loose, but I think that is misleading. Weeb was blind to Alan's productivity as a player. That's all he needed to judge Alan, or any player for that matter, but Weeb took it way beyond that.

"I'm sure Alan got a good bonus for signing a contract, and Weeb probably didn't like that either. I think Weeb thought Alan was paid too much and he had too much hype and reputation.

"There was just something about Alan Ameche that Weeb did not like. Whatever it was, it was so counterproductive it was unbelievable."

Ewbank may have won the battle with Ameche. In 1960 Ewbank effectively drove Ameche off the squad by making it clear that he was not wanted back after rehabbing his Achilles tendon injury. But the bottom line was that Ewbank's unfounded dislike for Ameche cost him and the Colts more than it hurt Ameche.

"The end result was, I believe, it cost Weeb his job," Berry said. "You know Weeb lost his job two years after Alan retired, and the reason was we got overbalanced throwing the ball. We really didn't have an effective running game after Alan retired.

"I don't know if Alan would have ever recovered from the Achilles tendon injury or not, because that injury was pretty uncommon those days, so there wasn't a lot of medical experience to go by in dealing with that injury. I just know that our offense totally changed from the time we lost Alan Ameche, and two years later Weeb got fired himself because he couldn't put a balanced attack on the field.

"We became overly reliant on Unitas throwing the football. You get out of balance in the NFL and you're butt is going to get handed to you. You'd better be able to run and throw and hurt people on the ground and in the air. We got to the point where we couldn't hurt them on the ground, so they pinned their ears back and took their pass rush to another level.

"When opponents are teeing off on your quarterback, obviously it affects your passing game. We struggled to be a contender after Alan retired."

Berry went on to have a very solid coaching career after his Hall of Fame playing days were over, coaching the New England Patriots from 1984 through 1989, including Super Bowl XX in 1986, and it's for certain that his role model for dealing with players wasn't Ewbank. Berry believed that Ewbank had picked up the destructive habit of needling his players when he was the offensive line coach on the staff of Paul Brown, the legendary coach of the Cleveland Browns.

"I think Weeb was influenced very much as a young coach working under Paul Brown," Berry said. "I don't think there is any question about that.

"And Paul Brown had a habit of needling his players; this was well known about him. He would needle his players with barbs and comments and verbal shots. Then Weeb comes to the Colts, and I know he was affected by Paul Brown's operation.

"I saw that myself, his need to needle players. My rookie year I was definitely on Weeb's list. I thought the needling was very counterproductive and to be honest, it hurt Weeb in his relationship with his players.

"I mean you can mark that down. That's exactly a big part of what was happening. Alan was on the receiving end of it. There is no question that he took a lot of needling from Weeb."

Art Donovan played next to Marchetti in the Colts' defensive line for years and like Marchetti and Berry is an NFL Hall of Famer. Donovan thinks there might be more to Ewbank's dislike of Ameche than the fullback's tendency to be tardy.

"To be honest with you, I don't think Weeb liked anybody who made more money than he did," Donovan theorized. "Weeb never liked the Horse from the beginning and it was because the writers were writing more about the Horse than they were about him.

"Don't get me wrong, Weeb was a helluva coach. . . . He had a great football mind. But he was a downright weasel. He thought he was something, and it was a lie from the beginning. But you better believe it . . . we all knew.

"How somebody couldn't like Alan Ameche is beyond me. He was the nicest fellow that ever lived. He was just a prince and I mean that seriously."

Marchetti's opinion of Ewbank is very similar.

"I once told Weeb that he was a great coach—a great judge of talent and I think that was his strong point," Marchetti said. "He was a good planner, too, but he was weak leader.

"He couldn't hold the team together because he had a double standard for some players, and I admit I was one of his favorites. But some of us would make mistakes, and he wouldn't say nothing about it. He'd let it slide. Other guys, like Alan, he'd be all over them for every little thing.

"What happens when a coach is like that is you eventually lose the team. Everybody takes advantage of the situation, and that's what happened with Weeb."

Ewbank inherited a weak Colts team, which was 3–9 in their first year in Baltimore in 1953. The Colts were also 3–9 in 1954, Ewbank's first season in Baltimore, but they began a steady ascent to the top after that. The team was 5–6–1 in Ameche's rookie season of 1955; 5–7 in 1956, quarterback Johnny Unitas's first season with the team; and 7–5 in 1957. With Unitas fully settled in, the Colts won back-to-back world championships in 1958 and 1959.

But mediocrity set in, and the Colts went 21–19 in the following three seasons. Whether or not it was because Ewbank "lost the team," as Marchetti put it, Ewbank was replaced by another legendary coach, Don Shula, in 1963.

"When you lose control of the team, you can be the best organized coach in the world, but it doesn't do you any good," Marchetti said. "After four or five years in Baltimore, he lost control of the Colts. You can look at Weeb's history. He had a great three or four years in New York [with the Jets] too, but then he lost control of that team, too.

"Most of the players didn't like Don Shula, but he had their respect. If they broke a curfew, they knew it was going to cost them 500 bucks, no matter who they were. Weeb wouldn't bother to fine certain people on the team, and you can't have a double standard like that."

Ameche may have been tardy to meetings, but he didn't have to worry about being fined for breaking curfew. He was not one of the "party boys" clique that exists on every NFL team.

"Alan and I were friends from the start, but we really didn't hang out that much," Marchetti said. "Some of us liked to drink a lot of beer after games, but Alan went home to his family. He smoked for a little while, but he quit that, too, but I never really knew him to drink.

"When we'd go on the road, a lot of us would go out and have some laughs, even some of the married guys would go along, but Alan hung out with the guys who went to the movies, when Donovan and [Bill] Pellington and me would go to a tap room and have a few beers.

"Alan just wasn't that type at all."

Despite their differences in what they considered an entertaining night out, Marchetti and Ameche became fast friends, and Marchetti remembers what brought them together at their first mutual training camp at Western Maryland College.

"I knew Alan was a good guy from the get go and I'll tell you why," Marchetti said. "My brother [Angelo "Itsy" Marchetti] tried out for the Colts the same year Alan was a rookie, and he and Alan made friends right away.

"Here's my brother, who had no reputation or anything, and Alan is the Heisman Trophy winner, big star coming in, and he and Itsy are friends right away. You don't usually see a superstar coming in to camp and hanging out with a guy trying to make the team who didn't really have a chance.

"Angelo had a slim chance of making it, because he had been out of football for a couple years. He was the type of guy who never wanted to leave Antioch [California]; just be around his family and go fishing. That's all he had on his mind.

"So I like Alan and we hung out a little, but I wouldn't say I took him under my wing or anything like that. We would talk about things that might happen [on the football field] or whatever. But on a friendly basis.

"We didn't hang out too much because he was married and I was batching it back then. He didn't need anybody to take him under their wing. He was a tough guy and he could take it."

Marchetti remembers his first face-to-face encounter with Ameche after the disturbing incident with Ewbank.

"The first time I ever really met Alan was at the fourth floor of a dorm at Westminster. I went up to see my brother, and there was Alan, playing cards with five or six of the other rookies. Alan got along with everybody. They all spoke highly of him."

Ameche may have been popular with his teammates, but not all of the NFL's talent scouts were unanimous in their praise of the rookie fullback. Despite the sterling credentials that Ameche brought with him from Wisconsin, there were still doubts how his skills would translate in the NFL.

In a story that appeared in the *Baltimore Sun* on January 14, 1959, John Steadman wrote:

> Despite what he had accomplished on a campus level, some of the more discerning critics said he wouldn't do it with the pros. Too slow, a straight-up runner who overpowered boys but couldn't do the same against men, no threat as a pass receiver and a big-money salary risk.
>
> A scout for the Green Bay Packers, in Ameche's home state, said his only chance might be as a linebacker. The Chicago Cardinals didn't think much of him. They preferred to take end Max Boydston of Oklahoma on the first round of the 1955 draft.
>
> That left Ameche for Baltimore, the second team to pick, and the Colts weren't about to look a gift horse in the mouth. The big fellow moved in as the team's starting fullback the first day in training camp and he's been there ever since.

But those doubts about Ameche, as chronicled by Steadman, might offer some insight as to why Ewbank had been so quick to pounce on the rookie. With the third pick in the entire 1955 draft, the up-and-coming Colts couldn't afford a clunker.

"To be honest with you, I think that's what Weeb had in mind for Alan . . . to play linebacker," Marchetti said. "You know Alan played linebacker in college.

"But it never got to that point because Alan did so well running the ball. He very seldom made a mistake. He did all the things a rookie should do."

Any plans Ewbank may have had for switching Ameche and his awkward-looking style to the defensive side of the ball were soon shelved. In his regular-season professional debut, Ameche ran 79 yards for a touchdown the first time he touched the ball in the game against the Chicago Bears in Baltimore.

Ameche rushed for 194 yards on that afternoon. Some consider it the greatest game ever by a Colts running back because he did it in just 15 carries—an incredible 13 yards per carry.

"I went over to congratulate him after the touchdown against the Bears, and you know Alan's dry sense of humor," Marchetti said. "He says, 'You know Gino, I didn't think it was going to be this easy. I never ran 79 yards in my life.'"

The only thing Ameche did wrong that day was repeat to the press after the game what he said to Marchetti. When asked about the difference between the college game and pro game, Ameche made a rookie mistake, albeit tongue-in-cheek, but he said he thought the college game was tougher.

The story circulated throughout the NFL ranks, and Ameche was soon a marked man. He was fed a steady diet of verbal abuse after absorbing the best shots of some of football's toughest defenders.

Years later he would tell the story to his Kenosha High School buddy Bobby Hinds.

"Alan told me that game was the worst thing that ever happened to him, so I asked him 'Why?' He said 'I paid for that comment every time I got tackled after that. They'd be getting off me and say, "How did you like that, college boy?"'"

According to Steadman's piece: "Ameche as a rookie used to hear defensive linemen taunt him with 'here Horsey, here Horsey.' But it never bothered him."

Apparently not. On his way to winning rookie of the year and All-Pro honors, Ameche carried the football 213 times for a league-leading 961 yards and nine touchdowns. Ameche also proved himself as a receiver, hauling down 27 George Shaw aerials for 141 yards.

"I didn't say anything to Alan [after the Chicago game], but we discussed it later over a beer," Marchetti said. "We really didn't get that close till maybe the third or fourth game of the season.

"I said to him, 'Alan, sometimes we have a tendency to talk too much, you know, you say things that don't really mean a helluva lot. But other teams will take them serious. And we don't like that.'"

Unfortunately, Ameche would make yet another press-related gaffe that would land him deeper in Ewbank's doghouse. The team was in San Francisco for the final game of the 1955 season, and Ameche needed approximately 60 yards to gain 1,000 yards for the season, a magical total in the NFL, especially in the days when teams played only 12 regular season games.

"We were standing in front of our hotel in San Francisco talking, and a newspaper man comes up to Alan and asks him how he feels about getting 1,000 yards. Alan is joking around and he says 'I'll have that by the second quarter.'

"Not many rookies have ever gained 1,000 yards, plus we were playing 12 games back then.

"So the next day we get to the locker room and Weeb is pissed. There was a huge headline in the paper about Alan saying he was going to go over 1,000 yards in the second period.

"Weeb felt that Alan gave the 49ers some ammunition to play us because they had nothing else to play for. To make a long story short, the 49ers set up their defense to stop Alan and it worked. He didn't get close to 1,000 and we lost the game [35–24].

"It wasn't like Weeb limited Alan's carries that day or anything. It was about eleven 49ers who were upset about his comments. They had nothing else to play for, so all their effort went into to stopping Alan."

Anyone who knew Ewbank, who considered himself a master of psychological ploys, understood how Ameche's loose lips would irritate Ewbank. According to Marchetti, Ewbank would lecture the team on how to manipulate the press to the Colts advantage. His favorite was flattering the other team with compliments, hoping they would believe them and that the Colts were truly terrified to play against them.

"Weeb always had a saying," Marchetti said. "'I'll tell you guys this. I'll build 'em up and then we chop 'em down. I'll say things about their team and get them all bigheaded. But I want you guys to know it's all a lie. I don't mean a word of it.'"

Any goodwill that Ameche might have built up with his spectacular rookie season was probably nullified by the San Francisco incident. Ameche's professional career would consist of six seasons in Baltimore with Ewbank as his coach, but their relationship was never repaired.

"To this day I don't understand it," Marchetti said. "I never saw anything about Alan that would make anybody, including Weeb, not like him. Alan was fun, he worked hard, and he was tough as hell.

"Guys would do things that you want Weeb to get upset about, but if he liked the guy, he'd ignore it. Yet with Alan, if he missed a block for instance, which happens to everybody, Weeb would be all over him. . . . He'd say stuff like 'You had bad footwork on that play. You should have done this.' But some other guy would miss three blocks and he would not say a thing.

"I can't remember when it was, but Weeb really laid into Alan one time and then it was Katy bar the door. We were in a meeting watching film, and Weeb told Alan, 'You know, the Bears were happy we drafted you because they didn't want to have to draft you,' or something stupid like that.

"It got pretty bad, because Alan didn't like Weeb either, and I can't blame Alan. He'd see guys miss assignments on the field, and Weeb wouldn't say anything to them, but he'd be all over Alan for the same thing."

Ameche wasn't one to bring his business home with him, but he couldn't hide his stormy relationship with Ewbank from Yvonne.

"I really don't know what the problem was, but I just knew that they didn't like each other," Yvonne said. "Whatever it was, it wasn't good. They just didn't mesh. Donnie [Art Donovan] said Weeb didn't like Alan because Alan was smarter than him.

"Honestly, I don't understand it. Everybody loved Alan. He didn't have one enemy on the team.

"I never heard Alan ever say anything negative about any teammate he had, whether it was Kenosha, Madison, or in Baltimore. Alan was a real team player. When Alan played, nobody cared who scored the touchdown as long as somebody scored it. It wasn't so much about money back then. It was a whole different ballgame."

Yvonne got a taste of how bad the relationship was when Ameche was laid up in the hospital with a torn Achilles tendon in his final season. She was in the room when Ameche heard Ewbank's voice in the hallway, as Ewbank was coming to visit him.

"He told me to tell Weeb he was sleeping," Yvonne said. "So Weeb came in the room and asked how Alan was doing and I just told him, 'He's sleeping, Weeb.'

"I don't blame him for not wanting to talk. He just had surgery, he was hurting, and he didn't like Weeb."

Despite their prickly relationship, Ewbank never lost respect for Ameche. According to Yvonne, Ewbank would send a check every year until his death in 1998 to the Alan Ameche Memorial Foundation, a scholarship fund for needy children.

"It was a small check, but Weeb would send a check every year," Yvonne said. "He would always attach a note and say, 'I never made the kind of money coaches make now.'"

Ewbank landed on his feet after being fired by the Colts in 1962, taking over as coach of the New York Jets the following season. The highlight of his career, other than the two championships in Baltimore, was coaching the Jets to victory in Super Bowl III, over the Colts, in 1969.

18

A New Leading Man

Rookies Raymond Berry and Alan Ameche were among the first arrivals at the 1955 Baltimore Colts training camp at Western Maryland College. Football was literally the only thing they had in common, but they talked. For hours they talked.

Ameche's father was an Italian immigrant factory worker from Kenosha, Wisconsin, while Berry's father Raymond was a legendary high school football coach from Paris, Texas. Ameche, from the University of Wisconsin, liked his mother's Italian cooking, and Berry was partial to barbecue; Ameche's taste in music was Beethoven, while Berry liked Hank Williams. Ameche was married with three children, Berry was single. Ameche was a Heisman Trophy winner, Berry was a converted defensive back, drafted in the twentieth round, trying to learn how to be a wide receiver. It is interesting that two men from the same country, playing the same sport, could be so different.

"As rookies we reported to camp a day early and Alan Ameche was the first player on the team I met," said Berry, one of six 1950s-era Colts to earn his way into the NFL Hall of Fame.

"I'd never met an Italian before," Berry said matter-of-factly. "The first day I met Alan, he said to me, 'Do you know anything about opera?' I said, 'You mean like the Grand Ole Opry?'

"He just looked at me and said, 'No, that's not what I'm talking about.'"

From that rather shaky beginning, a hearty laugh was had and a great friendship blossomed. Ameche, the gregarious natural, and Berry, who willed himself to be a Hall of Famer with hard work and perseverance, were fast friends from that day forward.

"Alan was one of the most intelligent people I've ever met," Berry said. "The thing I will always remember about him is how he was always laughing about something. He had that great sense of humor, and he was always joking around with people.

"I remember him trying to explain opera to me. He was married and I was single, so we didn't really socialize that much, but we got along really well."

While Ameche was almost immediately accepted as one of the team's star performers, it was a struggle for Berry, who was primarily known as a defensive back at Southern Methodist in Dallas.

"I was learning a new position, and you could have written a book about what I didn't know about playing wide receiver," said Berry, who didn't even start for his father's high school team until he was a senior and then caught only 33 passes in his career at SMU. "While the other single guys were out drinking beer, I was up in my room memorizing the play book. Heck, when I got to the Colts, I didn't know my butt from first base about playing wide receiver."

While Ameche was earning NFL Rookie of the Year honors in 1955, Berry was struggling to stay with the team. He had only 13 receptions his first season for a grand total of 205 yards and no touchdowns. But Berry was soon to be joined in Baltimore by a kindred spirit, a player whose career was also perilously close to crash landing in the NFL scrap heap. Legendary John Unitas was cut loose by Pittsburgh Steelers coach Walt Kiesling in what would prove to be one of the most wrongheaded personnel moves in the history of sports. Unitas would find his way to the Colts and go on to have a Hall of Fame career and be the dominant quarterback of his era.

The Unitas legend says that after being cut by the Steelers, he borrowed gas money to get to Baltimore and try out for the Colts. The gamble paid off and he made the team as George Shaw's backup. Four games into the 1956 season, Shaw suffered a broken leg against the Bears at Wrigley Field, and Unitas was thrown into the fray.

On his first pass attempt, Unitas threw an interception to Ameche's old college rival J. C. Caroline that the speedster from Illinois returned for a touchdown, and the Bears won the game, 38–27. The Colts had no choice but to stick with the Pittsburgh native, who had played collegiately at Louisville. Their patience was indeed rewarded. Unitas finished the 1956 season with a 55.6 percent completion mark, at that time a record for first-year quarterbacks.

What happened in 1956 was just a prelude of what was to come. By 1957 Unitas was the best quarterback in the league, passing for 2,550 yards and 24 touchdowns, both tops in the NFL that season. Unitas won the league's MVP award that season and in the process changed the course of Colts' history.

Unitas would not only resurrect his own career in coming to Baltimore; he made Berry perhaps the top receiver of that era. Maybe it was because they followed the same career path, but Berry and Unitas quickly developed a bond that would never be broken. They were the first Colts on the practice field in the morning and the last to leave at night, perfecting the timing of their patterns.

"I'm sure Raymond must have been a real pain in the ass to Johnny because he was always after him to stay after practice and throw to him," Gino Marchetti recalled. "But look how it paid off for them."

While there is no disputing that Unitas was the player who took the Colts from being a decent team to a championship team, his arrival did bring about changes. One of them was that the Colts would never again be a run-first, pass-second team. That meant that Ameche, who had been the focus of the team's offense as a rookie, would be relegated to a supporting role.

With Unitas demonstrating an uncanny knack for finding open receivers and throwing with pinpoint accuracy, the Colts would be a pass-oriented offense until his Baltimore career ended in 1972.

Ameche would only miss two games in his six years with the Colts. He missed the final two games of 1960 after suffering the Achilles tendon injury in the third-to-last game of the season against Detroit.

Despite his resiliency, his production would shrink with almost every passing season. His 213 carries and 961 rushing yards in his rookie season would remain the standard of his very productive of his pro career. Despite the reduced statistics, Ameche was still named All-Pro four seasons from 1955 through 1958 and voted to play in five Pro Bowls from 1955 through 1959.

In Unitas's first season, Ameche still had great statistics, 858 yards in 178 carries (8 touchdowns), but then the decline began. In 1957 he had 144 carries for 493 yards (5 touchdowns); in 1958 he had 171 carries for 791 yards (8 touchdowns); in 1959 he had 178 carries for 679 yards (7 touchdowns); and in his abbreviated final season he had 80 carries for 263 yards (3 touchdowns).

"Alan didn't run the football as much after Johnny Unitas came to the Colts," Yvonne said. "He never complained about it; he just did his job."

Ameche might not have brought his displeasure home with him, but his best friend on the Colts, Marchetti, knew Ameche wasn't happy with his diminished role.

"He told me, 'I should be a guard,'" Marchetti said. "'That's what I do now . . . block for John.'

"That's pretty much the way it ended up being. It was the way Weeb designed the offense. To be honest, Alan was lost out there. Weeb just put him aside. I'm sure he figured as long as John can do it, let him do it.

"I'm not saying that Weeb should have taken the ball out of Johnny's hands, though. He was a great quarterback. But as time went by, there were games when Alan would only get like 6 carries in a game. A running back can't get a rhythm like that. Sometimes it takes 15 or 18 carries for a running back to get warmed up."

As hard as it was to swallow at the time, Ameche apparently knew Ewbank was making the right decision by putting the ball in Unitas's hands. In the book *The Game of Their Lives*, by Dave Klein, Ameche looked back with resignation in 1976.

"I was bitter as hell when it happened," Ameche said, "but you can't argue with the success we had. I can't argue with what they did. I got to be a better blocker, and after all, how many times do you get a Unitas? But if I played with Green Bay or Cleveland or now with Shula in Miami, I could do as well as their fullbacks."

Berry fully understands Ameche's thought process, viewing his diminished role as a demotion. But Berry sees it more of a balancing act that transformed the Colts' offense from a one-dimensional running attack into one of the most potent offenses in NFL history.

"I understand where Alan was coming from," Berry said. "When he got to professional football, he was used to being the focus of the whole offense, and when he got here he was still the focus of the Colts' offense his rookie year.

"But when Unitas got here, that all changed. We started to get the balance that you need to win in the NFL."

Berry claims he learned about a balanced attack from his father and later applied that knowledge as head coach of the New England Patriots from 1984 through 1989.

"I was raised by a Texas high school football coach who was one of the best, and one of the things I absorbed from him, whether or not I realized it at the time, was balance," Berry said. "So my perspective on balance is totally different than someone like Alan, who with all due respect, is looking at the offense from the perspective of his position.

"Offensive players are all 'I want the ball.' That's just the way it is. They don't understand that it's a game of balance and you need to spread the ball around. To win a championship, you have to have a balanced attack. An offensive guy who wants the ball has to take his place in line.

"What very few people realize is that our peak years with the Colts were when Alan Ameche was healthy. Once we lost him, we went through a stage in Baltimore where we got overbalanced throwing the ball and did not pass effectively. It all coincided with Alan's Achilles injury that ended his career."

Although Berry understands why Ameche didn't like his new role after Unitas had arrived on the scene, he believes that Ameche's acceptance of his new role was one of the main reasons the Colts won back-to-back titles in 1958 and 1959.

"When Alan was healthy we had a totally balanced attack, and that's why we led the NFL in offense and were winning championships," Berry said. "We could throw to every receiver or run the football with Alan or L.G. Dupre or later Lenny [Moore].

"The funny thing is we didn't have balance in our first year before Johnny got here. Alan was definitely the focus of the offense, and we didn't have the ingredients to throw the football. Then in 1956, Shaw got hurt and Johnny replaced him and everything started clicking for the offense.

"The offense was totally balanced, and everything worked fine until Alan suffered the Achilles injury. Then we lost the balance again. Johnny couldn't throw the ball as effectively because we couldn't run the football like before."

Marchetti also doesn't second-guess Ewbank's decision to transform the Colts into a pass-dominated offense, but he says he has wondered whether Ameche's place in history would be different if he had been fed more carries. Marchetti even believes that Ameche may have been able to achieve Hall of Fame numbers.

"I've thought about that," Marchetti said, when asked about Ameche's reduced role in his final five seasons with the Colts. "If Weeb had kept giving Alan the ball, like he did his rookie season, and concentrated on the running game, you never know.

"I think Alan's potential was never realized. He got cheated out of four or five years of carrying the football. I think Alan would have gotten a lot of votes [for the NFL Hall of Fame] if he had played for a team that ran the football more. It just wasn't going to happen with the Colts, once Johnny got there. You can't argue with success."

Donovan agrees with Marchetti that Ameche had Hall of Fame ability if not numbers.

"I think the Horse was good enough [to be in the Hall of Fame]," Donovan said. "There are a lot of guys in there who weren't as good as he was. Look at me. I'm in the Hall of Fame and a lot of guys say I should be in the Hall of Shame.

"I was just talking with Jim Mutscheller [former Colts receiver] the other day, and we talked about the Horse. He and I both agreed that he was a much better runner than we ever thought he was. The Horse was right up there with the best of them. He was a good blocker, he could catch the football and like I said, he was a much better runner than he ever got credit for."

Mutscheller acknowledged his conversation with Donovan regarding Ameche's ability and agreed that Ameche had a Hall of Fame skill set.

"The more I think about Alan as a player, the more I think he could have been a Hall of Famer," Mutscheller said. "He didn't have that long of a career and I think he just didn't want to play anymore.

"But I was just looking at the movies of the 1958 championship game, and I really didn't realize how good Alan was. At the time things happen, you don't always see things you should see that are right in front of you. He was just a hard-nosed, tough son of a gun, not a prima donna by any stretch. He was a big guy and didn't look like he could run that fast, but he could."

Like the others, Berry buys into the notion that while Ameche had the talent to be a Hall of Famer, he didn't have a long enough career to rate serious consideration.

"Alan's career was too short," Berry said. "I don't think he had a chance to be considered because of the brevity of his career.

"Had he played 9 or 10 years, it would have been much different. Alan was a complete back and you just don't find that every day. Even today you don't find that kind of player often. He could do it all . . . catch, run, and block, and he brought tremendous intelligence to the game, which is something you always welcome."

Ameche played in the golden age of fullbacks in the NFL as a contemporary of Jim Brown of the Cleveland Browns (1957–65) and Jim Taylor of the Green Bay Packers (1958–67). Brown, who had the rare combination of speed and power, is considered by most football observers to be the greatest ball carrier of all time, regardless of position.

Taylor was more of a prototype utilitarian fullback, a straight-ahead power runner and no-nonsense blocker. Both are Hall of Famers. Where Ameche ranks in the history of NFL fullbacks is debatable, but certainly he isn't far below Brown or Taylor.

"Of course, Jimmy Brown was the best," said Marchetti. "I don't think anybody can argue that.

"But I would put Alan in a class with Jim Taylor from the Packers. . . . Taylor was one of the best, a really tough runner. I would say Alan was somewhere around the top five fullbacks when I was playing.

"Taylor and Ameche were both damn good blockers and both had good hands. And then there were guys like Hugh McElheny [1952–64, San Francisco, Minnesota, New York Giants, and Detroit] and Joe Perry [1948–63, San Francisco and Baltimore]; you've got to put them up there, too.

"Alan was a very upright runner, but he was so strong. If you went to tackle Jim Taylor, he'd hit you head on, like Alan, the same way. He couldn't outfake a lot of people, so when he'd get trapped he'd lower his shoulder and plow right into you. I know the defensive player had to feel it.

"Now, Jimmy Brown was different. You'd go to make a tackle on him and he wouldn't be there. But Taylor and Alan would go right after you.

"The point is when you compare all these guys is that Alan had the ability, but he never got to where he should have in his career. That's my main point."

Apparently Marchetti has revised his thinking somewhat over the years because in 1976 when he was interviewed for *The Game of Their Lives* he had said, "Except for Jim Brown, Horse was as good as any fullback then. And a damned sight better than any fullback playing today."

Donovan is a bit vaguer in his fullback rankings but is one of the minority who would take Taylor over Brown. While he agrees that Brown was the best runner, he preferred Taylor's all-around game.

"The best fullback I ever played against was Jim Taylor of the Packers," Donovan said. "I only played against Jim Brown twice. He was a great runner, obviously, but that's all he did.

"Brown was the best runner, no doubt, but Taylor was a better all-around player in my opinion. As a blocker, Brown would pat you on the ass on the way by you, but Taylor would knock the living shit out of you.

"The Horse was right there. He was more like Taylor, a good blocker, too. And like Mutscheller said, he was a better runner than we gave him credit for."

Steadman, writing in the *Baltimore Sun* weeks after the Colts' stunning victory over the Giants in the 1958 NFL Championship game, made some of the same points as Donovan in drawing a comparison between Ameche and Brown.

Jim Brown, the Cleveland Browns' fabled fullback, ran away and hid from the rest of the NFL's rushers this season. He had 1,527 yards in 257 attempts for a league record.

Runner-up to Brown was Baltimore's Ameche, who pounded out 791 yards in 171 tries. The New York club stopped Brown in the Eastern Division playoff the week before it encountered the Colts and Ameche.

In the two showdown games, the Giants put the brakes on Brown, holding him to eight yards in seven tries, but Ameche got away from them to rack up 65 yards in 14 carries.

There's no question that Brown is a better sprinter than Ameche, but take it from the Giants, and other teams. The Horse hits into the line with greater force and destruction. Ameche is also an outstanding blocker, something Brown isn't, and catches the ball with more assurance.

But to each his own. Brown couldn't block his shadow in the Giant playoff, consistently turning his hips into (Giants defensive end) Andy Robustelli and frequently missing. Ameche though has become one of the game's strongest blockers from the fullback spot.

When it came to Hall of Fame recognition, Ameche may have lost points for the relative shortness of his career—six seasons. And, of course, his awkward upright gait didn't win him any style points.

"They could have called Alan 'Crazylegs,' like [Elroy] Hirsch because his two feet were always going in opposite directions," Donovan said. "But he could run the football."

There were two other aspects of Ameche's game perhaps overlooked by most observers, but not by his teammates. He could catch the football as well as anybody coming out of the backfield, and he hung onto the ball once he caught it.

In his six seasons with the Colts, he had 101 receptions for 733 yards and four touchdowns. Somehow, at Wisconsin, he had managed just one reception in four years.

"It kind of makes you wonder what they were thinking of at Wisconsin," said Marchetti. "He was a great receiver, so I don't know why they never threw him the football."

The *Sports Illustrated* article written by Booton Herndon includes a telling Ameche quote. "'They think I can't catch the thing,' he said bitterly. It may have sounded like an off-handed remark at the time, but Ameche probably wasn't joking."

One thing that Ameche did very well at Wisconsin and in Baltimore was hold onto the football. In his 964 carries and 101 receptions, he fumbled just six times in the course of his six years with the Colts.

"An indication of how strong the man was, was that he almost never fumbled the football," Marchetti said. "He'd fumble the ball once or twice a year, that was it.

"To show you how strong he was, one time Alan, myself, Don Joyce, and Bill Pellington were out in California and we all went out and had a couple beers. Joyce is a 285-pound tackle and he wants an arm wrestling contest.

"Alan took him down like he was nothing. So Joyce is really hurt, getting beat by a 200-pound back and he says 'You cheated.' So they do it left-handed and Alan takes him down again like nothing."

In the final analysis, the only opinion that matters on how good a fullback Ameche was is Ameche's. In the 1976 Klein interview he gave a very frank assessment of how he felt he should be remembered as a player.

"Jim Brown and Jim Taylor were the best fullbacks. I'm down there somewhere in the next level. I knew my limitations. I worked hard and did things pretty well. Could I play today? Hell yes. I'm as good as anybody playing today."

The natural comparison for Ameche to make in 1976 was to Larry Csonka of the Miami Dolphins. Csonka was the focus of the Dolphins' offense at that time and generally considered the best fullback of his era.

> Larry Csonka? I hope this doesn't sound wrong, but I'm as good as Csonka. [. . .] I put myself close to Jim Taylor and about even with Csonka.
>
> You know, I don't like the way this sounds. It sounds like I'm blowing my own horn, and I don't like it. But Shula is a fullback-oriented coach. Maybe Csonka is Shula's Alan Ameche, maybe he built it the way he [Shula] learned it in Baltimore. You take Csonka and put him on a team geared to pass, and he'd have a hell of a time coming near to a thousand yards. He'd be working just as hard, but he wouldn't be getting so many chances to run it.

In the Klein interview, Marchetti supported Ameche's assertions. "Today they think a guy who makes a thousand yards in fourteen games is a big hero," Marchetti said. "But we used to say they made a third guard out of Alan, a blocking back. When Unitas got here, they had such confidence in his passing that it got so Alan would get the ball on third and one, third and two, fourth and one. They were the only times he'd even touch the ball. Sometimes he'd carry the ball six times a game, and before Unitas he carried the ball twenty-five, thirty times a game."

If it sounds like Marchetti was sticking up for his friend, he probably was. For Ameche, a truly humble man, to defend his football career was an extremely rare event.

"You know the kind of guy Alan was?" Marchetti said. "I asked him once what it was like to win the Heisman. It must have been a great honor. All he said was, 'It was okay.'

"Alan had a phenomenal career at Wisconsin. Some guys would have been bringing it up all the time, but I never recall him talking about his college career. He was just a very modest man who preferred to do his talking on the field."

19

An Unfortunate Situation

LENNY MOORE LOVES TALKING ABOUT HIS twelve seasons with the Baltimore Colts, from 1956 through 1967.

"Those were some great years, some great teams, Man," Moore has said on many, many occasions.

But he always includes a codicil when talking about those years. His favorite verbal appendage, and he uses it often, is "unfortunately . . ."

Unfortunate? Two world championships; a Hall of Fame career; Rookie of the Year in 1956; Comeback Player of the Year in 1964; 12,451 combined (rushing and receiving) yards; 63 rushing touchdowns; 48 receiving touchdowns; All-Pro five seasons; and an NFL record 18 consecutive games with a touchdown.

Where does "unfortunate" have a place in his vocabulary in the discussion of the spectacular career that Moore fashioned?

"Okay, Man, here's the way it was back then," Moore said. "On the field, you will never find a closer bunch of guys than the Baltimore Colts were back in those days.

"Everybody looked out for everybody else, we all protected each other. We all had the other guy's back. I actually feel very fortunate to have played for the Colts because not every team in the NFL was as united as we were.

"When the game was on, we were brothers to the nth degree."

But this is where the word "unfortunately" first rears its ugly head.

"Unfortunately, after the game, they would go their way and we would go our way. That's just the way it had to be back then. There was no way around it."

The "they" in this case were the Colt players who were Caucasians, and they made up the vast majority of all NFL rosters back in the 1950s and 1960s. The "we" in this case, were the African American players of the Colts and the NFL, who made up perhaps to 10–20 percent of most rosters in those days.

Obviously things are much different today, with African American players making up as much as 70–75 percent of some NFL rosters. But even more profound are the changes in the social climate of this country.

As the civil rights era began, positive changes were being felt in sports in general and the NFL in particular. Quotas were outlawed. Restrictions on what position a player could play were abandoned. Jim Crow laws and segregation of teammates on the road were ruled illegal in federal courts. Unfortunately, it was too late for Lenny Moore and many of the other pioneer black players of the NFL.

"I consider myself lucky that I played for a team like the Colts, because our guys were pretty close knit," Moore recalled. "I knew that they were there for me, if some of the guys on the other teams ganged up on us. I knew they were right there.

"A lot of teams of that era had a lot of problems with race, but we never had a lot of confrontation because the guys on our team were pretty much together. There may have been a few guys who didn't buy in completely, but most of our guys were very cool about it. They did what they could."

Moore, who was a first-round draft pick of the Colts out of Penn State in 1956, said one of his biggest regrets was not getting to better know some of his favorite white teammates on offense—men like Alan Ameche, Johnny Unitas, and Raymond Berry. While Moore still has great respect for all of those players, he says he wishes he had known them better. Perhaps his closest friend among the white players was Ameche.

"Alan was not only a great football player, but he was a great guy," Moore said. "Ameche was such a good guy, but we never got a chance to socialize. That's the bad part of what that does to people.

"We wanted to be friends off the field, but society wouldn't let us. It was a question of well okay, is Alan going to come down to Pennsylvania Avenue, where all the black players had to hang out in Baltimore at that time? Or was I going to go out to Towson, where the white players lived?

"See what I mean? Unfortunately . . .

"At that time, we couldn't hang out, black and white together. The black players couldn't go to downtown [Baltimore], and even where many of the white players lived, I couldn't go anywhere out there.

"If wanted to go out, I was kind of confined to Pennsylvania Avenue here in Baltimore, where most of the African Americans went for movies or any kind of entertainment. That was the only area where we could go into a club or whatever; we were very much restricted where we could go.

"It was the same for the black players who would come into Baltimore. Say the Rams would come in from L.A. There was nothing for the black players to do because the only place they could go was Pennsylvania Avenue."

The friendship of a few players was a nice gesture, but it wasn't enough to rectify the situation. It took an entire generation of Americans to change their attitudes before there was any meaningful improvement. But for Moore, it was nice to know that someone like Ameche appreciated his situation.

"[Ameche] would come to me and say things like 'Hey man, you know I'm sorry.' The guys would know we were being treated a little differently in some of these hotels. Alan would say, 'I just want you to know man, I'm sorry.'

"Guys like Ameche, you knew where they were coming from. You knew they were always open arms to you. We really had no problem on our team with inner player relations as far as race relations. We got along as best we could with a basic understanding of the times."

Alan Ameche Jr. remembers his father telling him how bothered he was by the inequities that existed between the races at that time.

"My father had a tremendous sympathy for the African American guys he played with," Alan said. "He would tell us stories about how heartbreaking it was to travel to certain cities and these guys had to stay in different hotels.

"I remember him talking to us kids about this. My father didn't lecture or pontificate, but he told stories to make his points."

Moore was good friends with not only Ameche but also Unitas and Raymond Berry. He claims that having white friends helped him keep things in perspective when there were negative occurrences.

"People like Ameche, to me, they were blessings," Moore said. "They *were* blessings.

"We needed that. We needed that support. It helped you keep your mind on where your mind needed to be, because football players have to keep their mind on their business.

"Football is a game where you have to reach down and pull to the nth degree of what you have to offer. You can't have anything interrupt those thought patterns.

"Now, I will tell you that there were guys on other teams who called me a nigger. There were defensive players who just tried to get me off my assignment and hope that I would maybe go after him and take a swing at him. Or maybe they just wanted to take me out of my game.

"I'll tell you this. It was very difficult for me to not go after somebody like that. But I knew I couldn't retaliate because the flags would fly and Lenny would be gone, because I'd be swinging.

"But that would take me out of what I was supposed to do out there. Not only that play, but it would carry over into the next play and the play after that. You'd still be thinking about that, when you've got to kick it, man."

Moore doesn't hold most of his teammates responsible for anything that happened in those years. Basically, he feels, it's just the way things were then.

"It was a tough situation for us, but it was tough for everybody," he said. "Some of the players were a little shaky on some of the racial stuff, but most of them were cool with it. Did it matter? Not really because we never had a chance to hang out anyhow.

"We'd come to the stadium on Sunday from all different directions and come together as a team. Unfortunately, then we'd leave on Sunday, and they went their way and we went our way.

"On the field, you couldn't find a closer bunch, but unfortunately we weren't able to have the kind of relationships that some of us wish we could have had off the field. Not all of the players were like Ameche or Unitas or like some of the other white players.

"But I had excellent relationships with those guys and would have liked to know them a lot better. Unfortunately, I didn't spend time with Ameche away from the field and get to know the guy better because of the racial situation at the time. Same with Unitas.

"But if I wanted to meet Johnny or Alan somewhere after practice, we would have had to figure out all the details of where. And you know what? That's a damn shame because I think we could have been even closer than we were."

"I don't blame those guys. What else could they do? That was the standard setup throughout the entire NFL at the time."

The "setup," as Moore described it, was this. In many of the cities the Colts would visit for road games, black players and white players would stay at different hotels and eat at different restaurants. Obviously, that wasn't a good thing for team building, but that's the way it was in those days. African Americans simply weren't allowed in some public facilities in those days.

"They would set up trips in advance, you know, where we would stay and where the white players would stay," Moore said. "We would usually stay at places that were outside of the city, way away from everything.

"I remember playing at Atlanta later in my career and that was a tough situation," he said. "But it was in the north, too. I laugh when people say that was only in the south where that happened. I remember having problematic situations in Detroit and Chicago, too."

Moore said the black players had no choice but to accept the second-class treatment if they wanted to play in the NFL. If they were deemed confrontational or "uppity," they would soon see that they were very expendable.

"One of the major conditions of black players in the NFL those days was that we don't get into any kind of negative situations, regardless of what it was," Moore explained. "If you did speak up, you weren't going to be around long. And if you tried to defend yourself to the degree that 'I didn't do this or that or whatever,' they considered that confrontational.

"'We'll get rid of him because he's too talkative.' That kind of thing. That's the whole scheme of what racism is all about.

"And we all knew what was going on. We talked to black players on some of the other teams. We shared our thoughts with Jim Brown and some of the other guys. We talked about how we were treated, the conditions."

Moore claims that the racism of the NFL in those days also manifested itself in less overt ways. It was there in ways that weren't talked about publicly, but everyone knew was there. Even though his career with the Colts lasted well into the 1960s, he never had more than a handful of black teammates with the Colts. Hall of Famer Jim Parker, Leonard Lyles, Eugene "Big Daddy" Lipscomb, and Milt Davis were among the most prominent black Colts of that era.

"It upset quite a few of the guys, but it was pretty evident that's the way things were," Moore said. "Every team was limited as to the numbers of black players that we could have on the team. Almost the entire NFL was like that.

"And then there were certain positions that black players were not allowed to play. You absolutely couldn't be a quarterback or a middle linebacker. You couldn't be an offensive guard, that was a little tough.

"Those were called 'thinking' positions, so none of the black players could be involved with those. So there were definitely not going to be any black quarterbacks or middle linebackers back then. They'd put most of the black players in the defensive backfields and let them compete against each other for jobs.

"[The teams] wanted to keep their rosters at four, five, six black players at the most and not that many more. We knew that, we had eyes. Plus we talked to players on the other teams."

Perhaps somewhat surprisingly, Moore credits Colts coach Weeb Ewbank for the relative harmony that existed between the races on the Colts. Although old-school in many of his views on players relations, Ewbank apparently didn't play favorites based on a player's race.

"I think the reason we had so few problems was that we had a great coach in Weeb Ewbank," Moore said. "He kept us all together as much as he possibly could, given the realities of that era. He was up against some things in certain cities, especially from a hotel point of view, but Weeb always did his best to make sure things were done as well as could be expected.

"Under the circumstances, I think we, as a team, did the best that could possibly be done."

Despite the fact that the Colts were, relatively speaking, ahead of the curve when it came to race relations, there were problems. Football is a contact sport, and tempers enter into the equation in nearly every practice. Fights are a regular occurrence, and sometimes they pit white players against black players.

"Oh sure, there were incidents," Moore said. "It's football and people have pride and they have tempers. And tempers are going to flare.

"So every now and then, you'd get a racial kind of thing. There were always fights and sometimes they involved a white guy and a black guy. But we were pretty good at breaking them up before things got out of hand."

One thing that helped keep the peace for the Colts was the presence of legendary defensive end Big Daddy Lipscomb. Although he was gigantic man (6 feet 10 inches and 310 pounds), Lipscomb was a peaceful man until agitated.

Lipscomb, who played for the Colts from 1956 through 1960, died tragically of a heroin overdose in 1963 at the age of 31. In 1999 William Nack wrote a profile of Lipscomb for *Sports Illustrated* in which he said of Lipscomb's death, "He is survived by a 1963 yellow Cadillac convertible, at least one fiancée and three ex-wives."

"Big Daddy wouldn't allow it," recalled Moore, one of his closest friends on the squad. "There was no racial stuff when Big Daddy was around.

"I remember one time, he gets up in front of the whole locker room and says it real loud so everybody hears him, 'I want all of you to know, I'll tear this whole locker room up. I don't be playing games. Any of you want to play any racial games, I'm just letting you know. Don't let me hear about it, or I'm going to tear something up. Anybody gets off the wall with me, and I'll do it. I just want all you to know that.' Big Daddy was a gentle giant, but he was not somebody you wanted to get mad."

Lenny Lyles, a black player who had two stints with the Colts—in 1958 and then 1961through 1969—said he saw an improvement in race relations in the NFL from the start to the finish of his career.

"[The Colts] drafted me in the first round, the year after they picked Lenny [Moore] in the first round, so I think that was a sign that things were changing," Lyles said. "But there were still problems. I remember we played an exhibition game in New Orleans, and they didn't want [the black players] to be there.

"Then we played a game in Texas, and we couldn't go to a hotel and eat with the rest of the team. There were all kinds of things that we didn't understand."

Like Moore, Lyles agreed that the presence of Ameche helped bridge the gap between the races.

"Some people felt that they didn't have to say anything or do anything because they didn't care, and that's okay," Lyles said. "We got through it as best we could.

"But Alan was always a straight up guy. I could never find anything negative to say about the man. He was always a gentleman and, as far as I'm concerned, a great athlete."

Lyles thought race relations in the NFL were starting to improve in his later years in the league.

"I think things were getting much better by the end [of his career]. Look at how different things are now. The majority of players are black now, and back then there were only seven of us on the team that were black."

Despite the fact that race relations were obviously starting to move in a positive direction in the latter stages of Moore's career, he claims they never got to where he was completely comfortable. He points to a team function at Bill Pellington's club late in his career with the Colts in the late 1960s, long after Ameche had retired from football.

"Milt Davis was in town, so I said, 'Man, let's go out there and stick our heads in,'" Moore said. "'If it gets tight, we'll cut out.'

"So, we're sitting there and chit-chatting with the guys, and the atmosphere was kind of cool. You could see the other guys were trying to be inclusive, but you could also see a little stiffness.

"Milt and I are sitting there and I said, 'Man, you about ready to cut out?' . . . Most of the stuff was done, so we got up to leave. All the other guys said, 'Whoa, where are you guys going? Hold on.'

"I told them 'We're going.' There is nothing to do but sit and drink and we were the only two [African Americans] in there.

"So at that point I got up and said, 'You know what fellows? I have to say this, and I have to be very honest with you guys. And, I'm sorry to say this, but I have to say it . . . I only wish that I could have known you guys a lot closer than what we were allowed to do, but so be it.'

"Unfortunately . . .

"'So have a good evening,' and Milt and I were out the door.

"And you know what? I really meant that. I wish we could have gotten to know each other better, to go to each other's kids' weddings, get together for dinner. But figuring it all out, that was the hard part. That's how tight it was.

"They went to their places and we went to Pennsylvania Avenue.

"Unfortunately . . ."

20

The Greatest Game

GINO MARCHETTI DIDN'T SEE THE END of the Greatest Game Ever Played, but at least he knows where the football from that game ended up.

Marchetti was in the visitors' locker room of Yankee Stadium when his buddy Alan Ameche crashed across the goal line on a 1-yard plunge to end the first overtime game in NFL history, the 1958 championship game. Marchetti was there, instead of on the Baltimore sideline, because he had broken his right ankle stuffing New York Giant halfback Frank Gifford short of a first down on a controversial play in the fourth quarter.

To this day Gifford contends he had the first down, but a recent review of the play with computer technology confirms that the referees had made the right call. The bottom line that day was that the Giants were forced to punt on fourth and inches from their own 40-yard line with just over two minutes left in the game.

That was just enough time for Johnny Unitas to march the Colts from their own 14-yard line 73 yards to the Giants' 13, where Steve Myhra kicked a 20-yard field goal to tie the game at 17 with seven seconds left, sending the game into overtime.

Marchetti saw the tying drive and Myrha's field goal. Although the Colts medical staff pleaded with Marchetti to retreat to the locker room, where his ankle could be properly treated, he was adamant about watching the game from his stretcher.

"I played on so many bad teams that when I finally got to a game like that one, the world championship, I wanted to see the finish. When we tied the game, I was on a stretcher and nobody knew what was going to happen next.

So the word comes down that we are going to sudden death, and they start to take me to the locker room.

"I stopped by the entrance to the locker room, and I made them put me down because I wanted to see the rest of the overtime. But the police came over and made them carry me inside. They were afraid because there were fans lining the field and if the game ended suddenly, they wouldn't be able to get me off the field.

"So I never got to see the overtime. . . . There was no closed circuit TV back then. Are you kidding me? I'm laying there and I hear all the yelling and cheering, but I had no idea what was going on. So finally [Colts linebacker] Bill Pellington comes running in and says, 'Yeah, we're the best! We're the World Champions.' So we all had our Cokes and celebrated."

What Marchetti missed was perhaps the most viewed play in the history of professional football. On third down, Unitas called the play known as 16-power, and Ameche, with his head lowered and both arms smothering the football, barreled off the right tackle and into the end zone from 1 yard out with the game winner. Ameche benefited from perfectly executed blocking from the likes of wide receiver Lenny Moore, tight end Jim Mutscheller, and right tackle George Preas, and the game ended at the 8:15 mark of the overtime period.

Marchetti has since viewed Ameche's touchdown plunge and the scramble for the precious game-winning football many times over.

"Alan gets into the end zone and instead of celebrating, he kind of nonchalantly shoves the football away from him," Marchetti said. "Alan wasn't a guy that wanted a lot of glory so he just kind of shoved it away. He was ready to just pick himself up and get off the field because by now, the fans were everywhere.

"Of course, a fan picks the ball up and starts to get away with it, but our center, Buzz Nutter, took it back from him. It was the championship ball, and Buzz went right after the guy and got it back."

Nobody was happier than Marchetti that Nutter had the presence of mind to retrieve the football. And where is the ball now?

"I know exactly where that ball is," Marchetti continued his story. "The team voted me the ball, I guess because I broke my ankle, and of course I accepted. But I'm not what you would call a real big collector of things like that, so I gave it away.

"I was voted into the Italian Hall of Fame in Chicago, and they asked me if I had anything I could donate to the museum. They wanted something to put in the trophy case, along with my jersey and all of that. So I gave them the ball. . . . If I only knew then what I know now, I would have kept it. That ball is worth a fortune."

The story was far from over at that point, however. It picks up around 2000, when Marchetti was doing an autograph signing.

"I don't remember where I was, but I was doing a signing, and a fan comes up to me and hands me a newspaper clipping and says, 'What do you think of this, Gino.' So I read the headline and it's about a guy paying $15,000 for the ball of that game and how happy he was about it.

"So I get a little upset. I'm thinking, What are they doing at that Italian American Hall of Fame selling my football? So the next time I was in Chicago I decided to pay them a visit.

"I went there and they showed me. The ball was right where it was the last time I was there. So I don't know what ball that fan bought, but it wasn't the ball that Alan Ameche carried over the goal line to win the game."

Obviously there have been volumes upon volumes of football played since that frigid December 28, 1958, afternoon in the Bronx. But there are so many ingredients of this game that have kept its memory alive and till this day allow it to retain its regal and rather presumptuous title of the Greatest Game Ever Played.

Comparing it to a classic movie isn't at all far-fetched. The 1958 game had a great plot—and four lead changes.

It had drama. Not once, but twice, Johnny Unitas marched his team down-field with near-perfect execution with the game on the line.

It had comic relief. Out-of-shape Weeb Ewbank trying to take a swing at Giants linebacker Sam Huff, one of the toughest men ever to play the game, was a funny sight, to say the least. Huff had infuriated the portly Ewbank by taking a cheap shot at Lenny Moore.

"We held Weeb back from taking a poke at Huff," Marchetti said. "We didn't want anybody getting hurt."

It had outstanding performances: Unitas (26–40, 349 yards passing); Ameche (14 carries, 65 yards, 2 touchdowns); Raymond Berry (12 receptions, 187 yards, 1 touchdown); Lenny Moore (6 receptions, 101 yards); Giants back-up quarterback Charlie Conerly (10–14, 187 yards); and Giants half-back Frank Gifford (12 carries, 60 yards).

And last, but certainly not least, it had more star power than many Holly-wood productions. The game was like watching the NFL Hall of Fame live. Both teams had six players who would eventually make it there: for the Giants—Rosey Brown, Gifford, Huff, Don Maynard, Andy Robustelli, and

Emlen Tunnell—and for the Colts—Berry, Donovan, Marchetti, Moore, Unitas, and Jim Parker.

Other future Hall of Famers in attendance that day included the Giants offensive coordinator, Vince Lombardi; the Giants defensive coordinator, Tom Landry; the Giants owner, Tim Mara; the Giants vice president and future owner, Wellington Mara; and the Colts coach, Weeb Ewbank.

"I think one of the really key factors to this game that nobody ever talks about is that the Giants had Vince Lombardi as their offensive coordinator and Tom Landry as the defensive coordinator," said Berry. "[Giants head coach] Jim Lee Howell was the smartest coach in NFL history because he knew enough to stay out of their way.

"The fact is nobody ever thinks that much about who the coaches were for the New York Giants at that time, but you had two guys who were two of the greatest coaches in the history of professional football. And in my mind, Weeb Ewbank was a match for both of them."

There was certainly plenty of unsettled business leading up to the championship game. The two teams had met once during the season, with the Giants handing the Colts their first loss of the season, 24–21, on November 9. The Giants contended that that victory made them the best team in football, but the Colts said it didn't prove a thing.

"It was a game when John [Unitas] was hurt and didn't even play," Marchetti recalled. "Then we got all the clippings from the New York Times and all the other papers where Frank [Gifford] and [Charlie] Conerly were saying, 'We outgutted them.' You know, talking about what a great job they did, so that made us want to beat them even more.

"We knew [the Giants] pretty well and I'll tell you, the game never should have been as close as it was."

Both squads entered the game with 9–3 records, but those were very different 9–3 records. The Colts' only loss in September, October, and November was to the Giants in the November 9 contest. But then Baltimore ended its regular season with a disastrous West Coast trip, losing to the Rams, 30–28, and the 49ers, 21–12. Considering that 1958 was just the second winning season in Colts' history, the late losses couldn't have done much for their confidence.

The Giants, on the other hand, had a veteran team and had been there before, winning the 1956 championship over the Chicago Bears with basically the same squad. They had started the season 2–2 but finished strong, winning seven of their last eight games to get to 9–3.

"I heard Gifford on an interview once, [. . .] that he thought they could have very easily won the game," said Ameche in the Klein book. "I really feel that we had the better team. If we had put in that third touchdown, it could have been the same rout it was the next year. But from a technical standpoint, I think it was a hell of a lot better game than any championship game I've seen lately."

The Colts came out ready to play that day, and in the Klein book Marchetti gives credit to Ewbank for that. He credits Ewbank's pep talk before the game for stoking the fire in the team's collective belly.

> Weeb gave probably the best pep talk he's ever given prior to the game. There's a lot of pep talks so shitty that, you know, you laugh at them. But he went down everyone on the roster, and he had something for them. For instance, Artie Donovan. He said, "Dunny, the Cleveland Browns didn't want you, they cut you. And the New York Yankees cut you. Now you're here, show 'em how good you are." And he had a thing about Alan and a thing about me. Everybody. I think that was the best pre-game speech he ever had. He's had some sickening ones, I'll tell you that.

Ewbank's pregame pep talk notwithstanding, both teams played horribly in the game's opening quarter. On the game's first possession, Sam Huff sacked Unitas, forcing a fumble that was recovered by the Giants' defensive back, Jimmy Patton, at the Colts' 37. The Colts got the ball back a play later, when Marchetti recovered a fumble by Giants quarterback Don Heinrich.

But the Colts soon turned it over again when Unitas threw the game's only interception to Lindon Crow. The Giants were forced to punt, however, and Unitas finally got the Colts moving. He teamed with Lenny Moore for a 60-yard completion, but Steve Myrha's 26-yard field goal was blocked by Huff.

Charlie Conerly replaced the ineffective Heinrich on the Giants' next series, and a 38-yard run by Frank Gifford put New York in range for the only points of the first quarter. Pat Summerall's 36-yard field goal gave the Giants' a short-lived 3–0 lead.

The Colts took their first lead early in the second period on Ameche's 2-yard touchdown run. The touchdown was set up by a Gifford fumble deep in New York territory that was recovered by the Colts' defensive end Ray Krouse.

The Giants were forced to punt on their next possession but got the ball back at the Colts' 10-yard line when Jackie Simpson muffed the punt. But again, Gifford fumbled, and this time defensive end Don Joyce recovered on the Colts' 14.

From there Unitas drove the team 86 yards in 15 plays for the team's second touchdown and a 14–3 halftime lead. Berry scored the touchdown on a 15-yard Unitas pass. The key play of the drive was a 16-yard scramble by Unitas on third and seven.

"Once a game started, [. . .] John was in complete charge of the offense," Ameche would later say in Klein's book. "You had to lock Weeb up at game time, I'll tell you that."

The Colts threatened to break the game open early in the third quarter when they got to the Giants' 1-yard line. On third and goal, the Giants stopped Ameche for no gain, but Ewbank decided to gamble and go for it again on fourth down.

Unitas apparently called the play, because he called almost every play, and the play he called was the 428—a pitchout to Ameche, who was to run a sweep to the right and lob a pass to Mutscheller in the end zone. Ameche got the sweep part correct, but not the pass part.

Ameche apparently heard the 28 portion of the play, which called for the fullback to take the pitch and run through the eight hole. But he missed the 4 part, which designated the pass. Ameche took the pitch from Unitas and was thrown for a loss at the Giants' 5 by linebacker Cliff Livingston, and the Giants took over on downs.

If the play called had been a run, as Ameche thought it was, tight end Jim Mutscheller's assignment would have been to block Livingston. Instead, he brushed Livingston and was waving his arms in the end zone, wide open and yelling for Ameche to throw him the football.

"I guess Alan didn't hear the play called correctly," Mutscheller said. "But I'm standing in the end zone, wide open, yelling 'Alan! Alan!'

"If he throws me the ball it's 21–3 and that would have probably ended the game, or at least put the Giants totally on the defensive. As it was, that turned things around for them."

The mistake cost Mutscheller his chance for glory, but he never complained.

"I don't believe Alan and I ever talked about that play. In fact, I didn't realize that I was so wide open till I looked at the game film twenty years later."

Berry also felt that Ameche just misunderstood which play had been called in the huddle.

"It was a special play and we didn't have many special plays," Berry said. "But that was a play that never should have been called, and it shouldn't have even been in the game plan. The theory behind it was all well and good, but you have to be able to execute it."

Marchetti claims that the reason the execution wasn't there was because the team hadn't practiced that particular play since training camp.

"We put in 300 plays in training camp, but once the season starts and they draw up the game plan, there are only 60 to 70 plays for an opponent," Marchetti said. "So we never used that play, but now, in the heat of the game, John calls it. Alan didn't remember the play, but if he had thrown it, we would have had them 21–3 and the game would have been over.

"We never practiced the play after training camp. We put it in the playbooks and forgot about it until that day."

In Klein's book, Ameche admits that not scoring in that situation nearly cost the Colts the victory. He was asked what sticks out in his mind about that game.

"There were so many dramatic events. For example, early in the game we had a chance to score a third touchdown in the first half. And we could have blown them out, but we didn't score from the one-yard line. Unfortunately, I was involved in three out of the four plays down there. Had we put it in there, I'm convinced it would have been a rout."

Certainly the failed opportunity was one of several clearly delineated turning points in the contest.

"I don't think there is any question about it," said Berry, when asked if that was the game's turning point. "We should have put the game out of sight at that point. It would have been a totally different outcome.

"It was a huge play and a huge mistake, but as a coach you come with the ideas, the special plays. What I learned in the coaching business is don't put the ball in somebody's hand who can't execute the play."

The Giants wasted no time in seizing the gift of momentum that the Colts had presented to them. They moved 95 yards in four plays, cutting the lead to 14–10 on Mel Triplett's 1-yard touchdown plunge.

The play of the drive, and most likely the play of the game, was a wild pass play from Conerly to Kyle Rote that covered a total of 86 yards. Conerly hit Rote, who was cutting left to right across the middle, and Rote broke an arm tackle near midfield. Rote then fumbled when hit from behind at around the Colts' 25.

Giants running back Alex Webster, alertly trailing the play, scooped up the loose ball and carried it to the 1-yard line before being shoved out of bounds.

"And it was a fluke, the way they came back from there," said Ameche, describing the Giants' quick strike. "It was a crazy play . . . a pass that was completed, a tackle, a fumble, a recovery and somebody running . . . and by the time it was over they were on our one [yard line]. . . . So instead of being twenty-one to three, it was fourteen to ten. And instead of us putting them away, we had to scramble from then on."

The Giants weren't finished squeezing out every last ounce of momentum, however. New York regained the lead at 17–14 early in the fourth quarter on Conerly's 15-yard touchdown pass to Gifford. The touchdown was made possible by Conerly's 46-yard pass to tight end Bob Schnelker.

The Colts were far from finished, but their next two possessions ended in frustration, when they were unable to tack on a tying field goal. On the first possession of the fourth quarter, they drove to the Giants' 39, only to have Burt Rechichar miss a 46-yard field goal.

The Colts got the ball right back, as Joyce made his second fumble recovery of the game at the New York 42. Baltimore penetrated to the New York 27, but consecutive sacks of Unitas by Andy Robustelli and Dick Modzelewski moved the Colts out of field-goal range.

The task of the Giants' offense at that point became to run out the final few minutes of the clock. But with just over two minutes remaining in the game, Marchetti stopped Gifford inches short of a first down at the New York 40. Marchetti's ankle was broken on the play when teammates Art Donovan and Big Daddy Lipscomb landed on top of him.

"First of all, it really surprised me that that they'd come our way," said Marchetti, who with Donovan formed a nearly impregnable right side of the Colts' front line. "During the whole game, they left us alone and ran more to the left side than the right side.

"But they toss it to Frank Gifford and I shed blockers, flowing with Frank. I had him in my sights. I tried to get him to cut back, so I made the tackle and he didn't get the first down. But Big Daddy Lipscomb was flowing over to help me, so he dives in and Big Daddy was the one who actually broke my ankle. They regularly weighed him in [Friday pregame] at about 280 pounds, but by game day he might have been 300 or 310.

"So I'm laying on the ground moaning and groaning. . . . It was painful and Gifford is yelling at me, 'Get up, Marchetti, the play is over.' I said 'Gosh Frank, I can't, my leg is broken. I can't get up.'

"Gifford has always claimed he made that first down, but he didn't make it. I always tell him, 'Frank, who's got the ring on?' Every time I walk I remember that play and that game. Something didn't heal right, so I've still got a bit of a problem with my ankle . . . my whole leg actually."

That play took the game out of the Giants' hands and put it in the very capable ones of the great Unitas. Rather than try again on fourth and inches, the Giants chose to punt, and Unitas and the Colts took over at their own 14-yard line.

"I remember trotting on to the field at that moment thinking that we had blown that darn game," Berry said. "I was very angry. I'm thinking we should have put the game out of reach a long time ago and was just stupid that we hadn't.

"Then I got into the huddle and I put all of those thoughts behind me."

And it's a good thing, because Unitas had big plans for Berry for the next two minutes. He was about to captivate a nation and add a new phrase—the "two-minute drill"—to the sports lexicon.

The drive started inauspiciously enough. Unitas opened with two incomplete passes, but then he hit Moore with a critical 11-yard pass on third down. After another incompletion, he and Berry went to work. They connected on three consecutive pass plays that moved the ball 62 yards to the Giants' 13-yard line.

"Johnny and Raymond had things going on, and Johnny took full advantage of it," Moore said. "Unitas was such a great quarterback, but I'll tell you, Raymond Berry made him even greater. Raymond Berry was a technician.

"Raymond came to me during the game and said, 'Lenny, you know what? You've got [Giants defensive back] Lindon Crow over there and he's afraid of your speed. Any time you're on the flank, he's giving you 10, 12 yards cushion . . . There are a lot of things we can do.'

"Raymond was so good about stuff like that. He and Johnny would work after practice and to be honest, we'd laugh at them. But look at what they accomplished together. They were so tight."

Ameche agreed: "You take a guy like Raymond. The beautiful thing about it was that this was like a culmination of everything for him, of all this guy's efforts. Because Raymond was a perfectionist.

"Everybody wondered what this guy was doing there. He had one leg shorter than the other, he wore contact lenses . . . he was barely a hundred and eighty five pounds, he didn't have speed, wasn't particularly strong. But just from hard work, he made it."

And this time, so did Myhra . . . make it that is. The man who no one had confidence in sent the game into overtime with an odd-angled 20-yard field goal with seven seconds left in regulation.

Ameche described the moment: "Then Myhra, who was always a little shaky as a field goal kicker anyway, comes through in as clutch a field goal as he ever kicked in his life. He's a hell of a guy, don't misunderstand. But he was a nervous-type guy, pacing up and down, and then he goes in and puts the ball right through there. We couldn't tell if it was good or not. He kicked it from a funny angle, like from the hash mark away from us, kicking toward us. But it was a hell of a moment there on the sideline with everybody standing still, watching, wondering if we'd tie it up or go home losers. Then he jumped up and down, and the holder—George Shaw, I think—began jumping around, so we knew it was good."

There was some confusion on both sidelines at that point because quite simply there had never been an overtime game before and no one was quite sure of the protocol for such an event. But word came down from NFL Commissioner Bert Bell in the press box that the game would have a sudden-death overtime.

"When the game ended in a tie, we were standing on the sidelines waiting to see what came next," said Unitas in later years. "All of a sudden, the officials came over and said, 'Send the captain out. We're going to flip a coin to see who will receive.' That was the first we'd ever heard of the overtime period."

With Marchetti out of commission, Unitas met Giants' co-captains Rote and Bill Svoboda for the midfield toss. Unitas lost the toss, the last mistake he would make that day, and the Giants chose to receive.

Hall of Fame wide receiver Don Maynard muffed the kickoff but managed to corral it at the Giants' 20. The Colts' defense held and the Giants were forced to punt.

The Colts took over with one thought in their minds. Touchdown.

"In overtime, that's all we were thinking was touchdown," Berry recalled. "People ask all the time, why not just kick the field goal when we got down there, but a field goal never entered our minds. We already had had one blocked that day, so we were just very confident we could take it all the way.

"When you have a field goal stuffed up your rear end, it raised a whole lot of questions with a lot of people. Weeb did not have confidence in Steve Myhra kicking the winning field goal, plain and simple. They blocked one and we weren't even sure how they did it.

"We just knew we could put it in the end zone."

Although Marchetti was by this point in the locker room and feeling extremely lonely, he knows what the Colts were thinking in the overtime.

"The process was that John could get it done," Marchetti said. "We knew he could complete the score. That was why they were thinking touchdown all the way. Plus, to be honest, there was a lack of confidence in the kicker.

"Somebody asked Johnny later in life, 'What would have happened if somebody had intercepted one of your passes?' He said, 'Nobody was going to intercept anything. I made sure of that.'"

Lenny Moore was a little more blunt about the Colts' strategy to take it all the way. He claims the coaches had zero confidence in the team's part-time, job-sharing kickers, Myhra and Bert Rechichar.

"Why didn't we kick?" said Moore, feigning shock. "Are you kidding? We didn't have the greatest kickers in the world. Steve Myhra was not a great kicker and they even used another guy in there. I don't know how they figured out which one to use. . . . I guess it was which ever one the coaches thought was more in synch.

"I know Steve Myhra made the kick [that tied the game in regulation], but that thing could have just as easily been 5 yards outside. It was a question of 'Oh, Lord, please, please.'

"But that kick went right through and the rest was all Johnny U."

As you might expect, the Colts' big three—Unitas, Berry, and Ameche—made the bulk of the plays in the winning drive. Ameche caught an 8-yard pass in a third-and-eight situation that kept the drive alive at the Colts' 33. Later he rushed 22 yards to the Giants 20 on a draw play.

Berry caught two passes for 33 yards on the drive, including a 12-yarder that took the Colts to the New York 8-yard line. Berry's final reception was his twelfth of the game, which still stands as NFL Championship/Super Bowl record.

Incredibly, at that point in the game, NBC, which was doing the broadcast, lost its signal, and the game's estimated 45 million television viewers were sent scrambling for a radio signal. It was probably no coincidence that at that time, a fan ran onto the field, delaying the game.

By the time he had been escorted off the field, the problem was discovered and the live broadcast resumed. It turned out to be a cable that had been inadvertently unplugged.

When play resumed, Ameche lugged the ball to the Giants' 7 on first down. On second down, Unitas connected with Mutscheller on a sideline pattern. Mutscheller appeared headed for a sure a touchdown, but his momentum on the icy turf carried him out of bounds at the Giants' 1. For the second time in the game, poor Mutscheller had been denied his piece of glory.

"Later John said to me, 'I tried to make you a hero and what do you do? You slide out of bounds,'" Mutscheller joked. "It was pretty icy out there, so I just slid out of bounds."

Added Berry: "I felt bad for Jim, but I think the footing was a little tricky out there at that point. He couldn't get his feet together and turn it up into the end zone."

As it turns out, Mutscheller's misfortune was Ameche's ticket to immortality.

"I'm not really sure why John called that [Ameche] play," Berry said. "Years later, John told me the only instructions Weeb gave him before the game was 'John, I want you to throw it and throw it a lot.' The Giants' defensive coordinator was Tom Landry, and believe me, they knew how to stop the run.

"But [Ameche's run] was totally and successfully blocked. Everybody got their man. . . . There was one guy that was unblocked, Jimmy Patton in the end zone. But there was no way he was going to stop Ameche when Alan had a full head of steaming coming at him.

"Lenny Moore blocked out on Emlen Tunnell; and George Preas and Jim Mutscheller blocked down on the defensive end and linebacker."

"Yes, I blocked Emlen Tunnell, took him right out of the play," confirmed Moore, laughing. "Thank God, too, because blocking wasn't one of my great strengths.

"Hey, it just happened and we won the championship. Ol' Ameche threw that shoulder down and he could have just walked in. It was beautiful."

Mutscheller admits he was skeptical when Unitas called the play in the huddle, largely because the Giants had stuffed almost the exact play in the ill-fated third-quarter drive.

"If you look at it, I thought it was a pretty unusual call," Mutscheller recalled. "Earlier in the game, Alan was running the ball straight up the middle when we were ahead, 14–3, and he couldn't get in. John came up with the play where Alan goes through the 6-hole [off tackle], which is fairly wide.

"I'm thinking, Hmmm, but it worked so well. I think maybe [the Giants] were overcompensating toward the middle, thinking we were going up the middle again and they guessed wrong."

For his part, Ameche barreled low through the 6-hole with both of his muscular arms uncharacteristically squeezing the football.

"He only had one yard to get, so I'm sure he was thinking he needed to have his left arm swinging free," Berry said. "He just rolled into the end zone."

Ameche would say later in life that the hole he ran through was "big enough that Artie Donovan could have run through it." Donovan could only dream of that happening.

"The picture of that touchdown is in every bar room in the state of Mary-land," said Donovan of the iconic *Sports Illustrated* photo by Neil Leifer. "What a play!

"All I know is I was on the winning team. We were the worst team in the league when I got there and all of a sudden we were the best."

Unitas explained his call years later. "That was a pretty basic play. We knew that with Ameche and our offensive line, they weren't going to stop us. You knew you could count on him in tough times to come up with the big plays."

In Steadman's *Baltimore Sun* article, Ameche was asked if that touchdown was the biggest thrill of his football career.

"You know, I can't think of a better one," Ameche replied. "But I can say too, that when those fans mobbed me in the end zone and took the ball away, I was probably hit harder than any time in football."

Thankfully, Nutter was there to reclaim the precious football.

"Nutter grabbed it right out of the kid's hands," Donovan said.

Of course, justice was served and Marchetti was served the winning football.

"Can you imagine being in a game like that and not being able to see the end of it?" Marchetti said. "We didn't have champagne like they do today, so we drank our Cokes. But it was one hell of a celebration anyhow.

"I was in pretty bad shape there, but when they came in and gave me that football . . . I felt much, much better."

21

Burgers, Burgers, and More Burgers

ALAN AMECHE NEVER GOT A RETIREMENT PARTY from the Colts. There were no halftime ceremonies, no retired numbers, and no testimonial dinners. He didn't get a gold watch from his boss. All he got from Weeb Ewbank was a swift kick in the ego.

As Ameche was helped off the field against the Detroit Lions on December 4, 1960, in the third-to-last game of that season, little did he know that he would never carry a football in earnest again.

Certainly a torn Achilles tendon is a serious injury. But is it a career ender? In most cases it isn't. With hard work, it is an injury that most athletes can come back from. For a 27-year-old athlete like Ameche, a man at the peak of his enormous physical capacity, it probably would have been a routine rehabilitation.

But at an off-season banquet following the 1960 season, Ameche wanted to test the waters. Apparently, he wanted to know if the hard work to get back to where he needed to be as a high-performance athlete was worth it. He wanted to know if he was wanted.

"We were at a banquet, and Alan goes up to Weeb and says, 'You know, Weeb, I'm thinking about retiring,'" said Gino Marchetti, who witnessed the exchange.

"You know what Weeb says to Alan? He says, 'Alan, I think that's a good idea.' That was it. That hurt Alan so badly to hear those words. That's what made him retire.

"It hurt Alan so much, I thought he was going to cry. He wanted Weeb to say, 'Wait a while, come to camp and everything will work out. We need you.'

But he didn't. Weeb told him it was a good idea to retire and that's not very encouraging, is it?

"Alan figured that was it, he wasn't wanted. That's not good when a coach makes up his mind that he is going to cut you. Once they decide, that's that. I think what really hurt Alan is that he worked as hard as he played in 1960. Then to be told he wasn't wanted . . .

"I'm sure that ruined his night because it ruined my night, too. He was a great teammate, and I would have loved to see him keep playing."

Art Donovan agreed that Ameche deserved a better ending to his career.

"I never heard that story about the banquet, but I think Horse just had enough of the way Weeb treated him," Donovan said. "Then, when he injured the Achilles tendon, I think he just felt he had the lucrative business, so he didn't need it anymore.

"But I definitely feel the Horse could have played longer. You know Weeb embarrassed him by starting Billy Price ahead of him a few games. Now that was really an injustice. You're a Heisman Trophy winner and a coach pulls that kind of bullshit on you? But Weeb was a little man in stature and a lot of other ways, too."

There is some mystery involving the injury itself. One story has it that Ameche's tendon snapped while blocking Detroit's perennial All-Pro tackle Alex Karras. But according to Marchetti, the injury occurred without contact.

"To be honest, I never heard that he got hurt blocking Karras," Marchetti said. "He wasn't blocking anybody. He just took off from his stance and he went straight down. He didn't hit anybody on the play. He jerked forward to get into position and he tore the Achilles.

"He always said to me, 'Damn it, I'd get hit 100 times a game, and now just taking off, I'm out for the season.' He was a little pissed.

"The thing about it is he was going to do the rehab and he always told me he planned to come back [in 1961]. He never talked to me about retiring, and I wouldn't have listened to him even if he did. Anybody can talk about retiring in January and February, but when it gets down to June and July, you decided you want to play another year. It's like Brett Favre . . . he always knew he was coming back.

"I don't know if it was so much that Weeb hurt his feelings as it was he was telling Alan he didn't want him anymore. And if a coach doesn't want you, nothing else matters.

"I don't know if too many people know that story because I don't think Alan told a lot of people. It was embarrassing. Alan had a lot of pride."

If Ameche had really wanted to continue playing, all indications were that he would have been welcomed elsewhere in the NFL. At age twenty-seven he was just scratching the surface of his potential as a football player. Apparently Don Shula contacted Ameche about making a comeback when Shula replaced Ewbank as Colts head coach in 1963, but by then Ameche was well into his next career.

"It didn't work out," Marchetti said. "Alan went into business and decided to take that route. But he often told me he wished Shula had been there before he announced his retirement. He would have loved playing for Shula."

Ameche did have other options, options that allowed him to work more with his very engaged brain rather than his brawn. By 1960 Ameche was fully immersed in the fast-food business.

"Don Shula called Alan to come back, but by that time we had the drive-ins, so Alan said no," Yvonne Ameche said. "Alan liked being in business, he liked being home, and the family was growing. He was just ready.

"I'm sure Alan had withdrawals from football. . . . He loved football. And he felt his career was cut short, but the business was growing and he just felt it was time."

The business began in 1957, when Ameche was asked to join Colts teammate Joe Campanella and his former teammate at Ohio State Lou Fischer in a fast-food venture. It was dubbed Ameche's Powerhouse and was strictly a ma-and-pa operation.

"The first Ameche's, Nan Campanella and I were the waitresses and Babs Fischer was on teletray," Yvonne Ameche recalled. "She was mad because we never shared the tips with her to pay the babysitters.

"Joe had already retired [from football] and he went into business with Lou, because they knew each other from Ohio State. They both had worked in restaurants before, while Alan had been working at Bethlehem Steel as a laborer during off-seasons with the Colts."

Ameche's Powerhouse was similar to Sonic today. Customers wouldn't have to leave their cars because waitresses, in some cases on roller skates, would take their orders. The specialty of the house was the Powerhouse, a double-decker hamburger that was served with shredded lettuce and a "special" sauce, not unlike today's Big Mac.

"Joe and Lou were great friends from Ohio State, and they wanted to go into business, but they didn't quite have enough money," Marchetti remembers. "So they brought Alan in with them."

Campanella, who went on to become the Colts general manager from November of 1966 until his untimely death in February of 1967, left the business when he rejoined the Colts management. Fischer loves to talk about how the original Ameche's came into being.

"Joe and I were thinking about going into business, and it just so happened that Joe was in an airport where he ran into a fellow by the name of Alex Schoenbaum, an all-American tackle at Ohio State, who was the founder of Shoney's Big Boy," Fischer related. "He thought it sounded like a good idea because nothing like that had ever been developed in the mid-Atlantic or the Northeast, so there was a lot of potential.

"We opened an Ameche's in Baltimore, and pretty soon we had four of them. We couldn't believe it, but we were doing more business than you would believe a little place like that could do. Everybody in our families worked in these places. It was very ma-and-pa and unprofessional, but it worked. As we grew, we became more and more professional."

At the same time that Ameche's Powerhouse was starting up, Marchetti was opening his own chain of hamburger joints. His concept was a bit different, however. He freely admits that his Gino's chain was a direct knockoff of the McDonald's concept, from the building to the burgers to the budget prices.

"I took a trip down to Washington [D.C.] to see one of the first McDonald's," Marchetti recalled. "They were selling hamburgers for 15 cents at the time. I got there about a quarter to 10, and people are lined up outside the door to buy these burgers. I'm thinking, What the heck is going on here?

"So, we copied the building exactly like McDonald's. I brought an architect with me and he copied it right down to the T. The first places we opened, I'd be there at night, after practice, flipping burgers in the window. It was a big attraction. . . . There would be 50 or 60 people looking through the glass, watching me flip the burgers.

"Baltimore didn't really have a college football team, so we were like their college football team. The fans really took to us. Almost every Colt player who went into business in Baltimore was successful.

"So after the first championship [1958], Carroll Rosenbloom [the Colts' owner] asks me what I'm going to do with the rest of my life. He said, 'I want you to move to Baltimore, you have a good name, people like you in Baltimore and I'll help you get into business.' So we decided to move to Baltimore, and that's when Campanella and Fischer and Alan asked me to join their group. The deal was they would use the Gino's name on a 15-cent hamburger, and within a few years there would be no more Ameche's.

"So, they converted the Ameche's into Gino's . . . Gino's food was a little faster and served a lot quicker. At their places, they needed car hops, and they were a pain to run."

Fischer, who would later become the CEO of the company, pretty much agreed with Marchetti's version of the merger.

"The decision from our standpoint was easy," Fischer said. "Gino's attracted volume, and there was no service. It was like an old Dairy Queen—two windows to order, no outside or inside seating. It was the most efficient system for getting hot food out hot and cold food out cold.

"It was right after the championship game in 1958, and Gino is in the hospital with his broken leg. . . . It's almost like fate. We are in the room visiting him, and in comes Carroll Rosenbloom. He wants Gino to move to Baltimore and not go back to California in the off-season.

"So we make a deal, name the company Gino's, and it took off like crazy. Gino was a terrific asset, and Alan was the best friend you could ever have— two true-blue, sincere, wonderful guys.

"It wasn't just that the price of the Gino's burger was less, it was that it was a far less complicated system. With Ameche's we had waitresses, a bigger menu . . . it was just harder to control. The Gino's setup was so uncomplicated you couldn't believe it."

Rosenbloom not only helped bring the two fast-food operations together, he also literally put his money where his mouth was.

"There was a location on Pulaski Highway that we wanted, but the landlord wanted a guarantee on the lease," Marchetti said. "He wanted $10,000 a year for 10 years. . . . He wanted $100,000 guaranteed. He had no confidence in 15-cent hamburgers.

"At that time we had just gotten our bonus checks from the 1958 title game. [The checks were for $4,674.] We put the money back into the business, but there was no way we had that kind of money.

"So I went to Carroll and he said, 'How's things going? What do you need?' I said I need somebody to sign for us, guaranteeing that if we go broke, somebody will pay off the lease. His exact words were: 'Will my name do?'

"I told him if the guy wouldn't take his name, he wouldn't take anybody's name. So we got the lease, and that store was phenomenal. That was the start of the Gino's chain.

"We opened the first Gino's in 1959, and pretty soon there are 12 to 15 stores around the Baltimore area. By the time Alan retired after the 1960 season, there were probably 15 to 20 stores. It was moving."

That is an understatement. The takeoff of Gino's was every bit as dramatic, on a regional basis, as the emergence of McDonald's was nationally. As Marchetti described it in Klein's book:

> They had served a fifty-five cent hamburger, a Powerhouse, and they wanted to go into a cheaper-type menu. At that time, our hamburgers were fifteen cents. They didn't want to use Ameche's name for both of them. This was like a pilot model, and they didn't want the people in Baltimore to say, "Gee, they're selling a fifty-five-cent hamburger here and the same thing for fifteen cents over there." They didn't want to connect the two, because people thought the fifteen was cheaper meat, which it wasn't.
>
> So that's when they brought me into the company to start Gino's.

The new Gino's menu couldn't have been more basic. Hamburgers were 15 cents; French fries were 10 cents; soft drinks were 10 cents; and milk shakes were 10 cents.

"Price was the big thing," Marchetti said. "We used to advertise 'Feed a family of five for $1.75.' For that price you could buy five hamburgers, five fries, and five drinks. That was the whole point. . . . It was top-quality beef and it went over.

"The hamburgers were 1.6 ounces, 10 patties to the pound. People liked the 15-center, they were damn good. They were exactly like McDonald's burgers. . . . The only difference was we didn't have golden arches. The food product was exactly the same.

"For a company-owned store we were right there with McDonald's. Pretty soon we had places in California, Boston, Detroit. We were spread out pretty good. The Baltimore fans got us off to a damn good start, they really took to us. At our peak, we had over 500 restaurants.

"They were all company owned too, not franchised. We had our own training, advertising, purchasing, the whole thing. We just hired managers for the stores."

In Klein's book, Ameche gave credit to Marchetti for helping the company take off.

"The company really started moving when Gino came in. I think we were the first of the chain-type fast-food operations . . . in the East anyway. McDonald's started out in the West, but they didn't get here until we had already been established."

After Campanella left Gino's to rejoin the Colts' management team, the roles of the three remaining partners were sharply defined. Ameche was in charge of purchasing, Marchetti handled personnel matters, and Fischer was the company's CEO.

"Alan helped the company in a lot of different ways," Marchetti said. "But mainly he was in charge of purchasing. Alan was a very scientific-minded guy.

"He would analyze everything from every different angle, using the most modern technology. And he was a very smart guy who just got along with everybody. He was just the most authentic man I ever met in my life. Whatever he said to you, you could take it to the bank."

Marchetti's official title was chief operation's officer.

"I liked to go in the stores and work with the kids," Marchetti said. "I did that right up till the time we sold out. I probably knew every manager of all the stores."

As time passed, the corporation diversified, adding Kentucky Fried Chicken to many of its restaurants. Also, with Ameche leading the way, the company began opening a chain of budget steakhouses called Rustlers.

But like all good things, Gino's run came to an end when the company, which now included 550 Gino's, 150 Rustlers, and assorted other properties, was sold to the Marriott corporation for approximately $150 million in 1984. Ameche had retired from the day-to-day operations of Gino's after his first heart surgery in 1980, but he was still a member of the board of directors and a major stockholder.

Incredibly, instead of retaining the proven Gino's brand, Marriott shut down Gino's and converted many of the stores to Roy Rogers drive-ins, which specialized in roast-beef sandwiches. Some of the Gino's were just closed.

"They made us an offer that we just couldn't refuse," Fischer said. "We had a great run, our stock went crazy, and quite frankly, we thought the fast-food market was getting saturated. Maybe that wasn't the case, but that's what we thought, so we cashed out. I think we got a great deal."

Not everyone was as thrilled with the outcome as Fischer, however.

"That's the $64 question. What happened?" asked Yvonne Ameche. "I really don't understand why Roy Rogers bought Gino's if they didn't want to use the name. I guess they didn't buy the name, just the buildings."

Marchetti said he still regrets the sale of the Gino's chain.

"What happened? Fischer was chairman of the board, and I think he made a few bad decisions," Marchetti said. "Marriott came along and made us a pretty good offer, so that was the end of it.

"But I've always had regrets. I probably had more regrets than Alan or anybody else because I was so hands on. I probably knew every manager of all 500 stores. I always made a point to spend a couple days in every store and get to know people. I was glad I had it when I retired from football, because it took the place of football for me."

As for Ameche, he was still too young a man to completely retire, so he tried his hand at a couple more ventures before retiring. He invested in several indoor tennis facilities to support his love of tennis, his favorite sport after retiring from football.

"After Gino's, Alan played a lot of bridge and tennis, and we traveled a lot, so he stayed active," Yvonne said. "I don't think he really liked the corporate world. He was a private person and a little introverted, so I don't think it was his cup of tea."

Ameche also invested in a bar/restaurant in Kenosha, partnering with his old high school teammate and good buddy, Mario Bonofiglio. He also dabbled in the world of sports agency. Neither venture ended well for Ameche.

Apparently Ameche originally tried to purchase a Madison landmark, known as the Brat Haus, with Bonofiglio as his partner. But the price was too high, and the two high school buddies decided to build a place on the northern outskirts of Kenosha, called Pub and Grub.

The place opened in 1975 and was centrally located to Kenosha's two colleges—the University of Wisconsin–Parkside and Carthage College. Since the drinking age for Wisconsin residents at that time was eighteen, the place was a gold mine in its early years.

"It's more of a bar and recreation room," Ameche told Tom Butler of the *Wisconsin State Journal* in a story on February 9, 1975.

Mario and I are partners. We built the first unit from the ground up and it's going very well.

It has fireplaces . . . an old English atmosphere . . . something fairly unique. It's near UW–Parkside and Carthage College. We are catering to the college kids.

It's something Mario and I have talked about and wanted to do for a long time. I told Mario to look around and research it. It's all Mario's baby.

Mario and I are like brothers and we always wanted something like this where we get into business.

But the business went south when Wisconsin boosted its drinking age back to twenty-one because so many teenagers were crossing the border from their home states, where that was the legal age. Wisconsin legislators rightly felt that the disparity in the drinking age between Wisconsin and its neighboring states created an unnecessary safety hazard.

"We were doing great for a while, but then they changed the drinking age and it was very hard after that," Bonofiglio said. "It just wasn't there anymore. I don't think we lasted a year after they changed the law."

When things started going bad, Ameche sent his second youngest son, Michael, out to Kenosha to try to save the business. Michael spent four years in Kenosha managing the Pub and Grub, but there was no saving it.

"The place started going downhill, and there was no turning back," Michael said. "It got a tough crowd in there. We got a lot of sailors from Great Lakes [Naval Training Center] in there, and they didn't get along with the Kenosha townies very well.

"There were a lot of fights in there. I hired eight of the biggest human beings you've ever seen to stop the fights, and things quieted down, but it was too late to save the place. I was there to run the place because nobody was ever there to run it. . . . The kids were running the place. I tried to clean it up. It was a learning process for me, too.

"The change in the drinking age was part of the problem, but it wasn't being run very well. I know that it created a problem in my dad's relationship with Mario. I don't know the specifics, but there was money that was not accounted for, money being spent frivolously. It wasn't run like a business should be run; it was more like a playground, and that put a wedge between the two."

Bonofiglio doesn't deny there was a problem but says that he and Ameche remained the best of friends till the end.

"Alan thought maybe we should have been doing a better business, but it was hard after [the changing in drinking age]. We had a meeting and I told him why things were slow. He called me a week later and said, 'You were right, I never thought of it that way.'"

Yvonne, who still owns the property and the vacant building in Kenosha (which suffered fire damage around 2010), recalls the meeting between the two boyhood friends a bit differently. She claims the failed business did everlasting harm to their relationship.

"I remember them coming out from the meeting and it was not a happy meeting at all," she said. "The looks on their faces were not happy."

Bonofiglio, who flew to Philadelphia for Ameche's funeral, denies there was a lasting rift in their friendship caused by the failure of the Pub and Grub.

"Do you know how many bars in Kenosha went under because of that law?" Bonofiglio asked. "Alan knew that. There was nothing we could have done differently.

"Alan and I were best friends till the day he died. He just thought that the business should have done better, but he understood."

Ameche's other ill-fated venture was a sports-agent partnership with another Baltimore legend, Brooks Robinson of the baseball Orioles. Attorney Ron Shapiro was the third member of the team, and the idea was that Ameche would represent football players while Robinson would advise baseball players. The corporation was called Personal Management Associates and was headquartered in Baltimore.

"It was very altruistic . . . Alan didn't need the money," Yvonne said. "They would set up contracts so that when the players were done playing ball, they would have money to retire on. Alan was going to deal with the football players, Brooks Robinson with the baseball players, and the lawyer would handle the contracts.

"It started out, it was a wonderful idea. It was an all-encompassing sort of plan. But then they found that a lot of players already had agents and, you know in college, you're not supposed to do that, so it didn't work out.

"Alan was well received by the players, but I think he was surprised by the things that were going on. So that was that."

22

Father Was a Fullback

Alan Ameche had a nickname around Malvern Prep School and it wasn't "the Horse."

At the Malvern, Pennsylvania, school, which all four of the Ameche sons attended, the senior Ameche was known respectfully as "the Owner," as in the owner of the football program. Technically, of course, high school football programs don't have owners, but *owner* pretty much described Ameche's role within the program.

After his premature retirement from the Colts, he had plenty of time on his hands—some might say too much time—and Malvern's football program was, to say the least, his pet project. Ameche did everything for the down-and-out-program, from supplying it with the best equipment to handpicking its coach. But perhaps his biggest contribution to the program was donating his four sons—Brian, Alan Jr., Michael, and Paul.

"I remember when we first moved to the Philadelphia area, it was about the time my older brother [Brian] was just getting ready to start high school," Alan Jr. said. "My dad knew he had four sons that were going to be playing football at Malvern Prep over what? A 10- to 12-year span, and Malvern Prep was not competitive in football at that time. The year before my brother got there, I don't think they won a game in the league, and they had a history of going winless.

"My dad had it in his mind that if his kids were going to go that school, that things had to change. He singlehandedly made that change."

One of Ameche's first moves was to get rid of the man who was football coach at Malvern at that time. After an 0–8 season in Brian's freshman year and two wins the following year, when Alan Jr. joined his older brother on the varsity, Ameche had seen enough.

Ameche lobbied to have the current coach replaced with successful local youth coach Jack "the Shark" McGuinn. It turned out to be a good move, because McGuinn coached at Malvern from 1969 through 1977, posting a 64–14–4 record.

"I remember we started two-a-days my sophomore year and one day we came to practice and we had a new coach," Alan Jr. said. "He got rid of the coach. . . . He was there one day and gone the next. There was a guy [McGuinn] my dad had in mind who was a very successful grade school coach and the next thing we knew, he was the coach.

"The new coach drove us relentlessly and made us win football games. The first year we were the co-champions of our league. That's what this guy did. He was such a tough coach that he took the same group the previous guy had and went on to establish a dynasty at Malvern. Malvern is still a dynasty."

But Ameche didn't stop with appointing his own handpicked choice for coach. He went after players.

"My father not only created a change at coach, he went to the headmaster and said, 'We've got to get some players in here,'" Alan Jr. said. "The teams we were competing against in our league were recruiting players, so he felt we had to recruit some players to keep up with them. They were bringing in kids to play for them and Malvern wasn't. My dad changed that."

To that end, Ameche started a scholarship program at Malvern. The program served a double purpose. It bolstered Malvern's football program while giving a quality education to underprivileged boys.

"My dad told the coach go out and pick five kids a year from the Catholic grade school system in Philadelphia, which is a very big system," Brian Ameche said. "By our junior year we were the league champions.

"My dad was known around the school as the owner of the football team. The game films would come to our house and be shown in our living room. The coaches would all come to our house to watch the films with our father before the players would see them.

"We had several universal gyms set up in our three-car garage, and players were actually required to come over to our place and work out on a regular basis. We were essentially the physical fitness center for the football program."

There was pressure on all the Ameche children to excel because that was the sort of parent that Alan, especially, was. It's clear that he mellowed over the years, but he learned the fine art of childrearing by trial and error. To be sure, there were trials and there were errors . . . many of both.

Unlike some fathers, he didn't have the advantage of being raised in the perfect home. The word *dysfunctional* may not have been part of the popular lexicon in those days, but Ameche's parents, Augusto and Elizabeth, were the poster children for that concept. There was constant turmoil at the Ameche home in Kenosha, and the only constant in Alan's home life was his strong bond with his big brother, Lynn.

In later years Ameche would be the first to admit that he had made mistakes as a parent. He understood that part of being a parent was learning on the job. There were times when he was too rough on the children, especially his sons, but at least he learned that about himself.

"He wanted peace and quiet, but he got neither in our house," Alan Jr. said. "That's just the way it is with six kids.

"And Dad had a lot of displaced anger because he had his football career taken away from him. He would be angry at everybody at times. The first question we'd ask when we'd come home is, What kind of mood is Dad in?

"His whole identity was being a Baltimore Colt and that was taken away from him when he was twenty-eight years old. He went from being a hero to an everyday person. He was extremely bitter and angry."

Unfortunately, sometimes that misplaced anger was projected onto the boys. There were times when the Ameche house was run more like a football training camp than a home.

"My brother [Brian] beat me up nearly every day of my life," Alan Jr. said. "Finally, my dad said, 'Alan, you have my permission to defend yourself any way you can. Grab whatever is nearby. If you break a lamp, you'll never get in trouble from me.' Twice, Brian went to the hospital for stitches."

Despite his very un–Dr. Spock methods, Ameche is universally loved by his children today. The living proof that he worked his entire life on being a better parent is perceptible today in Brian, Alan Jr., Catherine, Michael, and Beth (the sixth, Paul, died in a car accident in 1981). They unanimously share a deeply rooted love and admiration for their father that will never die.

There is no doubt that Ameche was a gentler, kinder, more understanding parent in his later years than he was while he was playing and in the immediate aftermath of his football career. As the oldest child, Brian, who was born between Ameche's sophomore and junior years at Wisconsin, was held to the highest standards.

Brian, who went on to be an all–Ivy League defensive end at Yale, also may have been the most headstrong of the Ameche children. He and his father butted heads often while he was growing up.

"I think my dad and I banged heads a little more than he did with my brothers," Brian said. "When we were younger, I think he pushed me harder than he pushed the others because I was the oldest.

"Plus, it was part of *his* transition into adulthood. You have to remember I was born when he was nineteen years old, so he didn't know how to be a father. It was something he had to figure out for himself.

"I played organized football from the time I was in second grade till I finished college. I was six years old when I started playing. Did I want to play? Who knows?

"I just knew it was a way to have my father's attention, some of it, at least, positive. It was a way for him to care about me and to appreciate me. And that was something important to him, so it was something I naturally fell into."

But, as Brian pointed out, not all of his father's attention was positive.

"Yes, he did put pressure on me, too," said the eldest Ameche son, now an architect in Connecticut. "He took my playing very seriously. I always had the feeling that the only person on the field he was watching play was me.

"And then our coach [in high school] would stand me up before the game and say things like 'Brian, if you play well today, we are going to win this game.' That was a lot of pressure to put on a kid. I was a tackle in high school, for God's sake, not a quarterback or halfback. I was what they called a pulling tackle. I'd lead the sweeps and people would stay out of my way. I was a very good high school football player."

Brian agrees that much of the reason his father was so rough on him might have been partially due to his father's unceremonious departure from the Colts.

"I think he took the end of his [football] career really hard and some of that, I think, got projected onto us," Brian said. "He was deeply involved in my football career, and I think part of that involvement sprang from the premature end of his own football career.

"At least I felt that was the case with me. He worked out some of his issues with the premature termination of his career by being so deeply involved with the Malvern football program. My response to my father's personality was basically to become my own man as quickly as possible.

"When I was eighteen or nineteen, he's still saying 'Go with God.' I had a pretty good feeling for who I was."

Alan Jr., who was much less defiant of his strong-willed father than his older brother, has nothing but admiration for Brian.

"I admire Brian so much for standing up to our father," Alan Jr. said. "That was not an easy thing to do, but Brian did it."

Brian remembers succinctly the turning point in his relationship with his father. Shortly before departing for Yale, he and his father took in Ohio State's season opener. His father's company, of which Ohio State alumnus Lou Fischer was the CEO, had donated the funds for the Astroturf at Ohio Stadium.

"Our relationship was very tough up until the time I was eighteen," Brian recalled. "I remember we went to the Ohio State game and we had a long talk.

"He said if I wanted to grow hair down to my ass that was my choice. He said if I wanted to smoke pot, that was my choice. If I wanted to screw around, it was my choice. And he said he'd be there to catch me if I fell.

"From that point on, I went to Yale and our relationship changed dramatically. My parents allowed me to choose where I wanted to go to school rather than getting involved. The interesting thing is that [he and his father] both grew out of this. Essentially I was on my own, three hours from home.

"He became far more loving and supportive and positive about my life than the years when I was living at home. It was the start of our adult relationship, something I have always cherished.

"He would come to all my games but no longer was able to stay involved the way he was in high school. He had a great relationship with my coach [Carmen Cozza], but that was as deep as he could get into my career, so he let go. My college career was just that . . . my career. I was on my own for the first time in my life and I found that a very exciting experience.

"He'd come to the games and laugh with me when we won, and he'd cry with me when we lost, but it was my career. He was very, very proud of me and the way I could play. That was a very important part of our relationship. Once it became mine, and I could share it with him as a choice, I loved playing football in college. I had a great experience.

"I didn't let my hair grow down to my ass, but I did have hair that was flopping around on my shoulders. I had long hair and a very loose attitude. I didn't understand why I was that way at the time, but I see it all pretty clearly now."

It's clear that Brian Ameche was able to put aside all his issues with his father growing up in the past.

"I remember the last time I talked with him," Brian said. "I was leaving after my sister's [Beth's] wedding and he came out to say good-bye. We were hugging in the driveway and telling each other 'I love you, I love you.' And he said, 'Stay in touch. You are so important to me.'

"We had some hard times, but some of the gifts he gave me as we went through that process have been enormously useful in my life. My basic perseverance, my fearlessness, my energy . . . I can go through a whole list of things I learned from him. I benefitted enormously from having him as my father."

Although Alan Jr. was just a year younger than Brian, he seemed to have a smoother go of it with his father. Perhaps it was that the elder Ameche was learning from his somewhat confrontational relationship with Brian, or perhaps it was just that father was learning from his mistakes. Or it could have been that Ameche didn't feel that Alan Jr., at 5′ 11″, 205 pounds, had as much potential as a football player as Brian had.

"Believe it or not, he never pressured us to actually play football," Alan Jr. said. "But he made it clear that if we did play, he expected certain things from us in how we approached the game. If we weren't living up to what he expected from us, it wasn't a happy home to be around.

"And by that I mean, it wasn't a pleasant home for anybody, not for my mother or my sisters or anybody. He was a very intense man, and when he wasn't happy, nobody was happy.

"If we didn't win or we didn't play well, it was no fun going home for me and [Brian]. We would drive around rather than go home, because we knew what was waiting for us if he wasn't happy. He let us know when he wasn't happy."

Yvonne Ameche agrees with Alan Jr. that the only pressure Alan Sr. put on his sons came after they committed to play football.

"[Ameche] didn't put pressure on them to play football, but there was always pressure to do the best they could," she said. "He would be at every game and he'd get carried away sometimes.

"One time the refs stopped the game and said to our coach, 'Who is that man on your side of the field?' The coach said 'I don't know, never saw him before.' The ref told him, 'Well, I'm not going to restart the game until he is back in the stands.'

"But that was just Alan being obnoxious. Nobody wanted to be near him at the games because he was yelling at everybody. He was emotional. He was Italian and they are all emotional people."

There were reports about Ameche hiding his Heisman from public display as his sons were growing up, but the boys say it wasn't really that.

"I really don't know if that was the case," Alan Jr. said. "My father was just very humble. He downplayed his success. He wasn't somebody who wanted to be defined by football. His whole thing was just this . . . if you're going to do it, be the best you can. Be in shape, lift weights, go at it intensely and seriously. It's not a sport you play at."

Being the son of a Heisman Trophy winner carried enough pressure in itself, but Alan Jr. claims his father did everything to downplay the whole Heisman and pro-football thing.

"I remember there was an event for the parents in my freshman year, and another kid's father comes up to us and goes on and on about what a great player my father was and if I could be just half the player he was. I remember my father kind of jerking me away from the guy and me not understanding why he was angry. But now I see that he was angry that I had to listen to that nonsense.

"I remember him telling me, 'You never have to listen to any of that nonsense. Don't worry about what I did or think you have to compete with that or measure up to anything.' He was more about lessons in life and goodness and kindness and generosity than he ever was about football.

"I remember as a very young kid and we were still living in Baltimore that people would always crowd around him in public. And if he ever came to school, my classmates would always crowd around and make a big deal. But he always downplayed that stuff and never wanted to put pressure on us kids, that we had to live up to anything."

Alan Jr., who is now in the insurance business in the Philadelphia area, went on to play football at Delaware, which at the time he played there was a perennial power in Division II football.

"I sort of played at Delaware, but it probably wasn't the right choice for me," he said. "I was very small for my position [defensive tackle], and they were so loaded with talent, winning the Division II championship every year."

When it comes to pressure, perhaps no young men have ever had more pressure to perform than the sons of Michael Cappelletti and Catherine Ameche. Cappelletti, who was the recipient of one of Ameche's scholarships to Malvern, is the brother of 1973 Heisman Trophy winner, John Cappelletti.

Thus, their sons, Michael and John, who are now grown, had the double-barreled burden of being the grandson of one Heisman Trophy winner and the nephew of another.

"I don't think they felt a tremendous amount of pressure, because football is the kind of sport you can't force somebody to play," Catherine said. "It's a sport you have to love. If they were really intense about football, there would have been pressure, but I don't think the intensity was ever there."

Michael played football at Saint Joseph's Preparatory in Philadelphia and was, by all reports, a solid defensive end. He was recruited by some Division III football programs but chose to attend Penn State and not play football.

"We enjoyed watching Michael play in high school, but when he decided he was finished playing, we were fine with that," Catherine said. "We certainly didn't force him to play."

John played football in the seventh and eighth grade and freshman year at Malvern Prep.

"He was a good player, but he realized he wasn't going anywhere with it and didn't particularly enjoy it," Catherine said. "He played lacrosse. As long as you find something you love, it doesn't matter what it is. He ended up going into theater, and he is now [2011] an acting and directing major at DeSales University.

"Michael and I are very sensitive to let them do what they want to do. You have to have a certain intensity to play football, and they didn't have that fire or aggressiveness. My husband was a very good football player, and I was a very good field hockey player.

"We always assumed that we'd have fabulous athletes, and both our sons are decent athletes. They just didn't have that competitive fire. I had it, my husband had it. . . . So what are you going to do? We laugh about it and say, 'It probably skips a generation.'"

Growing up in the Ameche household, Catherine didn't totally escape the wrath of her father when it came to sports, but it was mostly secondhand smoke. Her father came to all of her field hockey and basketball games in high school, but he wasn't as passionate or intense about it as he was about the boys' football.

"We had a very intense childhood," Catherine said. "I was the only girl in the house for eight years until my youngest sister was born, so it was a very male-dominated household. Your worth was measured by how fast you were and how tough you were.

"It was an interesting way for a girl to grow up. I had an intensity that other girls didn't have, and it served me well in field hockey because I scared the hell out of the other girls. But I think it was a lot harder for the boys to measure up, and they were all different in their approach.

"I was a very good field hockey player, very intimidating and very competitive, so he didn't have much to say about me. I loved having him come to my field hockey games because it was a sport I was very good at. I wasn't very good at basketball though, and I remember him yelling at me, 'Jump! Jump!' all the time."

Although she was pretty much immune from her father's critical eye, Catherine definitely felt sympathy for her brothers.

"I think he really did mellow out over the years, but for my brothers, it was a very intense experience," said Catherine, who still lives in the Philadelphia area and owns an indoor tennis facility. "Football at Malvern was very intense, and in a way that was unfortunate. When they lost, you would have thought the world came to an end.

"My father was not real patient, he was so intense. You could say he was a little over the top. I don't know, maybe he felt he was cheated out of playing, but it definitely was a difficult transition for him to make back in the day.

"There is so much aggression and intensity in professional football, I feel it was even more so when he was playing. So what do they do when they stop playing? I'm sure he was very frustrated. . . . He wanted to play longer than he was allowed to play. But his level of intensity was not appropriate for high school football. That made it hard on the boys.

"He'd get so angry that he would overreact to things. I'm married to man who was a very good athlete, but he has a very mature outlook on the value of sports. He never allowed emotions to get in his way. Dad had so much of his own emotions wrapped up in it, it was hard to separate. He let some of his anger show on the sidelines."

On the plus side, Catherine noticed a gradual mellowing of her father in his later years.

"He was just an absolutely wonderful man," she said "Yes, he was flawed like we all are. But over the years he learned to deal with his anger much better, and he was somebody always evolving, always growing.

"He was curious about so many things; he had so many wonderful attributes. He was just very special and so wonderful to be with."

Number-three Ameche son, Michael, came along at a time when Alan was definitely starting to mellow.

"Honestly, I don't remember my dad being too over the top," Michael said. "I just remember a dad who was really into it, but when I look back, I don't consider it negative."

Michael may have been the best pure athlete of the Ameche sons. Like his father, his position was fullback, and he starred at Malvern and later went on to play three seasons at Franklin and Marshall College in Lancaster, Pennsylvania.

"He was still very invested in my football career, but in a good way," Michael said. "I remember in grade school, my dad was yelling at me from the sidelines and then my coach yelled at me, 'Don't listen to your dad, listen to me.' It was pretty comical."

It wasn't so comical, however, when Ameche would pull aside Michael and Lou Fischer's son Mark, who was also a running back, during the boys' lunch break at Saint Aloysius Grade School.

"We were dressed in our Saint Aloysius outfits with the flannel pants and winged tipped shoes and ties, and he would take us off to the side and hand a football off to us, over and over and over again," Michael said. "He wanted to show us how to grip the ball and not fumble it.

"On the one hand, it was kind of awkward because your friends would be watching and say, 'What's going on over there?' But the older I've gotten, the more I appreciate that he took time to come over from work. When it was going on, I was almost embarrassed by it.

"My dad was a 1950s parent, so he was strict. There was one way to do things. He was tough. But he taught us. I really don't have a problem with anything he did. It was all out of love. I think when he left football, he had a problem channeling his aggression, because there is so much aggression in football. But he was tough in a loving way."

It's almost contradictory, because the elder Ameche was so invested in his son's football careers. But like his other brothers, Michael insists that his father went out of his way to alleviate pressure on him.

"I never felt any pressure [to play football]," Michael said. "His whole philosophy was 'I don't care if you are a trash man or a football player. Just do the best you can and do it with integrity.'

"I thought I should be starting as a sophomore, so I called my dad and told him I was thinking about quitting. He didn't try to talk me out of it, he just said 'If you're not going to give it 100 percent, then don't do it. Do what you think is right.'

"My dad did keep his Heisman in the closet until we were older, but I don't know if it was because he wanted to keep pressure off us. I think it was more just him being humble. It really wouldn't have made that much of an impact us, because I'm not sure any of us realized what a big deal it was until we were older. My mom was the one who finally dragged it out of the closet."

Michael, who was also heavily recruited as a baseball player, may have been the best athlete in the family, but he readily admits that he didn't have the best attitude. He seems to regret that to this day.

"I was a punky kid," he said. "My dad used to say I was the best athlete he ever saw for a kid my age, but I was a knucklehead. I was diagnosed with [attention deficit disorder] before it was fashionable. I was a bright kid and a great athlete, but I didn't focus the way I should, and that is one of my regrets."

Michael had a great career at Malvern and then played football for three years at Franklin and Marshall, but as he put it, "My head wasn't in it.

"I went there and floundered. I was probably a better athlete than my older brothers, but I was more of a knucklehead than they were."

Michael owned and operated his own bar and grill, Casey's Dugout, in the Philadelphia area for over two decades. He recently went to work for Gino Marchetti in the new Gino's restaurant in Philadelphia.

Beth, the baby of the family, didn't see the side of her father that the others saw. By the time she came along, he had mellowed considerably to the point where she almost wishes she could have seen some of the fireworks.

"I was the youngest of the six, the baby of the family, so I really didn't experience much of that," Beth said. "He was a different person, a different father by the time he raised me. He had really mellowed.

"I know it was definitely different for the boys. . . . It was old-fashioned back then. For me, he had been through open heart surgery and he was trying to lead a little different lifestyle. When you have open heart surgery at forty-four, you pretty much know you need to make some lifestyle changes. He still had intensity, but he was much gentler with me than the others."

Like her older sister, Catherine, Beth also was a field hockey player. But even that was a lower-key experience for her than it was for Catherine.

"He came to all my games, and I remember when he would pull up, all my friends would say, 'Mr. Ameche is here, Mr. Ameche is here,'" she said. "They were all comfortable with him being there, and they respected him, but they knew they had to be on their game because he was there.

"He would learn all of the girls' names and he'd call out their names during the game, but in a good way."

As it was with Catherine, music played a big role in Beth's relationship with her father. In her teenage years, she and her father shared "music exchange" nights in which Alan would share some of his favorite classical music with her and she would share her music with him.

"I tried to pick things I thought he'd like, like *Dark Side of the Moon* [Pink Floyd] and *Fragile* [Yes], and Steve Wonder's *Key of Life*," Beth said. "No Lynyrd Skynyrd or anything like that. He couldn't have been any kinder or sweeter about it.

"He picked out classical music for me, but I never appreciated it like my sister."

Ameche's love for Beethoven was well documented from the time his brother, Lynn, introduced him to the University of Wisconsin music library, when Alan, still in high school, visited him in Madison. He converted many of his friends, like Bobby Hinds, to classical music, but perhaps nobody shared his love of Beethoven like Catherine.

"You know, when I was young, I found classical music a little tedious to be honest," Catherine said. "But I really grew to love it. I became a music major in college, and I still sing in church for weddings and funerals, and I'm in a couple different choirs.

"I think classical music, and Beethoven in particular, was my father's escape. He was such an introvert, he loved his downtime. He loved to lose himself in his music.

"I think it spoke to him. It was very spiritual for him. . . . He found God in his music and in nature, and I inherited both of those passions from him."

But why Beethoven? What was it about the Teutonic genius that made him Ameche's idol?

"I think Alan loved Beethoven so much because he liked the fact that Beethoven overcame his handicap of not being able to hear and still created such masterpieces," Yvonne recalled. "He marveled at that."

Hinds was another Ameche convert to Beethoven.

"When we were in high school, we never had any money, so we'd go over to Simmons Library [in Kenosha] and check out LP albums," Hinds said. "Then we'd go over to Allendale [neighborhood] because we knew a gal over there who had a Victrola we could play the records on.

"It's funny, but Alan never could afford a record player until after he graduated from college."

Catherine has her own theory as to her father's love of Beethoven.

"Beethoven was very, very fiery . . . very emotional, stormy," Catherine said. "It's driving, powerful stuff. He was the first composer to have a full range of emotion.

"Before Beethoven, you had Mozart, and he was very sweet, pretty. But Beethoven was the first of the whole Romantic period who was into all that innovative stuff. Dad loved that about him. He loved the emotion and the passion that Beethoven had for his music.

"Beethoven's whole story was so amazing. There was nobody like him."

23

A Funeral and a Wedding

YVONNE AMECHE WILL NEVER FORGET the late evening of December 27, 1981. The doorbell rang at the Ameche home in Malvern, and she answered it.

It was a policeman, and he had news for her that most parents receive only in their worst nightmares. Her son Paul, the youngest son of the Ameche family, was dead at the age of twenty-one. He had died in a one-car collision about a mile from the family's home when his automobile left the road and he hit a tree.

"Paul was home from college, Ithaca College, for Christmas," Yvonne recalled. "He was coming home from a bar and maybe he had one too many, and he was coming home. He was a big, tall, handsome boy, such a nice, nice kid."

Hearing the news was horrific, but what she had to do next was even more terrifying. She had to tell her husband Alan that his son was dead.

"The policeman asked me if I wanted him to come with me when I told Alan, but I said, no, I would do it myself," she said. "I'll never forget . . . he was sitting up in bed, so vulnerable, so sleepy, so peaceful.

"I thought to myself that as great as my pain was in losing Paul, that it was doubly painful that I had to tell Alan. But I told him. He let out a sigh and a moan, and a cry that I think I will remember all the days of my life."

Six months after Paul's death, the entire Ameche family made a public service feature on dealing with grief. Paul's five siblings and Alan and Yvonne all spoke frankly about their loss and how they were attempting to cope with the tragedy, each in their own way.

"To lose a son is the most painful thing I have ever experienced," Alan Ameche said in the short featurette, produced by Group Two Productions out of Baltimore. "I suffered complete destruction . . . physically and mentally. I doubt that I will ever forget the moment I heard the words of Yvonne, telling me of Paul's death."

Just as Yvonne said the hardest part for her may have been passing the news on to Alan, the hardest part for him may have been watching the suffering of his five surviving children.

"Part of the problem is seeing your own children grieving," he said in the documentary. "That adds to your own grief.

"I remember I cried almost constantly those first three days. It really came out."

Ameche was able to pull himself together, however, and speak at Paul's funeral mass. Alan Jr. will never forget his father's words that day.

"I remember him speaking at Paul's mass," Alan Jr. said. "I have never been in a church as crowded as that one was that day. I remember my father having tremendous courage and getting up and speaking in front of all those people.

"He told the people, specifically the fathers who were there, to love their children and never be afraid of telling them that you love them. He talked about a recent conversation he had had with Paul and how he was so glad that he had told Paul how much he loved him."

Paul Ameche was the youngest of the Ameche sons and by all accounts nothing like his rough and tumble older brothers. The words that pop up most frequently in describing Paul are *gentle* and *sensitive*.

Paul played football at Malvern and was a decent player, but his heart was never in it, apparently. He thought about playing football at Ithaca but literally decided not to play as he was driving to the campus in his freshman year. He made up his mind on the drive to Ithaca, but not before pulling over his car several times to call his brothers and ask their advice.

"Paul was just kind of feeling his way through the world at that point of his life," Brian said. "He was more gentle and sensitive than the three of us. He was more sweet and generous than the three of us—I know that's something I didn't have when I was in high school . . . that's for sure.

"By the time Paul played football at Malvern, our father had let go entirely. Paul was a tackle and he was a good player, but he didn't like contact, and that's the real measure of whether or not you are a good player. He was just a really good kid."

Paul seemed to be closest to his sisters, Catherine and Beth, especially Beth.

"Paul and I spent a lot of time together, just playing games and doing things together," Catherine said. "He was very competitive . . . I hated to lose to him because he was such a terrible winner. But he was a little softer than the other boys; he was very sweet. He was the biggest of the boys, but he really didn't have the intensity to be a football player.

"That's why he called so many times on his way up to Ithaca. He ended up deciding not to play. He was a very gentle soul."

Paul was perhaps closest to Beth, who was four years his junior. She would graduate from high school in the fall of 1982 and she planned to join Paul at Ithaca College, where she had already been accepted at the time of his death.

"Paul and I were very close, and I wanted to go to Ithaca College to be with him," Beth said. "I had visited him there and I liked the school, but mostly I just wanted to be near Paul. He was a gentle giant. He couldn't have been kinder, gentler, and easy to talk to. He was just so supportive and mellow, a very relaxed person.

"But after he died, I didn't want to go there. I had no other schools in mind because that's where I always planned to go. I was floundering a little bit. But I had a friend who was going to Fairfield University. . . . She said, 'I love it. Go there.'

"So I went there, sight unseen. The first time I saw it was the first day I was there for classes. Thank God, I went there because that's where I met my husband."

Beth's meeting and eventual marriage to Sean D'Arcy wasn't the only bit of fate that was a direct result of Paul's death. Catherine would reunite with her old high school sweetheart, Michael Cappelletti, at Paul's funeral.

"They dated in high school and were reunited at Paul's funeral," Beth said. "Apparently Michael went home and told his mother that he was going to marry Catherine.

"If for nothing else, [Paul's death] gave meaning to a tragedy. I feel so horrible for people who live through a tragedy and aren't given any meaning for it.

"But as I look back, I'm very comforted to know there was a reason for it. It really made things easier for us. It was such a mess. Just to get through it is all you can do."

Unfortunately, getting through it was easier said than done for the Ameche parents. They both suffered and grieved in their own ways, which was problematic for the couple.

Alan's period of public grieving was perhaps more intense, but briefer, than Yvonne's. It took her much longer to put aside her grief.

"I believe my father grieved openly, deeply, and honestly, and I admired him for that," Brian said. "The only thing that comes close to the madness of grief is jealousy. My dad keened in his own way. He made this deeply disturbing noise, like an Arabic woman would make at a funeral, sound. But I was impressed by his outpouring of feelings."

Added Alan Jr.: "My father handled [the mourning] like he handled everything else. He mourned deeply, he cried hysterically, like we all did, and he was inconsolable, like we all were at times."

The difference between Alan and Yvonne was that Alan decided to move on with his life much more quickly than Yvonne. Michael, who was living at home at the time, remembers the day his father seemed to accept Paul's death.

"At first, he was like any other parent," Michael said. "He was very full of faith. He'd take long walks with the dog on the golf course, sometimes power walks and sometimes just ambles.

"He came home from his walk one night, maybe it was a couple months later, and he told me, 'I just had this overwhelming feeling that Paul's okay.'

"After that he was a lot calmer, a lot better with it. He seemed to really come around with that. I don't want to say he was okay with it, but he seemed to accept it more."

Indeed, Ameche's strong faith seemed to give him the strength to proceed with his life much sooner than Yvonne. He talked about Paul being in a better place and reuniting with Paul up until the day he died in 1988.

"I talk to Paul just about every day, and there are many times that I really feel his presence," Ameche said in the 1982 documentary. "I do believe there is a life hereafter and that we will be together again. I really feel that we will be together again and that makes it all better."

Ameche touched on how everybody in the family dealt with the grieving process differently, and in particular, he talked about how Yvonne dealt with it.

"There is a great deal of difference in the grief of a mother and a father," he said. "The mother is the life giver. Yvonne is in a different place. . . . There is a big difference in how mothers and fathers react. There really is a difference, a vast difference."

Their children noticed the difference in their parents' grieving. It worried them about their mother and, quite frankly, about their parents' marriage to some extent.

"My mother still grieves for Paul, but that first year was just so horrible," Catherine said. "It was like she just went away. She was so caught up in her grief.

"My father had a very, very strong faith, and I think he really believed that Paul was in a better place and took comfort in that. He grieved, but not like my mother, and maybe that's the difference between a mother and a father, or maybe it was just their personalities.

"My father had a lot of interests, things to do, a lot of passions. My father was distracted by his music, his love of bridge, his love of tennis. He had a lot to do. My mother was all about the family. She didn't work, she had no structure. When you are grieving and you don't have distractions, it really adds to it."

Alan Jr. remembers the pace of his parents' grieving well, and frankly it was very distressing to him.

"My mom was just a wreck about losing Paul and that made it incredibly hard on him," Alan Jr. said. "My father dealt with Paul's loss the way he dealt with most things. When Paul was buried, it wasn't a time to forget, but it was time to get on with living. . . . My father chose to do that.

"My mother was constantly bringing up Paul, no matter what was said or done, she would bring it back to Paul. Then she would cry. I'm not talking about weeks or months either. Paul's death possessed her."

Alan Jr. felt the different mourning styles of his parents created a serious problem in their marriage.

"I watched her and my father struggle, and they dealt with it such opposite ways that they were basically in conflict with one another," Alan Jr. said. "My father would get angry with her because she would constantly bring it back to Paul, the grief, the crying, the emotion. . . . She wasn't trying to get over it.

"With him, it was like when he came back from his triple bypass surgery. He was playing tennis right away, a lot quicker than the doctors wanted him to. He was someone who was 'Hey, let's get back to normal.'

"There is an incredible percentage of marriages that break up after the loss of a child, and that was the only time in my entire life that I was worried about their marriage. They actually were not good for each other, the way they were dealing with Paul's loss. I was really worried for them.

"My mother is aware of it, and she did some grief counseling. Two years after Paul died, she woke up one morning, and it was like saying, 'It's time to get on with my life.' It was like flicking a switch.

"She was transformed from being Yvonne Ameche who lost her son Paul, to being Yvonne Ameche Alan's wife and all of our mothers. For her, it was going to bed one night, still feeling the same way, not being able to get over Paul. And then, waking up the next morning, and whether you want to call it realization, an awakening, whatever you want to call it . . . she was a different person."

Catherine agrees that there was a definite rift between her parents but doesn't think it was as dire as Alan Jr. describes it.

"I remember going to lunch with my dad," she said. "They never discussed their relationship. . . . They kept it sacred, but one time he shared with me that he was really concerned for her, because they were grieving along different lines and that was scary for him.

"Dad tried to keep Mom busy, but it was hard because she was so remote at the time. But to be honest, I never worried about it as far as the long term."

Yvonne, of course, wasn't the only Ameche family member who struggled to get their life back on track. They all seemed to come at their grief from different angles, yet it was something very tangible to all of them.

"I remember being very upset . . . I felt so guilty that I found myself going through an entire school day and not thinking once about Paul," said Alan Jr., who was teaching school in Philadelphia at the time of Paul's death. "I always thought that if ever I were to lose a family member, it would be the end of me.

"But I was amazed that I could go back to school ten days after Paul's death and be so involved [with school]. I talked to my father about this, and he said very gently, 'Alan, that's what you should be doing. Don't feel guilty. Don't beat yourself up. Get on with your life.'"

Michael and Beth were the only two Ameche children still at home during the mourning period. Michael was bartending at the time.

"I was the oldest child living at home, and when all the hoopla died down, it was my little sister and me having dinner with my parents every night," Michael said. "I was the one trying to make jokes and lighten things up every night.

"It was just really, really difficult. There were times when I wished it had been me instead of Paul. It was just indescribably terrible to lose your brother."

24

A Houston Finale

I N WHAT CAN ONLY BE DESCRIBED AS classic irony, Alan Ameche died at the Houston DeBakey Heart Institute on August 8, 1988. There laid a man whose heart was never questioned, a man whose courage and fortitude had never failed to carry the day. *Heart* when used in the context of sport, was never an issue with Ameche. He was a man of immense heart. But when his playing days were done, tragically his heart failed him.

"We first realized there was a problem when Alan was forty-seven," Yvonne said. "He used to say his Rosaries while he walked the golf course where we lived in Malvern. God love him.

"He came in one day and said, 'My heart's not right.' I told him, 'You are just imagining things,' but he insisted. He said, 'It's not beating right, Yvonne.'

"Within a week he was in the hospital, and they found he had congestive heart disease—arterial sclerosis. Who knows how that happened?"

While Ameche was still a very active and seemingly healthy man at the time, playing tennis and handball and taking daily walks, there were warning signs.

"Alan loved food and he really didn't watch what he ate," Yvonne said. "He was pretty heavy for a while, but then he lost it too."

So, in 1980, Ameche made his first trip to visit the pioneering heart specialist Dr. Michael DeBakey at the renowned DeBakey Institute in Houston, ostensibly for an angioplasty. The doctors at the institute decided, however, that triple bypass surgery was needed.

"He came through it fine, and we thought that was the end of it," Yvonne said. "He did really well."

Ameche started to pay attention to his diet. Unfortunately, all was not well. Eight years passed, and it was discovered that Ameche's heart valves were dysfunctional. Again, it was decided that Ameche would return to the DeBakey Institute for surgery.

"He just had a very bad heart," Yvonne said. "Whether he had rheumatic fever when he was a child and it went untreated, I really don't know. I'm not sure if he had rheumatic fever as a child or not."

Before Ameche could go to Houston, there was some family business to be taken care of. The Ameches' younger daughter Beth was about to marry Sean D'Arcy. Yvonne suspected that Alan's impending surgery would be much more serious than the last one.

"Alan knew," she said. "A dear friend of ours, Alice Schrieber, asked him how he was at the wedding. He shocked her a little and told her, 'I'm just waiting to die.'

"Alice told him, 'Dear friend, I'm not ready for you to die. Have you talked to a priest?' Alan told her, 'No, I don't have to.'

"I think Alan was satisfied that he had led a good life. But again, that's just the way Alan was. He always had an answer for everything."

Ameche delayed his trip to see DeBakey for a week because of Beth's wedding. Some of his children and friends may have suspected, but no one knew for sure that it would be the last time they would see Ameche alive.

"I would say he didn't look good toward the time of the wedding," his daughter Catherine recalled. "He was pale and not as strong as he usually was. He was starting to lose his energy, but honestly, it didn't occur to me that he was about to die.

"We knew the surgery was risky, but I was totally shocked that he didn't survive."

Brian recalls his father taking up golf shortly before his death. An episode on the golf course around the time of his sister's wedding led him to believe that something was seriously wrong with his father.

"He couldn't even walk down the fairway without being out of breath," Brian remembered. "He would have to drop to his knee to catch his breath. This happened right around that time. We all knew then that it was very serious."

Beth's future husband, Sean, was golfing with the group that day, and Beth remembers his horror of the event.

"My brothers told Sean that whatever he did, don't let our father walk the course," Beth recalled. "Sean was driving after him [in a golf cart] all day, saying, 'Please, Mr. Ameche, get into the cart.' He'd have to kneel down on almost every green to catch his breath."

Michael didn't see the signs that the others noticed but admits he perhaps wasn't as in tune with his father as he should have been at the time.

"We knew how serious things were, but deep down, I think we thought everything would be okay," Michael said. "And then when it got so serious at the end, I was kind of taken aback.

"I saw that he was on edge at the wedding, but he was very in tune with his body, and he went for checkups all the time and they told him he was okay. Personally, I don't think he knew he was dying, but I was in my own world back then, being a knucklehead, bartending, and staying out late."

Beth had returned to the family home to live in the month leading up to her wedding, and she noticed a change in her father.

"He seemed to be more short tempered than he normally was in that month before the wedding," she said. "I think he wasn't feeling well and he was afraid.

"I'll never forget on my wedding night, he came up to me at around 10 o'clock and said to me, 'Can I go home now?' He was such a sweet man."

Ameche's former business partners, Lou Fischer and Gino Marchetti, were guests at Beth's wedding, and both had telling moments alone with their long-time friend that told them that things were not right.

"Alan wasn't himself at the wedding. . . . He knew it wasn't going to work," Fischer said. "He told me that by his actions. He was very despondent, just not feeling himself. They had a big Rottweiler named Zeus, and Alan would take him for a walk, and he would stop after a half a block to rest.

"At the wedding, we walked into the yard, just the two of us, and I said, 'All of my prayers are with you.' He was very bleary eyed. He turned and walked away. I knew it wasn't good."

Marchetti recalled that Ameche's classic, droll sense of humor was with him till the end.

"I knew he wasn't feeling well and that he was going in to get his heart taken care of," Marchetti said. "When I saw him at the wedding, Alan said, 'You know, Gino, we have got to get together more. The only time I see you now is at weddings and funerals.'

"Then he says, 'I think I'm beginning to like the funerals better.' That was his way of making a joke out of everything. He had that dry sense of humor. A week or so later, he was gone.

"He died too young."

After a discussion with Alan prior to the trip, Yvonne knew that this trip to Houston might not end as well as Alan's first one.

"He said 'If something happens to me, it will be okay. I'll be with Paul and I'll get to meet Beethoven. And I'll see if my mother has changed at all.'

"I said, 'Well, hope springs eternal. I'm not even sure she'll be [in Heaven].' I was kidding when I said that, but he was deadly serious. He knew he had a valve issue and he knew how serious it was."

Most of those in Ameche's inner circle knew of his heart problems, but very few knew exactly how severe the problems truly were. Not even Bonofiglio, his old friend from Kenosha, had any idea that Ameche was in a life-and-death situation.

"I knew Alan was going to Houston for surgery, but I had no idea how serious it was," Bonofiglio said. "I knew he had had trouble in the past and came out of it, so I figured it was just more of the same.

"When I heard he died, I was literally shocked. I remember just sitting there, crying and crying. I couldn't believe it happened."

Alan and Yvonne arrived in Houston on the Tuesday after the wedding, and he was immediately admitted into the hospital where the gravity of the situation was soon apparent. Yet till the end, Ameche never lost his trademark sense of humor.

"It was summertime and Alan had a great tan and just looked way too healthy to be there," Yvonne said. "One of the nurses said to Alan, 'What are you doing here? You look so healthy.'

"Alan, always the joker, quipped, 'It all started when I got on the wrong plane.'"

But very soon, the laughter subsided. Ameche was examined on Wednesday and the news was not good.

"They take the most urgent cases first so when Dr. DeBakey said, 'We're going to operate tomorrow at 6:30 a.m.,' I knew we were in trouble."

Unfortunately, Yvonne proved to be very perceptive. Ameche suffered a heart attack on the operating table, and the only thing that kept his heart beating through the weekend was the roller heart pump that DeBakey had invented. It was determined that a heart transplant was the only course of action, and by Friday he was a candidate for a new heart.

"That heart pump was the only thing keeping Alan alive," Yvonne said. "He was a candidate for a heart transplant, and they told us that Alan was the number-one candidate for a heart transplant in the United States that weekend.

"I'll never forget, the transplant team doctor came in and said, 'We've got the jet and we're ready to fly it out to wherever a heart becomes available.'"

It was at that point that Dr. DeBakey urged Yvonne to gather her five surviving children in Houston. All of them, including newlyweds Beth and Sean, who cut short their honeymoon in Ireland, made it to Houston. Unfortunately, there were no good-byes because Ameche never regained consciousness.

"At least I called him the night before he went into surgery," Brian said. "We had the same sort of conversation that we had in the driveway before he left. I had a feeling at that point he wasn't going to make it."

Both Brian and Catherine used the word *surreal* to describe their experience in Houston.

"I spent four days in Houston, and talk about a surreal experience," Catherine said. "The hospital was connected to the hotel by a tunnel, and it was so hot out that we never went outside the whole time we were there. We never got any fresh air. It was just very odd.

"It was a horrible four days. They wouldn't let us go see him because they didn't want him to know we were there. But I had a Sony Walkman, so I sent him my favorite Beethoven symphony, the *Pastoral*.

"That would be my way of letting him know we were all here for him. I had the nurse put the earphones on him, but they said he got a little agitated. He knew the *Pastoral* was my favorite so maybe he knew I was there, I don't know. I still have that tape in my special drawer."

The Catholic priest on duty that weekend just happened to be an Italian American, and like Ameche, spoke his native tongue. He spoke with Ameche just prior to the operation.

"It was great to hear Alan speaking Italian one last time," Yvonne said. "I don't think I heard him speak Italian since we visited Italy.

"I'll never forget that the priest told me we were lucky, that 'We get more hearts on the weekends. If there is a heart available anywhere in the United States, we'll get it.'"

But the heart that Ameche so desperately needed to survive never arrived in Houston. It was the longest weekend of Yvonne Ameche's life. When she returned to the hospital on Monday morning, she knew the end was near.

"They couldn't close Alan's chest back up [after the surgery] because there was so much fluid," she said. "The transplant doctor told me he had held Alan's heart in his hand and 'it was a very bad heart.' That's when I pretty much knew it was over."

Another of Ameche's teammates, Art Donovan, recalled the shock he received when he called Houston to get an update on his pal's condition.

"I called the hospital and they put me in touch with the waiting room and one of the Horse's daughters got on the phone," Donovan said. "I said, 'How is your father doing?' She said he just died five minutes ago.

"I didn't know what to say," said Donovan, a man who is rarely at a loss for words. "So I just started crying. We lost a great man that day. You couldn't have a better friend than Alan Ameche. He was just a wonderful, wonderful person."

Before she was willing to let go, Yvonne had some words she needed to tell her long-time soul mate.

"I don't know if he could hear me or not, but I think he still had brain cell activity. I could see he was still swallowing.

"I had just read a book, *Love, Medicine and Miracles* [by Dr. Bernie Segal]," she said. "The book said that sometimes it helps if you give permission . . . if you say it's all right.

"So I told Alan, 'It's okay if you're ready to go. It's all right, we'll be fine. You were a wonderful husband and a marvelous father.'

"I told him that the sun will never shine so brightly, and I will never laugh so hard again. But I will know I've had the best life has to offer and that will sustain me all the days of my life.

"And then I kissed him."

Epilogue

ALAN AMECHE AND GLENN DAVIS had two things in common: both were Heisman Trophy winners and both were married to Yvonne Ameche-Davis.

Yvonne thought she would never marry again when Ameche died in 1988, but then Davis—or "Mr. Outside," as he was known when leading a great Army team to a 27–0–1 record in 1944 through 1946—came into her life. Davis was runner-up twice for the Heisman before winning it in 1946.

As you might guess, the Heisman had everything to do with Davis's and Yvonne's meeting.

"I always try to get to most of the Heisman ceremonies and I was at the Heisman ceremony in 1995 with Ruby Horvath [widow of 1944 Heisman winner, Les Horvath], and there was a big birthday party that we were all invited to," Yvonne recalled. "So Ruby and I decided to go and we saw Glenn sitting at the bar [at the Downtown Athletic Club] by himself so I said, 'Would you like to come with us?' and he said, 'Sure.'

"Well, we all went to the party and had a good time, and then Glenn calls me from the plane on his way back to California. I told him, 'I can't get involved. . . . You are way out there and my kids are here.'

"He said, 'Yeah, Yvonne, your forty-year-old kids will really miss you.'

"Well, I went home, and the guy who does my hair says to me, 'So, did you meet anyone at the Heisman?' I remember telling him I met this guy, 'But he's too short and too old.' The next thing I know I was married to him."

After a whirlwind courtship, Yvonne and Davis were married in 1996. They split time between his home in California and her home in Philadelphia until he died March 9, 2005, of prostate cancer at the age of 80.

"Glenn was nine years older than me and he had cancer, and I knew he had cancer when I met him," Yvonne said. "But he was convincing. He said, 'I know you've buried a lot of people and I know you're worried about burying me and you probably will. But I'll tell you what. We will have one helluva good time before you put me in the ground.'

"And we did."

Yvonne is the first to admit that the two men who were her husbands were total opposites.

"There was a great difference between them," she said. "Alan came up the hard way. He was street smart. Glenn was just sweet, he grew up in California with the house with the little white picket fence.

"Everybody loved Glenn and it was a joy to be with him. He had this sweet life which made him a very sweet man. He had wonderful parents; Colonel Blaik [legendary Army coach Red] loved him. Glenn never swore and he was just such a gentleman that everybody loved him.

"Alan was rougher. He grew up in a home that wasn't real happy, his brother left home at an early age, and that was all very traumatic for Alan. He got married right after high school . . . Alan just had a harder life.

"Both were very gentle, sweet men, but Alan was much more streetwise. He came from a much rougher background."

Yvonne remembers both men fondly, but she admits that being married to two Heisman winners made her more than an answer to a trivia question. Sometimes it could be a bit of a nuisance.

Ironically, when Ameche found out he had won the 1954 Heisman, he said one of the greatest benefits was that he would get to meet Davis's partner in the Army backfield, Felix "Doc" Blanchard, the 1945 Heisman winner. Blanchard played Mr. Inside to Davis's Mr. Outside.

"In Glenn's last December, I had to fly back to New York for the fiftieth anniversary of Alan's Heisman in 2004," Yvonne said. "My whole family was there and I spoke at the event.

"I was given a huge portrait of Alan in his football uniform and wearing a cape. When I brought it home, Glenn wasn't well. He said, 'What are we supposed to do with this? Hang it over our bed?'

"Glenn was a competitive man, too. We were golfing in California, and my son Michael got a hole in one. They go into the bar afterwards and Glenn didn't congratulate Michael and he never mentions it to anyone.

"Michael, to this day, says 'Mom, can you believe that? He was mad because he never had [a hole-in-one].'"

Yvonne said that having two Heismans in the family (three, if you include John Cappelletti's) gave her greater appreciation for what Alan had accomplished in his life.

"One of the biggest regrets of my life is that I never really appreciated what Alan did," she said. "I thought anybody that wanted to play football could play football. It wasn't until I had four boys that I realized how rare it was [to win a Heisman].

"I went to his games in college and I was a cheerleader in high school. But I think that the fact that he was a football player was a very small part about what I loved about him. As I aged and saw my sons play ball and became involved with the Heisman, I realized how rare it was for someone to have the sort of ability he had.

"If I had to do it all over again, I would have followed more closely. I was Alan's number-one fan, but not because of football."

INDEX